W9-BCQ-705

WHAT AMERICANS

REALLY WANT

...REALLY

The Truth About
Our Hopes, Dreams, and Fears

WHAT AMERICANS
REALLY WANT
...REALLY

The Truth About
Our Hopes, Dreams, and Fears

DR. FRANK I. LUNTZ

HYPERION
•••••
NEW YORK

Library of Congress Cataloging-in-Publication Data

Luntz, Frank I.
    What Americans really want—really : the truth about our hopes, dreams, and fears / Frank Luntz.
        p. cm.
    Includes bibliographical references and index.
    ISBN 978-1-4013-2281-6 (alk. paper)
    1. Social psychology—United States.   2. Consumption (Economics)—United
States.   3. Public opinion—United States.   4. National characteristics, American.   I. Title.
    HM1206.L87 2009
    306.30973'090511—dc22

                                                        2009023228

Hyperion books are available for special promotions and premiums. For details contact the HarperCollins Special Markets Department in the New York office at 212-207-7528, fax 212-207-7222, or e-mail spsales@harpercollins.com.

Design by Sunil Manchikanti

FIRST EDITION

10 9 8 7 6 5 4 3 2 1

THIS LABEL APPLIES TO TEXT STOCK

We try to produce the most beautiful books possible, and we are also extremely concerned about the impact of our manufacturing process on the forests of the world and the environment as a whole. Accordingly, we've made sure that all of the paper we use has been certified as coming from forests that are managed to ensure the protection of the people and wildlife dependent upon them.

CONTENTS

ACKNOWLEDGMENTS

As we express our gratitude, we must never forget that the highest appreciation is not to utter words, but to live by them.

—JOHN F. KENNEDY

In one sense, the origin of this book began a decade ago. I scoured dozens of memos, hundreds of polls, and thousands of pages of analysis that I have written since 2000, but it still took the expert hand of others to fashion these words into text worth reading. Clearly most important in this effort is Sandy Johnson, who had to read those memos, polls, and analyses, suffering in silence as she consumed the material and spit it back out without ideology or bias. Six other people accepted the burden of reading and reacting to the prose—often with a candor usually reserved for an estranged spouse after the divorce settlement—as the book slowly took shape: Lowell Baker, Liz Bieler, Jonathan Karl, Amy Kramer, John Patterson, and Mike Phifer. Finally, thanks to my intrepid researcher Alyssa Salvo for finding so much in so little time.

My editor at Hyperion, Gretchen Young, was once again my guardian angel, only this time she was fully prepared for my eleventh-hour phone calls begging for just a few more . . . months . . . weeks . . . days . . . hours . . . whenever a deadline approached. And if I knew the request was beyond reasonable, my selfless agent Lorin Rees reluctantly made the phone call and took the heat.

There are many people who have entered my life and in some way either made me particularly proud to be an American or helped me better understand and interpret life in these trying times. I only have room to acknowledge a few:

Roger Ailes, the visionary chairman of Fox News, who gave me the opportunity to translate the hopes and fears *of* average Americans *to* average Americans and kept his promise to change my life forever.

Eric Cantor, a congressman of strong faith and philosophy, for all that he has done for his community and country.

Stephen Cloobeck, CEO of Diamond Resorts, who has proven to me again and again that customer focus should be a way of life, not a marketing slogan.

Jim Gray, sportscaster extraordinaire, for teaching me the finer points of interviewing and challenging me to challenge the world.

Tom Harrison, chairman and CEO of DAS, an Omnicom holding company, who taught me in his groundbreaking book *Instinct* to appreciate not just my own business DNA but to study America's as well.

Mr. Lawrence Kadish, the only person in my life whom I still address as Mr.—out of respect—who helped me understand the importance of never giving up and never giving in when it comes to the defense of our country.

Jon Kyl, the definition of senator extraordinaire and Washington's best-kept secret.

Bill Margaritis, senior VP of worldwide communications for FedEx, who forced me to examine, define, and then explain the importance of corporate reputation and rewarded me for it.

Mike Milken, one of the most powerful economic players in our lifetime, for dedicating his life to curing cancer in my lifetime.

Ian Rafferty (Fox) and Tom Bernthal (MSNBC), for turning my focus groups into watchable television. And an extra thanks to Tom for coming up with the idea of *"100 Days, 1000 Voices"* that took me to twenty-six states in three months.

Herb Simon, the co-owner of the Indiana Pacers, for demonstrating that success, decency, and civility can and should coexist.

Steve Wynn, for never accepting second best in anything and for allowing me to help him name the finest hotel in the world.

And most importantly, my grandfather, Benjamin Luntz, a second-generation American who passed his love for his country, its history, and its people down to his son and grandson. It was his influence that turned me into a political junkie and history freak, and for that I dedicate this book to him.

PREFACE
75 STEPS

It's not just Joe the Plumber and the Maytag Repair Guy who have lost their jobs. Entire swaths of corporate middle management are gone. One-third of my college roommates have seen their positions eliminated or had to declare bankruptcy in 2009. It really feels like we've entered the Hobbesian state of nature out there: "nasty, brutish, and short."

—JOHN PATTERSON (HARVARD CLASS OF 1994)
SENIOR VP, KETCHUM PUBLIC RELATIONS (LAID OFF 3/2/09)

An economist walks past a hundred-dollar bill on the sidewalk and doesn't pick it up. His friend asks why. *"If it were worth something, someone else would have picked it up already."* And that sums up what Americans think today, the worst economic era since the Great Depression. Words like "devastation," "carnage," "crisis," and "crash" have been thrown around like dimestore cigars, but they accurately describe not just what has happened to Wall Street but also to Main Street. They articulate not just what has happened to wealth but also to confidence.

The word "credit" comes from the Latin word that means "to believe." The crisis in America and for 300 million Americans is the *lack* of credit, the *lack* of credibility, and the *lack* of confidence that has rocked our nation to its very core. At its worst, twenty-one thousand employees a day became unemployed, and the country's jobless rate now sits at a numerical high Americans haven't seen for many years. Shopping malls are now places for walking, not for shopping. Car dealerships are empty—if they're lucky enough to still be in business. Sales of books like this one are down 10 percent. Simply put, nobody is spending because nobody has money anymore.

This economic upheaval hit with full force during the writing of this book, and it required almost a complete rewrite as bad news tumbled into worse.

The average American family had lost 9 percent of their household worth in just the last three months of 2008—the fastest disintegration of wealth in more than seven decades. In fact, a majority of families were reporting a drop of more than 25 percent in their household worth over the past year alone.

Pretty pessimistic stuff, and you're going to read a lot of it on the following pages. But this book isn't designed to bring you down. On the contrary, it has been written to help you identify and take full advantage of the numerous silver linings in even the darkest clouds. As you read this, an increasing number of Americans believe the bottom has been reached and that tomorrow will once again be better than today. At least they hope so. Fortunes are already being made by people who are able to spot an opportunity and seize the initiative. This book is filled with those stories—the marketing and advertising anecdotes that launched products and grew businesses in good times and bad. These success stories all had one thing in common: a genuine, accurate, and comprehensive understanding of the American people.

Know America and you will know the limitless opportunities waiting to be discovered. Ignore America and you will know difficulty, distress, and failure.

Perhaps the most remarkable characteristic of the American mindset is the spirit and passion of its people to change and improve the human condition. As Bobby Kennedy said some forty years ago, "Some men see things as they are and ask why. I dream of things that never were and ask, 'Why not?'" When I first envisioned this book several years ago, Americans were still among the most optimistic, forward-looking populations on the globe. No longer.

In our new reality, we need a new road map to help us figure out where we are going and how best to get there. This book is that road map—a snapshot of who we are, what we believe, and where we hope to go both as individuals and as a nation. I've opened my research vaults and utilized more than a decade of public-opinion polling to help explain and illustrate the American condition. Most of the public opinion cited in this book comes from my own personal experiences, having now polled and conducted focus groups in all fifty states. Many of the results and recommendations you will read appear here in print for the first time.

I see these next few years as an arduous journey through uncharted waters to a future that is as undefined as at any time in post-WWII America. I'm still confident we will arrive safely at our destination, but I'm less confident that the America of tomorrow will be as hopeful as the America of yesterday.

This book, as well as my life, has been enriched by the opportunity to explore the *hows* and *whys* of excellence from the eyes of those who are at the pinnacle of their careers. The highlight of that exploration may well have come on June 28, 2007. All the candidates for the Democratic nomination for president had come to Washington, DC's Howard University for a forum sponsored by PBS and hosted by Tavis Smiley to address the issues of importance to people of color.

What the candidates didn't know was that less than 100 feet from their stage, I was moderating a focus group of thirty-five undecided voters of color that would appear the following evening on PBS. What the focus group participants didn't know was that MoveOn.Org had been leading a massive Internet, e-mail, and telephone campaign against my hosting of the event because of my previous association with the Republican Party. I have to give them credit. They had generated more than fifteen thousand calls and e-mails in protest. But thanks to the courage of Tavis Smiley, PBS didn't balk, and the focus group went on as planned.

After the debate, I slipped over to the stage where the Democratic candidates, their staffs, and several journalists were still milling about and cajoled them to come walk the seventy-five steps it would take to talk to my focus group. Two of them said yes. The first to arrive was then-Senator Joe Biden, who walked right over to the participants and began shaking hands and taking pictures. You could see how moved he had been by the forum, at one point embracing an African-American woman, gently touching his head to hers, and whispering, *"I understand. I'm with you."*

Moments after he left, I brought over the second candidate. Barack Obama had not been in good form that evening, and he knew it. "The campaign is like a decathlon," he told me, "and these debates are my worst event." But despite his disappointment, and against the urging of his advance team, he took the seventy-five steps to meet with the focus group, announcing to the startled but dazzled participants the words that adorn the back jacket of this book. His debate skills, lacking that evening, would dramatically improve in the months ahead.

You can learn a lot from listening to accomplished individuals talk about their craft. As Duke Basketball Coach Mike Krzyzewski explained to me when I asked him about the ongoing pursuit of excellence, "There's a big difference between being a winner and a champion. Many people reach that bridge, but only one or two get to cross it." In essence, this book is about listening—and learning from—the American people. Unlike the remarks of exceptional achievers like Coach K and Barack Obama about their professional experiences, the singular thoughts of any one American are not enough to provide true insight into the public hopes and private fears of the people as a whole. But over a career of talking to—and more importantly, *listening* to—thousands upon thousands of Americans, I have been able to study, aggregate, and appreciate the wisdom of an extraordinary people. Through this book, I can share that wisdom with you.

Among the most memorable conversations of my career was one with Jason Kidd, one of the great basketball point guards—not just of our time, but of all time. He had three simple words to explain his success on the court: "read, react, execute." Read the basketball court not just as it looks at that instant but as it will look a split second later; react to the opportunities in front of you as they develop; and execute so that those opportunities are realized. That's a good metaphor for *What Americans Really Want . . . Really*. But more important, that's a good metaphor for life itself.

As of the closing of this book, the markets have stabilized, consumer spending has begun to return, and the danger signs are subsiding. While our individual financial condition may not be getting any better, at least it has stopped getting worse. But while the short-term economic outlook has improved, the long-term national pessimism remains— and that is the basis of this text. The psychological destruction caused by the meltdown of the housing market and an 18 percent plunge in the stock market in a single week—the worst collapse in American history— isn't repaired overnight. These are core components of the American Dream, and it will take years, if ever, for the unbridled optimism of the 1980s and 1990s to return.

This book is not meant to be a simple snapshot of the American psyche on a particular date and time. Rather, it is meant to show just how radically our outlook has changed, and how it is essential to reset assumptions and expectations for the future.

DR. FRANK I. LUNTZ
JULY 4, 2009

INTRODUCTION
DO YOU REALLY KNOW WHAT AMERICANS REALLY THINK?

Cut through the management-speak, and the key to success is simple:
Observe people going about their daily lives, identify their unmet needs, and
come up with new products.

—A. G. LAFLEY
CHAIRMAN OF THE BOARD, PROCTER & GAMBLE[1]

Do you *really* understand America?

Do you *really* know what your country thinks, how its citizens behave, and what they do when no one's looking?

Companies live or die based on what researchers like me know and how well they respond, if at all, to what we tell them. Thanks to my work for dozens of Fortune 500 companies, hundreds of "Instant Response" dial focus groups, thousands of hours of face-to-face interviews with about 25,000 customers, employees, and voters, and telephone polls with more than one million Americans since 1992, I have had an unprecedented perch above the bedrooms, the living rooms, the boardrooms, the conference rooms, the operating rooms, and the classrooms of this great nation. From photo booths to voting booths, I have had the good fortune to observe and assess our habits, our interests, our hopes, and our fears. For anyone who ever asked the question, "What do Americans really want . . . really?" you'll find the answers on these pages.

This book is written for the voyeur in all of us—the person who reads the survey graphic in *USA Today* before anything else . . . the person who takes polls online because they want to see what everyone else is thinking (and why they're wrong) . . . the person who writes on a Web post that "everyone I know agrees with me" or starts off every political argument with the words "Americans don't think that . . ." There's a reason why polling dominated much of the 2008 political focus and why more media outlets do more political and cultural polling than ever before—it sells. And it sells because we're intrigued. We want to know the dirty details; and we want to see where we stand relative to our neighbors, our friends, and our peers. We use polls we agree with to validate our point of view, while polls that challenge our assumptions are dismissed for their methodology or their inaccuracy. You know it's true. How many times have you said to yourself, *"Well, they didn't poll me . . ."* when you realize that some poll has you in the minority on some issue or behavior? What we say to pollsters is not always what we believe or how we behave when no one's looking.

This book is not about lists of mind-numbing numbers. It's about reality and the day-to-day contradictions that govern our lives.

Yet for all of the talk about "public opinion," there is a stark lack of understanding about what Americans *privately believe*. This book will give you a peek inside the lives of Americans from the moment they open their eyes in the morning and pour that first cup of joe, until the moment they turn off the TV and slide back between the sheets at night. You'll know what they do in their cars, in their offices, at home, and on vacation. This book will tell you how people think, how they feel, and how they make decisions at every moment of the day. It's the true-life story of 300 million people and what makes them tick.

We've all heard the phrase "time is money." This book operates under a stronger principle: "knowledge is wealth." It is written with the often painful realization that in these incredibly difficult times, success in virtually any profession demands that we either understand what Americans *really* want or suffer the consequences.

And if you ask the average American what he or she *really* wants, the answer today is radically different from the heady optimism of the 1990s: *freedom from fear.*

Fear arrived on September 11, 2001. On that day, we learned the meaning of the phrase "Ground Zero," first used to describe the devastation caused by the atomic bombings of Hiroshima and Nagasaki. It was a perfect metaphor for the instantaneous psychological and emotional impact that still continues to reverberate nearly a decade later.

But just as we were dusting ourselves off and getting back on our feet, Americans were once again struck by massive misfortune—only this time it was economically based. The slow but systemic destruction of wealth that had begun in early 2008 reached crescendo proportions over a ninety-six-hour stretch beginning September 14 with the bankruptcy of Lehman Brothers, the fire sale of the venerable Merrill Lynch to Bank of America, the impending collapse of Washington Mutual, and the ongoing bailouts of Fannie Mae, Freddie Mac, and AIG. By the end of the year, trillions of dollars in corporate valuations and 401(k) savings had been washed away, and with it faith in the future. And in its wake came the rise of "Generation Zero"—the tens of millions of Americans who have lost all confidence in the political and economic institutions that have governed this country since its founding. For most of the past 230 years Americans have embraced their personalized Declaration of Independence as their own, and have engaged in the active pursuit of happiness. But for a population once almost incurably optimistic—aspirational in life and certain that tomorrow would be better than today—we are less happy, less secure, less confident, and less trusting than any generation since the Great Depression.*

The subheading on the lead story of USA Today's June 12, 2009, issue said it all: **"Workers fare worst since Depression."** The average employee is working just thirty-three hours a week—the fewest hours than at any time since the U.S. government began keeping these statistics in 1964. If you're lucky enough to have a full-time job, forget even asking for a raise. Businesses slashed salaries 6.2 percent in the first quarter of 2009. And for those out of work, the average time since their last regular paycheck is 22.5 months—a post-Depression record.

It's ugly out there. By the time you read this book, general economic conditions are likely to have improved. But the damage to our individual hopes and dreams will take years to repair.

So how do we rejuvenate and revitalize our lives as individuals and as a nation? Let me give away the answer in this introduction and use the rest of this book to explain how. We are desperate for the political-economic-social elixir that will restore our "peace of mind" or at least protect us from further harm. We definitely want those words—those

---

* Or in the words of humorist Dave Barry, "All of us are born with a set of instinctive fears—of falling, of the dark, of lobsters, of falling on lobsters in the dark, of speaking before a Rotary Club, and of the words 'Some Assembly Required.'"

exact words. But more important, we want that feeling of safety, security, and intergenerational improvement once again. It is a national imperative.

"What do Americans really want?" is an even more basic, fundamental question than "What do Americans want to hear?" which was the focus of my previous book *Words That Work: It's Not What You Say, It's What People Hear.* "What do Americans really want . . . really?" is the ultimate question that faces all of us who seek to provide products and services, govern communities, or simply help make life worth living for ourselves and for others on a daily basis. I put the emphasis on the word "really" because this book is, in essence, written by and for the American people. It has no ax to grind and no ideology to sell. What it does offer is the application of public opinion to address what genuinely matters most to most Americans:

- If you're a parent, you'll learn things about your kids you never knew, and you'll find out what they're doing when the door is closed. (If you still don't know about "Twittering" or the meaning of the phrase "friends with benefits" or if the term "sexiled" scares you, you may want to skip Chapter Six.)

- If you're an employee, you'll realize why your managers don't really understand you and why it's so hard for you to communicate with them. In good times, you'll know how to get a raise. In bad times, you'll know how to keep your job.

- If you're one of America's 17 million small-business owners, you'll discover the reasons why people buy and the reasons why they don't—not what they may tell *you*, but what they say to *me* about you and your products and services when they have no incentive or need to be polite.

- If you're a typical consumer, you'll find out why the fresh produce is always at the front of the grocery store, why hotel registration is increasingly stuck at the back of the lobby, and why service personnel should stop asking "Can I help you?"

- And if you're one of the tens of millions of Americans in their sixties and seventies, you'll be comforted to know you're not alone in realizing that the word "retirement" doesn't actually mean "retired" any longer.

The truth is, individual Americans have no clue what we actually think as a country or where we stand within a population that's increasingly segmented and separated by language, culture, and customs. Consider the following amusing examples:

- 90 percent of Americans think they're smarter than the average American. That means tens of millions of people are flat-out *wrong*.
- 61 percent of Americans think they're more attractive than the average man or woman. *Wrong* again, though who would have thought that people are more likely to overestimate their intelligence than their appearance?

Our perception of *who* we are, *what* we think, and *how* we behave is determined in part by where we grew up, how we grew up, our current socioeconomic status, and our access to the outside world. It's hard to have a good handle on what Americans believe and want because the United States is so *diverse*. There are 300 million of us, and we are more like a vegetable stew than a melting pot: lots of different ingredients, each separate and distinct. With that in mind, consider this your recipe book—for understanding the American people.

Even with increasing mobility, global awareness, and interaction (thanks to the Internet as well as cheaper airfares), a working-class family in Mississippi doesn't know what life is like for the residents of the tony Upper East Side of Manhattan, and vice versa. The assumptions are wrong and the stereotypes unfortunate. A number of years ago, I did a project for Southern Company, one of America's great electric utilities, headquartered in Atlanta with operations throughout Georgia, Florida, Alabama, and Mississippi. I asked a focus group of middle-class residents from suburban Chicago to give me one word or phrase to describe a company of that name. The responses: "hick," "dumb," "backward," and my personal favorite, "dueling banjos." As a people, Americans tend to look down on individuals with a pronounced Southern accent, and yet some of the most innovative corporations and cutting-edge technologies are bursting out of Atlanta, Charlotte, and the North Carolina Research Triangle. Business executives from Dallas and Houston may sound like good ol' boys, but they're brilliant with oil and gas, and they've outsmarted many a Yankee who tried to take advantage of them. The South may yet rise again.

I wrote this book in part because I'm tired of all the stereotypes and erroneous assumptions that we have absorbed through pop culture, television, movies, and the media. I've spent the better part of the last two decades getting to know this country more intimately than I ever thought possible, and I've had enough of our simple ignorance of what exists beyond our own little worlds.

I have heard too many business executives who earn more than half a million dollars a year claim to be middle-class.

I have seen too many politicians ignore the obvious signs of discontent among their constituents, telling friends that their reelection would be "a cakewalk" hours before they were thrown out of office.

I have watched too many teenagers beg for more adult attention in their lives to give them a reason to stay off the streets, and their parents surprised when the kids just give up and disengage or, worse, engage in behavior hazardous to their health.

I have been moved to tears when grandparents in their late sixties have to return to work because the promise of the American Dream lost out to the reality of their financial nightmare.

I have witnessed the ruinous behavior of senior vice presidents in Fortune 100 companies willfully ignoring *facts* presented to them because they don't want to look bad to their CEOs.

Keep making those daily decisions based on bad information. Keep ignoring what is *really* happening in your neighborhood, your state, and your country. If you don't understand what Americans think, then you don't understand the future of America—or your own future. And you will keep making the wrong decisions based on bad information every time.

But there are exceptions.

Media mogul Rupert Murdoch wasn't even born in America, but he sees and hears things that other Americans do not.

Owner of *The Wall Street Journal, The New York Post,* the *Times* of London, Fox News, 20th Century Fox, and a dozen other newspapers, television stations, and online giant MySpace, Murdoch is constantly on the prowl for more ways to reach more consumers. At a secluded weekend retreat for his top executives in 2006, Murdoch listened intently to presentations about how various parts of his News Corp media empire planned to connect with customers, expand their reach, and deliver more profit. The Pacific Ocean was only steps away, but the idyllic setting could not mask the anxiety in the room. Jobs were clearly on the line.

Early on day one, a focus group of late teens and early twentysome-things I had convened attacked Murdoch's companies—and Murdoch himself—for being completely out of touch with their generation and lack-ing any content worth paying for. At one point, one of the kids, a visual throwback to the 1960s, yelled out, *"You don't know us, and we don't need you!"* Murdoch leaned over to former News Corp president Peter Chernin and whispered, *"They're right, you know."* His various news outlets were challenged by the focus group participants for being pro-Republican, pro-conservative, and anti-youth, but it was only the last criticism that raised any concerns in the room.

By the third day, Murdoch was in full boil. Exasperated by what he believed to be a dangerous disconnect between his team and what he called "the emerging consumer," he interrupted a presentation from one of his editors and belted out:

*I know you people think I'm too old. Well, after listening to you, I think **you're** too old. I don't want to hear what you want. I want to hear what your consumers want, and I expect you to give it to them!*

Murdoch was furious that his management team was so out of touch. Here was a septuagenarian who had a better grasp of what a twenty-one-year-old really wants from the news than managers half his age or younger.

To be successful, you have to be willing to set aside what you know, even if it took you a lifetime to learn it. You have to listen, constantly, to a cacophony of information and learn to synthesize the bits and bytes that will help your business grow today, so you can prepare for and pros-per in the future. That's the mission of this text.

The aerospace industry is a perfect illustration of a business sector that's fallen out of touch and out of love with America. In the 1960s and early '70s, we admired the astronauts not out of respect for the incredi-ble science or the fact that they were able to explore outer space or walk on the moon, but because of a personal relationship with them. Kids knew the astronauts' names. Adults named their children after them. We all drank Tang because the astronauts drank Tang, even though it was virtually undrinkable. For several years, young people most wanted to be an astronaut when they grew up.

But that was then. Being an astronaut has long since fallen out of the top ten most desired occupations. Americans no longer appreciate or even recognize that computerization and miniaturization came right out of the space program. Aerospace engineers created the technology that contributed to the development of microwave ovens, satellites, MRIs, CAT scans, and computer chips that can store this book on your laptop in a small fraction of its capacity. For all that they have done and continue to do for America and the world, aerospace should be just as intriguing to us today as when man first landed on the moon four decades ago. Yet the aerospace industry is failing to connect because it has failed to explain its relevance to the American people—how its successful experiments and innovation factor into so many of the modern conveniences and high-tech advances our society has made in the last half century. Today's space station may yield tomorrow's new MRI technology, but no one cares. It just doesn't matter anymore, not because people don't care about the origin of new technology but because the aerospace industry doesn't relate that technology to their day-to-day lives.

Another form of information failure is willful ignorance. There was a time in the 1970s and 1980s when driving a Cadillac was a symbol of status and success. Or as Baseball Hall of Fame slugger Ralph Kiner once said, "Hitters of home runs drive Cadillacs, singles hitters jalopies." Today, nobody wants a Cadillac (other than the Escalade), except maybe Morty Seinfeld—and that's in reruns, no less. And who can blame them? American cars are out of style because the car companies failed to listen and respond to what Americans really wanted. My first job out of college was for the Wirthlin Group, pollsters to Ronald Reagan, Margaret Thatcher, and General Motors. I remember listening to a GM executive proclaim during our presentation that "GM is back" when he saw that young people gave their vehicles their highest ratings of any age group. What he didn't acknowledge, even though the data was right there in front of him, was that young people gave *every* automotive company high ratings, but that new drivers ranked GM at the bottom compared to all the other car companies. I scribbled the word "idiot" on a legal pad. I wish I had saved the note. Great information. Bad analysis.

For twenty years, Americans asked for cars that were reliable and long-lasting. That's what they really wanted. For twenty years the U.S. auto industry heard the public outcry for more fuel-efficient vehicles, yet they ignored it. When Toyota launched its bold Prius hybrid in Japan in 1997 and worldwide in 2001 to great fanfare, Detroit scoffed. Said an auto executive at the time, Americans wouldn't buy it because the hybrid "didn't have the kick" of a traditional engine. They were wrong. Horribly wrong.

Toyota, on the other hand, knew the days of cheap gas were numbered and did something about it. That smart, forward-looking strategy paid off when gas prices hit $4 per gallon in 2008 and SUV sales took a nosedive. For years you had to put your name on a waiting list to buy a Prius—that's how badly the Big Three auto execs misunderstood the public. By the time they finally started listening, the public had given up on them.

I'd like to tell you that for every business horror story, there is a success story that quantifies the value of knowing what Americans really want, but that's actually not true. There are many more business failures than success stories, which is why it is so important to understand what people really want.

As someone who spends more nights a year in a hotel room than at home, I can tell you the Westin Hotel group made a brilliant move with its "Heavenly Bed" concept, launched in 1999. Most midlevel business hoteliers believed in the bargain basement Red Roof Inn philosophy, that the amenities in the room didn't really matter because people spent such a short time in it, and most of that time with the lights off anyway. Westin, seeking to raise the bar and appeal to upscale business travelers without a Four Seasons expense account, conducted extensive public-opinion research only to discover that the bed *does* matter—because people spend eight hours in it. The CEO of Starwood Hotels at the time, Barry Sternlicht, modeled it after his own bed at home because that's what consumers said they wanted most from a hotel—*"a bed just like the one they slept in at home."* After testing literally hundreds of mattresses and linens, the *Heavenly Bed* was born—"10 layers of pure comfort, one extraordinary sleep experience"—and the Westin brand spiked in popularity.[2]

The bed isn't the only hotel room amenity that *really* matters. Can you guess what comes in second? With more than 23,000 beds at 150 properties in 23 countries, Diamond Resorts is the largest privately owned vacation ownership company in the world. In a global research study, they found that "relaxation" was the number one priority of their members and the most common definition of a good vacation. Digging deeper, the most important component of relaxation wasn't the nearby attractions or the comfort of the lobby or the great dinner they had the night before. It was how well they slept. And after the bed, the single greatest factor in sleep was the pillow. So the CEO, Stephen Cloobeck, had a box with about thirty pillows from all over the globe delivered to his home in Las Vegas, and he tested each one over a two-week period for length, weight and, in his words, "puffiness." The winner—a thirty-five-ounce pillow that guests now beg to buy. Not surprisingly, his resorts frequently have the highest customer satisfaction levels of any in the travel industry because he delivers what travelers *really* want.

In the skies, Southwest Airlines ranked number one in a December 2008 survey of business and opinion leaders,[3] despite the fact that only a fraction of business executives actually *fly* Southwest regularly. Why? The airline has a great reputation because it delivers the two things Americans want most from flying: a guaranteed cheap ticket and a highly likely on-time arrival (a safe plane is assumed). True, the flight attendants are actually pleasant, compared to the surly service on the legacy airlines (*"No, you can't have another minuscule package of peanuts, and don't even think about asking for a free soda refill"*). Dig deeper into the public psyche and you'll learn that the emotional truth passengers want more than anything else when flying is the confidence that comes with *predictability*. People know exactly what they're getting with Southwest—the guarantee of a cheaper flight. They're willing to put up with slightly longer lines and group seating because they're absolutely, positively saving money. These customers don't care about first-class; they couldn't afford it anyway. Sure, they'd like more leg room, but as American Airlines realized the hard way, they're not willing to pay enough for it to justify the financial loss of several rows of seats in the back of the plane to accommodate more room up front. Southwest realized before anyone else that gone are the days when flying was about glamour, privilege, and even comfort—so why fight it? Market toward what consumers expect from a product *today*, rather than trying to recapture the past. Flying is today's mass transit. Much like on subways and buses, customers will accept airplane crowding and a distinct lack of glam as long as it is cost-effective and reliable. (For those taking notes, *reliability* is the number one American wish for products and services.)

Similarly, JetBlue is an upscale adaption of the Southwest model. If Southwest is for working-class, slightly older Americans, JetBlue, founded in 1999 on the premise of "bringing humanity back to air travel," targeted the more youthful and upwardly mobile middle class.* These people can't afford first-class either, but they appreciate the sense of exclusivity that JetBlue offers. In addition to comfortable leather seats and inexpensive tickets, JetBlue recognized the *boredom* of air travel—the number one complaint about flying—and built TVs into every seatback to overcome it. Each passenger can surf thirty-six free channels of DIRECTV, a simple but welcome diversion. For six years in a row, *Condé Nast Traveler* readers recognized JetBlue as the "Best Domestic Airline."[4] No surprise. Consumers talk. JetBlue listens.

Las Vegas has figured out a path to success—twice—all because it knows more about its customers than its customers know about themselves. Vegas businesses invest heavily in polling and research—more than any other vacation destination—to help them understand what consumers truly want. And then they act on it. The gambling mecca transformed itself into a family destination when family travel was the big thing in the 1980s and 1990s. Excalibur and Treasure Island were created to give the kids something to do. Soon, every casino had to offer some sort of indoor theme parks, outdoor roller coasters, world-class circus acts, and 4-D experiences with SpongeBob SquarePants.

But when the family vacation idea began to lose steam, Vegas invented a concept that became one of the best-known television slogans of all time: "What happens in Vegas stays in Vegas." It's entertaining, with a bit of tongue-in-cheek intrigue—what naughty thing did you do? The ad campaign gave adults permission to be adults, to be a slightly different person after sunset in a city that truly never sleeps. As life became more stressful, people needed a place to let loose and let go. Vegas provided the escapist climate and experience they craved at a price they could actually afford.†

---

* There is a caveat. The CEO of JetBlue had to conduct an embarrassing mea culpa press tour after days of massive last-minute flight cancellations, extensive runway delays of as long as ten hours on planes with no heat, food, or clean toilets, and otherwise horrific customer service in February 2007 nearly destroyed its flyer-friendly image. Their public relations efforts included a first-ever "Customer Bill of Rights," which sounded great until another series of flight cancellations the following month caused flyers to question whether it was humanity or hell that JetBlue had brought to air travel.

† True, the 2009 recession hasn't been kind to Las Vegas. Stations Casinos slipped into bankruptcy, and several other companies, most notably MGM Mirage and Las Vegas Sands, had the fight of their lives. With virtually no warning, the extraordinary extravagance of the Vegas lifestyle was exactly what individual tourists and business conventions actively sought to avoid. As of this writing, it is possible to get a room that sold for $300 at Wynn Las Vegas in 2007 for $109 a night.

My first experience going undercover for a client was for Las Vegas impresario Steve Wynn to understand what Vegas consumers really want from a hotel and casino experience. I poked around resorts, looking for designs or amenities or services and then asked customers whether any of them were worth emulating. But let me be clear: Wynn never *copies* anything. He wants to know if anyone else has anything worth *surpassing*. His properties may not have the largest rooms, but they are the most tastefully designed. He may not offer the most amenities, but his are always the best. His rooms are stocked not just with luxury shampoos and lotions but with toothbrushes and razors—the things you'd expect at a Four Seasons—only Wynn's are of an even higher quality. Steve Wynn's goal is simple: to make your stay *memorable*. His latest hotel, called Encore, is a $2 billion resort featuring a mosaic made from red and orange Swarovski crystals.[5] Now that's memorable. And even Wall Street has recognized the excellence of Wynn—the only major publicly owned casino company in Vegas not fighting off bankruptcy.

This is part of differentiating what Americans want from what they *really* want. When it comes to travel, we'll choose the low frills price option to get where we're going, but we'll pay more to get more when we arrive.

As you can already tell, much of this book comes from my own personal experiences. I have lived by the maxim A. G. Lafley talks about at the beginning of this chapter. You might not know it to look at me, but pudgy people can still be quite stealthy. I know the American people at home and at work, and I know what they want and what they don't. I have driven routes with a FedEx driver and walked the distribution centers of Lowe's. I've played $1,000 hands of blackjack (with the casino's money) to learn what high rollers in Vegas really want, and I've been behind the counter at McDonald's (with snacking privileges). I know exactly how long it takes to board a 747 aircraft—thirty-eight minutes—and how many hotel rooms I could clean in a day (thirteen, though the industry standard is closer to sixteen). I am the ultimate secret shopper, and my job is to watch, listen, and learn. I've personally observed how companies interact with their customers and treat their employees. Then I took note of the unfiltered reactions of these everyday Americans. And in this book, I have woven these observations together with the threads of focus-group research and polling to display the true fabric of American sentiment.

My favorite undercover assignment was to hunt for apartments in New York, Washington, and San Francisco as a prospective renter on behalf of Stellar Management. I watched for whether the rental reps actually knew the apartment's amenities, whether they called me by my first name, whether they allowed me the time to explore on my own, and whether they asked me more questions than I asked them. Most important, did they seem to *love* showing the apartment to show me how much I would *love* living there? Rob Rosania, a principal in the company, had more passion for his properties, his renters, and their well-being than anyone I had ever met in real estate, and it helped his company weather the economic storm better than most. Never *underestimate* the power of passion in the sales and customer satisfaction process, or *overestimate* the success of the hard sell.

Not long ago, Kroger sent me to "secret-shop" at some of their grocery stores. Not surprisingly, lighting is one of the critical factors for shoppers. People want to see the food before they put it into their carts. They want to examine it, make sure it's clean and fresh. They want to check the expiration dates. They want to know what they're getting. We may eat in dimly lit restaurants and drink in dark bars all week long, but we want bright light in our grocery stores so we know we're getting what we paid for. If your supermarket is dark, customers will wonder about the produce and they'll take their business elsewhere. And what do people want most from a grocery store? Fresh produce. How do you make fresh produce look fresh? Spray it gently with a slight mist to give it a just-picked, dewy look. Lighting, misting, perfuming—it's all staging to spell "fresh" to the shopper because that's what the shopper really wants.

Presentation is important in retail, but customer interaction matters even more. With all due respect to the management of almost every store in America, listen up: You teach and train every employee to ask "Can I help you?" Big mistake. We've been socially trained to push strangers away, so the simple offer of help by someone you don't know most often elicits a no-thank-you. If you want to deliver what Americans really want, your opening line to your would-be customer can and must be a great deal more personalized and humanized. More on this later.

Timing also matters. The next time you find yourself at the grocery checkout, notice how the clerk asks if you found everything you needed.

Think about it. Why do they ask you at checkout? There are three people behind you, everyone is looking at what you bought, and the social pressure to keep the line moving is so great that no customer would *dare* stop the process to get that jar of dill pickles they couldn't find or the carton of cottage cheese they came to the store for in the first place and then forgot. If you had been asked while you were still cruising your cart down aisle three, it would have been a lot more helpful to you and more profitable for the store.

Often the customer is looking for "expertise." Throughout much of the 1990s I was a secret shopper for financial services at Merrill Lynch, with disastrous results. Most of the brokers—they are currently "financial advisers"—had no clue how to connect on a human level with a potential customer. They had all read the employee manual about how to sell Merrill Lynch services without really understanding that you can't sell retirement and finances with a script. After a few weeks of listening, I advised them to throw away the canned lines and instead to "individualize, personalize, and humanize" their approach. Money is too personal and too important to people to generalize the approach. They also had the wrong job title with "financial adviser." Anyone can give advice—and anyone can get advice from the personal finance section of the bookstore or on the Internet these days. But an "investment specialist" has specific training and is therefore more trusted because it suggests a higher level of expertise and wisdom, not just run-of-the-mill advice. A specialist is, well, special. They never did change their lexicon, and it's too late now.

When I first sketched the concept for this book in mid-2007, the U.S. economy was on a roll—an upward roll, that is. The Dow Jones Industrial Average reached a record 14,164 on October 9, 2007. The financial meltdown since then has devastated our trust in institutions, shattered our confidence in the future, and thoroughly undermined our economic and emotional equilibrium. This book had to be completely rewritten because we're just not the same people today that we were in October 2007, and we don't have the same priorities. Ask Americans, and most will tell you they're worried, anxious, even angry about the world around them and angry with America. Our financial system now has the dubious distinction of weathering the worst slide since the Great Depression. Records were being made as fast as money was being lost—worst one-week drop since 1933, worst October in twenty-one years, and so on. And in this economic deluge, the average working American has less than sixty days' savings put away for a rainy day—and one-fifth of us have no savings at all. That's a lot of people in a lot of pain.

President Barack Obama may come to regret his stunning political success. He inherited an economy in crisis and a people hungry for leadership. Americans are still angry about gas that once cost them $4 a gallon and the taxpayer-funded bailout of Wall Street that lined the pockets of too many CEOs as they were laying off thousands of workers and buying million-dollar commodes. America's unbending belief in the American Dream is waning, along with their belief that government and business will do the right thing. They don't like anyone. They don't trust anyone. And for the first time since the early 1940s, the future looks even bleaker than the present.

Remember Ronald Reagan's classic question to the nation during his 1980 debate with then-President Jimmy Carter: *"Are you better off today than you were four years ago?"* Almost no one can answer in the affirmative in 2009. Nine out of ten people say they have been personally affected in some way by the economic crisis—often tragically. Worse yet, they think it'll take years to dig out of this financial hole—one-third think it will take a decade or longer. And 11 percent even say, *"We'll never fully recover."*

Remember the now-famous words bellowed by Howard Beale in the 1976 movie *Network? "I'm mad as hell, and I'm not going to take it anymore!"* Turns out he is in good company. For the first time ever, a majority of the country now fears the next generation will inherit a world worse than this one. Simply put, these people are mad as hell.

Our national confidence is in pieces, our personal expectations shattered. We've seen bad things happen to our friends and family, and we feel hopeless to prevent it. Our horizon is narrower than ever before. We can only look ahead to the next day, the next month, and if we are thinking "long-term," next year. Defining the future as being twenty years from now—that time span died years ago. Our quality of life has become a day-to-day proposition. From the moment we wake up until the moment we go to sleep, we're desperately looking for

proof to suggest an improvement—any improvement—in our condition. We want evidence that our lives will be better—social life, political life, economic life, cultural life. Maybe that's why so many millions
of Americans got stung by day-trading in the 1990s and house-flipping
a few years later. The exploration for the proverbial light at the end of
the tunnel has become a day-to-day struggle—only now we believe
that the approaching light is actually a train that is going to hit us
head-on.

Even "trust" has collapsed. We have little tolerance now for promises
that were meant to be broken and pledges that were never meant to be
kept. People used to trust their spouses, their kids, their employees, and
their neighbors. We don't trust anyone anymore—just ask the booming
private detective industry. We have no faith in political leaders, no faith
in business leaders, and no faith in institutions. We are even losing
faith in faith itself. There was a time when the clergy was the most
trusted profession in America. But thanks to the Catholic Church sex
scandal and subsequent cover-up—as well as scandals among Protestant and Jewish leaders—there was a meltdown that affected everybody's faith in organized religion, Catholic or not. It was a seminal
moment that caused real damage to our psyche.

The person we trust most is "the American people." It's why Joe the
Plumber caught on during the 2008 presidential campaign (until his
story was beaten to death by the media). We assume the Average Joe is
more capable because he's less likely to be corrupt. Frankly, he doesn't
have time for corruption. He's just trying to keep his head above water.
So strong is this belief, that when the truth came out about Joe the
Plumber—that he wasn't really self-employed, that he didn't earn anywhere near $200K a year, that he wasn't a licensed plumber, and that
his name wasn't even Joe (it was Sam)—it really didn't matter! Joe the
Plumber had become an icon for the angry American small-business
owner. His story took on a life of its own because it was their story, even
if it wasn't actually his.

So what do Americans really want?

It is the ultimate question that faces businesses every day. Will we
pay money for a parking meter or drive an extra few blocks to find free
parking? Will we still pay $4 for a cup of coffee at Starbucks or make it
at home for a fraction of the cost? When did our lives get so hectic that

we can't even slow down to order fast food? Why do we get anxious waiting for a microwave dinner that takes just five minutes to cook? If you understand how people think, live, and behave, you can predict the next great consumer breakthrough.

We have become a prickly, schizophrenic society with contradictions and hypocrisies that would make even *Eliot Spitzer* blush. We claim we want Social Security saved and strengthened, but then we vote against those who try to reform it. We say we want less-expensive health care, but then we rebel when it doesn't give us access to all the treatment we want. We claim we want quality, but then we buy the cheapest item on the shelf. So how do we prioritize in this tough economic, political, and cultural environment? The more you know about how people think and feel, the more comfortable you'll be in making either ten-dollar choices or ten-million-dollar decisions.

This book is about understanding priorities, not trivialities or frivolities. It is about all the contradictions, large and small, between what we want and what we really need.

Consider this an invitation—an invitation to view the American psyche as it actually is, not as it once was or as we wish it would be. Allow me to disassemble the preconceived notions we have about one another. Let's lay all the pieces of the American condition out in front of us, openly and honestly. And then let's put the pieces back together in a way that actually resembles the society in which we live. If you're looking for a real discussion of our public hopes and private fears, wants, and needs, you've come to the right place.

There is practical information in this book that will help you make key business decisions. It is for business owners and executives who want to learn how to improve their services, grow their companies, and connect with their customers. It's also written for elected officials who must understand that the responsibility is on them to restore their credibility and rebuild America's optimism—and make the right sort of changes for people who voted for them and those who will follow generations from now.

But even if your job doesn't require you to guide corporate policy or seek reelection every two years, there is plenty in here for you, too. We all share a continuing responsibility to better understand one another. Understanding is an essential underpinning for our community. The more we have of it, the better—especially at a time when our public institutions are wavering.

My hope is that this book brings you closer to your neighbors and them closer to you. This isn't about the guy next door who sprays grass clippings on your yard or the kid across the street who rides his bike onto your lawn. This book is written for the Salt Lake suburbanites who want to know more about their inner-city neighbors in Detroit. It's for the latte lovers at Pike Place in Seattle who are interested in the lives of their Wrangler-wearing neighbors in West Texas.

Your neighbor is every American who resides from sea to shining sea and all points in between. Take this opportunity to meet them, listen to them, and learn from them. This is your chance to understand what they really, *really* want out of life.

WHAT AMERICANS REALLY WANT RIGHT NOW

CATEGORY	WINNER	NOTES
Airline	Southwest	For the fifth consecutive year, Southwest carried more domestic passengers in 2008 than any other American airline.
Beer	Bud Light	Bud Light actually wins both the light beer category and the overall beer category as the best American seller. The student has surpassed the master, as Budweiser ranks second overall.
Soft Drink	Coca-Cola Classic	At 17.2% market share in 2007, Coke leads the pack, followed by Pepsi-Cola at 10.7% and Diet Coke at 10%.
Overall Vehicle	Ford F-150	Ford sold 515,513 of these trucks in 2008, particularly impressive considering the spike of the price of oil in that year. Americans still love their pickups. The Chevy Silverado placed second overall, with 465,065 sold.

CATEGORY	WINNER	NOTES
Nonpickup Vehicle	Toyota Camry	Toyota sold 436,617 Camrys, followed by the Accord, Corolla, and Honda Civic, and Nissan Altima respectively. The highest-selling American-made sedan was the Chevy Impala at 265,840.
Breakfast Cereal	Cheerios	Average annual sales account for around $268 million.
Mobile Phone	Apple iPhone 3G	The iPhone is on the march. It finally surpassed the Motorola RAZR as the leading handset purchased by adult consumers in the United States in the third quarter of 2008.
Notebook Computer	Hewlett Packard	HP had a market share of 20.8% in the first quarter of 2008, with second place going to Dell at 15.1%
Evening News	*NBC Nightly News with Brian Williams*	*The NBC Nightly News* has consistently won the ratings battle since Brian Williams took the helm in 2004, with the exception of a brief time in 2007 when ABC took the lead.
Morning News	NBC *Today* show	As of early March 2009, the *Today* show had notched 690 consecutive weekly wins.
Top Rated Prime-time TV Show	*American Idol*	Averaging 28.75 million viewers on Tuesdays and 27.78 million on Wednesdays in the 2008 season, *Idol* dominated. *Dancing with the Stars* was the next most popular, followed by *Desperate Housewives* at 18.21 million. The highest sitcom was *Two and a Half Men*, ranking 17th overall at 13.64 million.
Website	Google	Based on total hits. Google, at 293 million hits per day as of March 2009, is followed, in order, by Yahoo!, YouTube, Facebook, and MySpace.

CATEGORY	WINNER	NOTES
Talk Radio Show	*The Rush Limbaugh Show*	At 14.25 million average weekly listeners, Rush remains king. With 13.5 million apiece, NPR's *Morning Edition* and *All Things Considered* are next.
Retail Store	Walmart	Walmart by far generates the most global revenue among retail stores, totaling $374.5 billion in 2008.
Credit Card	Visa	Visa had a 46% share of the U.S. credit card market in 2008, compared to Master Card's 36%, American Express's 12%, and Discover's 6%.
Restaurant	McDonald's	Americans like their food fast and cheap. In 2008, McDonald's had 13,918 restaurants in the United States. The closest "sit-down" restaurant is Denny's at 2,500 locations.

1

I CAN SEE CLEARLY NOW:
What Americans Really Want in Their Daily Lives

What women want: To be loved, to be listened to, to be desired, to be respected, to be needed, to be trusted, and sometimes just to be held. What men want: Tickets for the World Series.

—DAVE BARRY

Be glad that you're greedy; the national economy would collapse if you weren't.

—MIGNON MCLAUGHLIN (AUTHOR)

The alarm buzzes insistently, pulling us out of bed and into the maelstrom of daily life. On comes the television so you know whether your company has gone bankrupt the night before or if today is going to be a wet one, and if traffic is going to be a nightmare or just the usual morning hassle. Set the shower temperature to exactly the same degree, use the same soap, same shampoo and conditioner, reach for the towel hung exactly in the same place it was the day before and the day before that. Stumble to the kitchen for a quick breakfast, or maybe grab coffee at exactly the same place on your way in to work. You leave the house at the same time each day and take the same route to work—unless you're running late, which you probably are.

Breaking into the morning ritual is for business what teenagers are to new-product development: the earlier you hook 'em, the more loyal they become. Mornings are about habits; at night, you have time, and that means choices and decisions. Every night can be a different experience. But in the morning, people are creatures of a routine that can last for years. Once people develop those habits, it's almost impossible to break them. And for business, once you're *in* their morning routine, it's almost impossible to be dethroned.

Americans have bedrock favorites. Hamburgers are our favorite food, far more than apple pie and hot dogs. Our favorite vehicle is still a pickup truck. Our favorite sport is football (even though people still call baseball America's pastime). We salute the American flag as the ultimate symbol of our American-ness, and gaze in wonder at the Statue of Liberty, the structure most symbolic of America's pride and patriotism, despite having been designed and built in France. We consider the Fourth of July as the most "American" day of the year. Hometown parades, barbecuing in the backyard, fireworks—all in honor of the birth of our nation. Two sporting events come next: the Super Bowl and the World Series.

Other American hallmarks are more subtle, but just as impactful. This chapter will help you understand the daily habits of Americans, from morning to night. We'll follow them as they commute to work, eat in restaurants, and we'll even peek into their bedrooms. For those of you in the business of selling products, you must *understand* people and their habits in order to *become* their habit.

GETTING OUT OF BED

A majority of Americans now begin most of their days in the dark. I'm not making a judgment on their level of awareness; I mean it literally. People who live in the far suburbs and beyond in the newly developed exurbs are up before the sun rises because they want the bigger homes with the larger lawns and are therefore saddled with the longest commutes. More than one-third of working Americans are awake by six a.m. and out the door by seven a.m. for a commute to work that is an hour or longer. In fact, more than 3 million Americans travel fifty miles or more *one-way* to get to work. The opportunities for connectivity and product placement in these early hours of the day are limitless—

and essential—for any business seeking to establish itself as a daily need rather than just an occasional desire.

In that first encounter with consciousness, people want to know what's going on in their community, their state, the country, and the world. For those first few seconds, the morning news isn't a luxury—it's a lifeline. Television beckons us first with what matters most to us—weather (to determine what we wear) and traffic (to determine when we leave and what route we take). The radio isn't relevant unless and until we get into our cars.

And the newspaper that once sat at your front door isn't relevant at all. Are you one of the 2,733 people who gave up reading *The New York Times* last month? At just about the time you read this book, the daily circulation rate for the so-called "newspaper of record" will sink below one million people for the first time in decades. They're not alone. Other than *The Wall Street Journal,* all 25 of the most read daily newspapers across the country lost print readership in 2008.[6] While print readership has declined for several years, the pace of collapse is accelerating. The fact is, people under age thirty don't read the print edition of newspapers anymore, and almost no one reads the classifieds, help-wanted, or full-page color advertisements that paid for the reporters, the photographers, the graphic artists, and the small profit for the owners. If you want to buy, sell, lease, or rent anything, it's all done online—and that's not going to change. For example, 85 percent of all apartment referrals that come from advertising are now generated from online sources. Put another way, less than 15 percent of all apartment rentals were in response to a newspaper ad.[7]

So how do you find out what part of the world blew up the night before—and which city is in flames right now? The answer matters, because we want to know what everyone else will be talking about at work so we won't seem uninformed or disengaged. But no longer is it necessary to hold the news in our hands or settle for news that is ten hours old. You can get the weather, traffic, and a dollop of news from multiple sources without leaving your bedroom thanks to the Internet.* And now the

---

* More than 73 million unique viewers click on a daily newspaper website each month in 2009, according to Nielsen Online. That represents a sizeable 10% increase in just one year.

LESSONS FROM AMERICA

A warning to marketers and merchandisers: Just because people are watching and listening to morning programming doesn't mean they're paying attention. On the contrary, we have done studies to test the recall of consumers to advertisements and product placements, and the results are horrible. The size of the audiences tuned in may be increasing but their attention span is not. A better strategy is to sell morning-related products at the end of the evening (ten p.m. or later) when people are paying attention and planning for the next day's activities.

news comes to you courtesy of news alerts that are sent directly to your phone—a popular application among twentysomethings who care enough about the world around them to stay informed.

For everyone else, there's the *Today* show, *Good Morning America,* and the other wake-me-up-but-not-too-loudly breakfast television programming. But these programs need to be available when viewers want to watch. The three cable networks have discovered the early nature of their viewers and now start their programming at six a.m. Sure enough, some of the highest ratings on the East Coast are at the 6:45 a.m. quarter hour, just before people head out the door. By the time the *Today* show and *Good Morning America* come on the air at seven a.m., much of their would-be audience has already left the building. Another note to programmers: simulcasting the network morning show on the radio is a way to build audience—remember all those minutes spent in the car? The morning-show hosts may not want to get up any earlier, but the rest of America has to, and at some point in the next five years you'll see the networks adjust their schedules accordingly. Six a.m. is the new seven a.m.

One caveat about morning habits in a family: the traditional gender roles still hold true. In two-parent families, it's Mom who wakes the kids, gets them dressed, throws together breakfast (it's a stretch to suggest that breakfast is *"cooked"* anymore), feeds the pets, and gets everyone out the door. Rightly or wrongly, women are responsible for the home and family—and that means getting the children ready for school or day care in the morning. Dad, for the most part, only has to motivate himself to get out of bed, get ready for work, and perhaps drop a family member off at a convenient location. Women have the additional stress of self and family—multiple showers, multiple breakfasts, multiple lunches. That means they have the most powerful voice in those morning products and services, and because they are loyal to what works for them, they rarely break from habit and tradition.

GETTING TO WORK

Watch the average American in the final moments before they leave for work.

Cell phone? Check, hooked on your belt or in your pocket or in your bag or purse.

Laptop? Check, in the briefcase.

BlackBerry? Check, in your pocket, bag, or purse.

Wallet? Check. Or at least a debit card.

Keys . . . oops, most likely to have gone missing because they matter less to you than your other gadgets. (Note to marketers: it's time to pitch a Never Lost system for car keys.)

Even before you leave the house, you've probably been online, checked your e-mail, made or received a cell phone call, and if you're thirty or younger, received a text message.

But the transition to work begins the moment you step outside your home. At that moment, you're out in the World and girding for what the World is going to throw at you. It's the second-most unpleasant moment of the day (after waking up) for many Americans, and yet we do it day in, day out for decades. Put your key in the ignition, start your car, back out of the garage, and head off to work. It's a painful daily occurrence that has become even more excruciating in recent years. But since we spend so much time in cars, and because we are so thoroughly dissatisfied with the experience, there are ample opportunities for businesses to meet unmet commuter needs—and for Americans to live their daily lives as clean and green as they talk.

Americans are quite good at supporting "bold action" for the greater good, but their actual record of personal participation and self-sacrifice is spotty at best. Our collective intentions are clear, but our individual follow-through is inconsistent. Nowhere is this more evident than in issues involving the environment.

THE COFFEE CONUNDRUM

"The Best Part of Waking Up Is Folgers in Your Cup."

"Coffee is for closers." Go ahead and chuckle, but coffee is serious business. Americans drink more coffee than anyone on the planet—400 million cups of coffee every day.[8] More than half of all Americans (57 percent) have at least one cup a day, and a majority of them start their mornings with coffee and keep up their caffeine intake well into the afternoon. The average twentysomething drinks *three* cups of coffee a day, and 17 percent of all adults drink a *"gourmet"* coffee every day. All this coffee consumption isn't just about thirst. People think it improves their mental focus and actually believe coffee is healthy for them (hold the whipped cream and caramel . . .).[9]

Coffee used to be simple—a pot brewed at home with the old standby Maxwell House, or an even simpler approach—Taster's Choice instant coffee. For those who wanted their coffee on the run, every diner and deli offered a standard 99-cent cuppa joe. Then Starbucks exploded this routine daily beverage into an upscale, $4 "coffee experience." By building the company "one cup at a time," as founder Howard Schultz likes to say, Starbucks rang up huge profits with its double-shot-low-fat-mocha-cappuccinos, and then introduced drinks that had *no* coffee at all to lure the no-caffeine crowd—and even those who don't like coffee at all. Every drink had its own unique name; even the coffee makers were called "baristas." And if you had time to relax, Starbucks stocked its small shops with small tables and chairs. It mimicked the Parisian café scene. Sure enough, people overlooked the sky-high prices for the atmosphere sadly lacking at the average corner diner. Even the accoutrements of drinking coffee have evolved. It used to be that coffee cups didn't have fancy lids or cardboard sleeves to hold them. Now you can't buy a cup without them.

Then some old-fashioned brands got into the game. Dunkin' Donuts, which has been making coffee for six decades, crowed about surveys claiming their coffee handily beat Starbucks in blind taste tests. Smart. Very smart.* The Dunkin' campaign went a step further, urging their loyalists to bring their Starbucks friends back to earth with messages like "Friends don't let friends drink Starbucks."[10] It worked. Dunkin', having lost the doughnut wars to Krispy Kreme, reemerged stronger and more profitable as the place for coffee.

McDonald's has also entered the coffee wars, selling convenience and pro-

---

* While it's a real challenge to convince Americans that taste tests aren't rigged, it is one of the most powerful and surprisingly underutilized methods of communicating a superior product. Providing names of participants, locations of trials, and even the date of the event helps build credibility for television advertising, and giving the exact percentage results builds credibility for print ads.

moting price in an ongoing advertising campaign more costly than all the other coffee companies combined. You can see their logo-branded vehicles and their blow-up cups of coffee up and down the California coast, an in-your-face marketing effort much too pedestrian for Starbucks (though I must admit it makes me instantly thirsty for an ice-blended mocha every time I see it).

And let's not forget the newest challenge to the Starbucks franchise, The Coffee Bean & Tea Leaf stores, connecting the laid-back Southern California experience with *hand-crafted beverages* and salespeople who really seem to enjoy serving customers. At a time when Starbucks is closing stores and shrinking presence, The Coffee Bean is still growing. One reason is the corporate culture—particularly important to younger coffee connoisseurs. Whereas Starbucks is corporate, regimented, and cookie-cutter, The Coffee Bean is more individualized and customer-focused—you can actually create your own unique blends of coffee, tea, and frozen beverages. And while Starbucks is a publicly traded company, Coffee Bean is family-owned—and proud of it. As Coffee Bean President Mel Alias likes to say, *"We serve customers, not shareholders."*

Then McDonald's joined the coffee wars, launching its "McCafe" coffee campaign in Seattle, the sacred birthplace of Starbucks, and suggested McDonald's coffee drinkers stage an "intervention" with friends who were paying too much for their coffee. Sure enough, McDonald's breakfast food sales increased as a result.

The purpose of this discussion is not to detail the coffee wars. It's to suggest to business how to benefit from them. Consider two lessons:

1. Position your product to benefit from the American love affair with coffee, even if your business isn't selling cups of joe. The cup holders in your car (one of the most popular automotive innovations) were invented for people who wanted to take their coffee on the road with them (as well as for people who were sick of their kids spilling soda in the car). The coffee shops that are opening in bookstores encourage patrons to stay longer and buy more. It's not the coffee you should focus on—it's the experience surrounding the coffee that is going to make businesses successful. Americans *love* coffee. If your product helps them love it all the more, then they'll love your product just the same. Share the love, then share the profits.

2. Follow the example of Dunkin' Donuts and McDonald's and *refuse* to play follow-the-leader. Starbucks blazed a trail that advanced the American addiction to coffee, but then forgot what it was they were actually selling—coffee—and what Americans were actually buying. Their competitors had room to maneuver because they focused much more on the product and far less on the experience. Lesson: You don't have to be the first, but you must constantly reevaluate how to be the best. Identifying unmet needs and filling them is a constant process—but the core product or service offering always matters most.

We have come to the collective decision that it is socially and morally unacceptable for people, governments, or corporations to pollute the air or foul the water—regardless of the economic consequences. Most readers will take this as a given, though it wasn't so long ago that a majority of Americans prioritized tangible jobs and lower prices over less tangible environmental standards. Even today there are exceptions. For example, Americans are more concerned about the consequences of continued dependence on Middle Eastern oil than the long-term environmental impact of drilling and burning that oil.

It boils down to a single word: consequences. To understand the shifting American public opinion about the environment is to understand the shifting prioritization of perceived conflicts and *consequences* of various public policies. The environment has never been the top issue or even somewhere in the top three in any presidential contest simply because there have always been other more immediately pressing priorities: war, jobs, cost of living, energy, health care, etc. Until the latter half of this decade, any political call for precipitous action to improve the environment was perceived to have negative consequences on a more important public priority. Efforts by environmental organizations to address the specific consequences of environmental decline were either too hot and emotional, undermining their credibility, or too scientific and wonkish, limiting their public appeal.

Two events changed everything: Hurricane Katrina and *An Inconvenient Truth*. The emotional impact of watching a great American city literally drown on live television combined with the intellectual impact of former Vice President Al Gore's ninety-minute glorified slide show made awareness of global warming and climate change universal—and changed our perceptions and expectations about the environment forever.* On its own, Katrina would still have left an indelible mark on the public psyche, but because *An Inconvenient Truth* gave an academic, scholarly rationale to the greatest natural disaster on American soil in modern times, it screamed for immediate action—even if no one quite knows what to do, or how to do it.

---

* What was different about Katrina as compared to all other man-made or natural disasters was the worsening plight of the victims over several days, the ability of television to bring the plight home in graphic detail, the inability of anyone anywhere to do anything about it, and the fact that it was happening right here on American soil.

International corporations have borne the brunt of shifting attitudes. American consumers fully expect Corporate America to be "committed to preserving and protecting the environment," and they demand tangible evidence that it is repairing whatever damage it has done, but that doesn't necessarily translate into a personal willingness to pay for it, sacrifice for it, or change their daily lifestyle for it. Two-thirds of Americans want Corporate America to take an active, leading role in making environmentally friendly behavioral decisions, but only one-third even *claim* they would pay more, give more, or get less.

It is intellectually insufficient to address the environment without raising the topic of energy, since energy exploration and energy usage have a greater impact on the environment than any other human activity. Fully 92 percent of Americans agree with the statement "More energy production and a clean environment can coexist." A similar percentage agrees that:

> *By using fewer resources to produce more energy, we pollute less and can help reduce the pace of global warming. By conserving our energy resources, we ultimately conserve and preserve our environment.*

Americans see energy policy as a genuine opportunity to look to the future in order to prevent the mistakes of the past—from environmental tragedies like the Exxon *Valdez* to the energy shortages that are simply unacceptable in our twenty-first-century economy.

Let me be clear about this: What Americans really want is more than just lower prices at the pump or the meter. When it comes to energy and the environment, we are more than just consumers. Sure, it may have taken four-dollars-a-gallon gas prices to shock the country into action, but the impact of soaring energy prices is lasting. We are seeking a permanent partnership between public policy and corporate technology that will take us boldly through the twenty-first century, much as the automobile and airplane changed our twentieth-century lives. Americans trust technology. The more futuristic the science, discovery, and technology, the greater the public embrace.

The current buzzword in pop culture is "conservation," and it is often articulated by Hollywood celebrities just before boarding their private jets to whisk them to Vegas, Aspen, or Cabo. But in reality, what

ENVIRONMENTAL
WORDS THAT WORK

So what do Americans really want when it comes to environment and energy?

- As far as process, nothing matters more than "progress."
- In terms of strategy, "a step-by-step approach."
- In terms of outcomes, "cleaner," "safer," and "healthier."
- In terms of technology, the most "advanced," "breakthrough," "twenty-first century," "state of the art."
- What do they really want from government and corporations? "Accountability" and "responsibility." And don't talk about "vision." Americans want "bold action." NOW.

Americans really want is *energy efficiency*. Allow me to insert the voice of the people here. In an early 2008 survey we conducted, Americans picked energy efficiency over energy conservation by a sizeable 67 to 28 percent margin. Similarly, the public is seeking "better use of natural resources" rather than "conserving natural resources" by an equally substantial 55 to 19 percent margin. In plain English, they expect government policy and the energy industry to **"do more with less."** In that same 2008 survey, when gas prices were at three dollars a gallon, Americans still prioritized "more efficient energy" over "less expensive energy" by a healthy 3 to 2 ratio. Why? Because efficiency addresses our national energy needs and leads to lower prices without making us change our individual, personal behavior. It also addresses the *long-term* problems of increasing energy demand, fewer natural resources, and increasing dependence on unstable or even dangerous regions of the world for the power we need. *More efficient energy* is a *cure* to the disease. *Less expensive energy* is just a way to mask the pain we will eventually feel.

Similarly, a policy that emphasizes research and addresses every form of energy—including "alternative fuels"—in a truly expansive fashion will be welcomed and embraced. It may take years, or even decades, but

ENERGY
WORDS THAT WORK

Conservation matters most to Americans with regard to energy and the environment, but there are six words that are uniquely energy-oriented in focus and desirability:

DIVERSITY, so that we are not too dependent on any single source or single region of the country or world for our energy supply.

EFFICIENCY, so that we can get more energy with less effort, and get more out of the energy we use.

SUSTAINABILITY, so that the energy we depend on today will be available tomorrow.

RELIABILITY, so that we know that the energy we need will be there *when* we need it.

LONG-TERM, which means twenty years or more.

COMPREHENSIVE, which means oil, gas, electricity, renewables—*everything.*

the public wants to hear from and will reward companies and policies that are pushing the technological envelope right now. *"We must depend on oil and gas today, but we are searching every day for better alternatives for tomorrow."* Automobiles such as the wildly successful Toyota Prius "Hybrid" are exactly what Americans want and are willing to pay for because they offer a clean conscience along with clean energy.

The cost of gas is the biggest concern with the daily commute. In fact, it's transcended the commute and is now a top political issue. When gas prices go up, driving leaps to the top of the heap of concerns for Americans. It is not just a topic of water-cooler conversation. It changes how people live (for the worse) and causes lasting anxiety and real anger.

When gasoline prices were in the $3 range and climbing, I convened a focus group of working moms in Los Angeles for the American Petroleum

CORPORATE ENERGY
WORDS THAT WORK

"We have the best scientists, the best engineers, and the best technicians in the world. It's time to put them to work to develop a twenty-first-century energy program that frees us from dependency on hostile OPEC nations, unleashes the power of American innovation, and protects our precious environment for our children and for generations to come."

Institute. These were all committed Southern Californians, jaded by their long commutes and snarled freeways—and all had the added responsibility of children. They had to leave home earlier and earlier in the morning to get to work. They had no idea how long it would take to get home at night. They had chauffeuring responsibilities that added to the stress. And now they were paying more for gas than many could afford. Some had already modified their behavior, giving up their cherished solo commutes for carpools, while others had given up driving to work altogether, settling on mass transit. Others had changed jobs to be closer to home. Some quit going to the movies or driving to Las Vegas for weekend getaways. They talked about trading in the gas guzzlers and buying hybrid cars instead (although as discussed later on, this car-swap trend has been slow). And when gas hit $4 a gallon during the summer of 2008, these moms told me with venom in their voices that it caused them to stop driving, stop shopping, and stop spending. The meltdown in consumer optimism in 2009 was in great part caused by gas prices in 2008.

Once you get into the car in the morning and head for work, prepare for a long drive. America is a nation on wheels. To get where they need to go, fully 90 percent of Americans say they usually drive, reporting an average of 87 minutes a day behind the wheel. For car commuters, it's an average of 100 minutes; for parents with children at home, an average of 104 minutes (compared with 77 minutes for people without kids at home). Less than 5 percent of the population takes public transportation to work and only 12 percent carpool. That means about 100 million people *drive alone* to work each day.

It is nearly impossible to make driving a truly pleasant experience for Americans. The joys of driving on the open roads are something of our nostalgic past, because today our roads are not exactly open and thus the experience falls far short of joyous. Too much about driving pisses us off: gas prices, road conditions, traffic, trucks, fast drivers, slow drivers, rude drivers, kids screaming in the backseat, the weather . . . you name it. Americans are looking for something—anything—that can either help them forget the frustrations of driving or help them feel *productive* during that time. It's no wonder car amenities like satellite radio, iPod docks, Bluetooth accessories, and built-in cell-phone chargers are hot sellers. Build a useful car accessory, and you've got an instant audience.

Look around the next time you're stuck in rush-hour traffic. The roads and bridges we drive on are in terrible shape. The 2007 bridge collapse in Minneapolis and the levee failures in New Orleans in 2005 and Cedar Rapids in 2008 are tragic reminders not to take infrastructure for granted. But let's agree to bury the word "infrastructure" beneath the tons of concrete it represents. The word smacks of bureaucracy. There's nothing that benefits you personally from infrastructure. If you talk instead about "highways," "bridges," "reservoirs," and "schools"— then it becomes a number one priority for the public because it becomes *personal.* You have to put it into human terms before it can really make sense. We don't want potholes destroying our cars. We don't want chemicals or junk pouring into our sewers because it'll harm our drinking water. If the schools are crumbling, it makes us fear for our children. We want air clean enough that we cannot see it, and water that doesn't have particles in it. The overwhelming majority of Americans consider clear air and clean water a right, not a privilege. And so is getting to work without the day-to-day hassles of unsafe roads, unsafe cars, and four-dollar-per-gallon gas.

But while gas prices may have made us sick, they didn't turn us green (pardon the pun). Although the trend toward fuel-efficient cars is growing—and growing at enough of a pace to put a serious hurt on Detroit—the trend is probably slower than you think. The average household owns two cars, trucks, or sport utility vehicles—and one in four owns three or more. Americans are still more likely to drive American-made cars, and it's likely to be a four-door sedan. If they have a second vehicle in the family, it might be a pickup truck or SUV—particularly if they live west of the Mississippi or south of the Mason-Dixon Line. If you're fifty or older, the brands in your driveway are most likely to be Chevrolet and Ford. If you're younger than thirty, it's a foreign car (though it may have been built in America), and it's most likely a Toyota or a Honda.

Americans would like their cars to be a little more fuel-efficient, and they appreciate any innovations that make the commute easier or less boring. But so far, there has not been a nationwide ditching of SUVs and mass purchasing of hybrids. Four-dollar gas might have affected our car-buying and -driving habits forever, but the change has not been wholesale or immediate. Since gas prices look more like an EKG than a straight line, it is unclear whether people will really buy the more fuel-efficient, four-cylinder boxy car rather than the more convenient SUV they've been chauffeuring their family in for a decade now. In today's economy, it's still not cost-effective to junk a still-functioning American gas guzzler to buy a relatively pricey new foreign hybrid. When it comes time to buy the *next* car, many Americans *are* downsizing, but the process will be slow, and that's why the average American family's car situation hasn't changed much. But American car companies, and people's perceptions of them, have certainly changed.

The bankruptcy of two of the Big Three auto companies would have been unimaginable just a decade ago. Not long ago there was a time when most people felt what was good for General Motors was good for America. No longer. I conducted a research project for GM several years ago that is still valid today. At the time, half of the car-buying public felt GM was "trapped in the past," and "no longer makes cars that people want to buy." They wanted GM to focus on the next generation of *innovative* cars and trucks that are *safer, more environmentally friendly*, and *require less gasoline.* The results were presented to senior management. Nothing happened. Instead, GM kept churning out big trucks and SUVs, each generation bigger than the last. When they created a hybrid Chevy Tahoe, it appealed to SUV drivers who were willing to consider 21 mpg a fuel-efficiency victory. Why do people buy it? Because people really want energy efficiency even as they insist on driving SUVs the size of a small bus.

Contrary to popular opinion, size does really matter—to some car owners. So does guilt for destroying the environment. This is not a case of hypocrisy—both attributes matter. Consumers found themselves trapped between two competing and contradictory values: a healthy environment and a safe vehicle. The challenge, then, was to develop a big car with decent gas mileage. So Cadillac rolled out a hybrid version of its Escalade SUV with a televised appeal that managed to work the word "luxury" into an eighty-eight-word ad no less than four times, underscoring one of the prime reasons people will (or won't) pay $50,000-plus for this vehicle. Luxury used to be enough to sell to almost everyone. But now Americans expect a little more:

- absolve us of some environmental guilt *so that* our friends don't think worse of us
- buffer us against tumultuous gas prices, *so that* I never have to think twice about filling the tank *and*
- let my entire family ride in comfort, *so that* the kids aren't complaining in the backseat

Yes, some Americans (with some means) will pay $50K for all that! But most still won't.

The problem for GM is that it always forgot the "so that" in its promotions. For them, the marketing was always about the attributes of the car rather than the quality of life of its occupants. They pitched their cars to the way people *think*, when people actually buy cars (and most products and services) for the way it makes them *feel*. After two decades of decline, GM finally figured out what Americans really wanted, but they didn't and still don't have a handle on how to communicate it back to us. Whether they unlock this newfound potential and unleash a more personalized, humanized approach to their marketing will determine whether GM is still around when you read this passage. That, or making better cars that people actually want to buy.

This communication lesson applies to almost any moribund industry with deep U.S. roots and the moxie to produce real innovation and change. Here are the five simple communication principles that the embattled American business community needs to articulate every day:

WORDS THAT WORK: REBUILDING TRUST IN AMERICAN CORPORATIONS

"Rebuild" the company reputation one credible step at a time. People will not buy the products and services of a company they think is going bankrupt and won't be around to service any guarantees. Consumers think in terms of years, not quarters. If people don't believe you have a future, they won't include you in theirs.

"Renew" the commitment to consumers and those who might be interested in your products. This is not just about making great products or providing exceptional service. It's also about making a genuine commitment to the communities they serve. Starting about a decade ago, Europeans began to stop buying products from companies they felt weren't good corporate citizens, even if those products were a little cheaper or a little better. That same behavior is heading to America.

"Revitalize" the image of the brands and products. We are more future-focused than ever before, and we want things that are up-to-date and modern. While we appreciate tradition and definitely applaud a "back to basics" approach, we would rather have the product benefits of the future than the products of the past.

"Refresh" the advertising and communications effort. With more distractions than ever, companies that market the same old way won't even capture the same old eyeballs. Historically, automotive ads consistently finish at the bottom of the Super Bowl ad contests because they're—in a word—boring. Without refreshing the marketing, you won't refresh the product or get the customer interested.

"Restore" the faith and confidence of the people in all that the company does. This is about "buzz," and it is both internal and external. Bad buzz leads to brand equity collapse. Taking billions of dollars in taxpayer money leads to brand equity collapse as well, only more slowly and painfully—unless it is paid back quickly and with interest.

Returning to the automotive example, GM needed to remind consumers about the company's long track record of innovation and success. For example, people were unaware that the still-popular Corvette is a GM brand. Most important, they didn't know that GM created OnStar, the incredibly innovative emergency-response device that has helped

100,000 crash victims and more than a million passengers and counting.[11] The point is that companies can *never* assume that consumers ever know enough about your brands. Customers can easily compare features and prices of products for themselves. It falls on *you* to teach them about what you offer them and their community beyond the bounds of the sticker, label, or box. And it falls on *you* to tie the value of your products back to your company so you get the credit you rightfully deserve.

One caveat: it's the *quality* of the features that matters, not the *quantity*. If you focus on the cornucopia of choices, you'll start to sound like a low-rent buffet.

GETTING *CONNECTED*

The most important aspect of the morning routine isn't a behavior, and it's more than just about the availability of new technology. It's an attitude. From the moment we wake up in the morning until the moment we go to sleep at night, we are on a never-ending search to be *connected*. Whether it's news and information when we first wake up or the cup of coffee we share when we arrive at the office, from the plans we make with friends and colleagues for lunch to how we plan our dinner and evening entertainment, from checking voice mail to checking e-mail, our daily lives are basically one long, continuous effort to connect to the people, places, and things that matter most to us. Keeping up in a fast-moving world can leave people feeling disconnected. The right products, pitched in the right package, can reverse that feeling.

A *connection* isn't just rational or physical. The most powerful connections are in fact emotional. That very first Coke, the first Budweiser—people remember where they were and who they were with. It's a rite of passage. Maybe it was a friend or relative who first shared a soft drink with you; a father or older brother who bought you your first beer; your first friend who met you for coffee. These powerful emotional memories last a lifetime, and emotional connections work in marketing. Ads that show a grandfather and granddaughter sharing a peanut-butter sandwich trigger a connection or a memory or an emotion. Same with buddies watching football and hoisting a beer together. For moms, it's ten-year-old children playing with a puppy. Simplistic? Yes, absolutely. But it's a connection that works.

I've seen the power of an emotional connection with my own eyes.

MORE WORDS THAT WORK

When it comes to automobiles, Americans know exactly what they really want. Note how different words and phrases ring with people:

"Our vehicles are dependable"—18 percent said this was good.

"We stand behind our cars"—56 percent said this was better.

The second phrase is more powerful because it gives consumers more than just a fact. It paints a picture of value with depth and meaning. *Good* language helps make a point. *Better* language helps tells a story. A couple more:

"Fuel savings"—15 percent good

"Fuel efficiency"—56 percent better

Savings is a one-time benefit, and it's just about dollars and cents. Fuel efficiency is the gift that keeps on giving through the life of the car, and it suggests good behavior as well as financial benefit.

"Automobile companies"—13 percent good

"Automobile manufacturers"—49 percent better

A company is bland and lifeless. A manufacturer actually crafts and creates something worth buying.

My focus group dial sessions are noted for their intensity, but rarely do they evoke tears. The rare exception almost always involves a sudden rush of memories.

I was in Atlanta, home of Coca-Cola Enterprises, the largest bottler of Coke products in the world, to study the attitudes of moms toward soft drinks. Few brands can claim to be an American institution like Coca-Cola. It's been around since 1886, and while it may not be about *change*, it has successfully positioned itself as *choice*. There is a Coke product for everyone—Coke, Diet Coke, Caffeine-free Coke, Coke Zero, Diet Coke with Lime, Diet Cherry Coke, Coke Vanilla, etc. By the time you read this book, they will surely have invented yet another taste that needs fulfillment. My job that night was to listen to moms and try to reconnect them to the soda they once loved but were now buying in decreasing quantities.

While the session took place more than a half decade ago, I still re-member it in great detail. A brightly clothed African-American woman in her mid-fifties broke down when I asked her to describe her first memories of having a Coke. In a sweet Southern accent, she said she was six or seven years old, and she had been instructed to meet her un-cle secretly behind the family barn. He had hid a bottle of Coke under his jacket so that her parents wouldn't find out. Her voice began to crack as she described how special that moment was in her life, how much she loved and missed him, and how his slipping her that first Coke was symbolic of her relationship with him—and her feelings toward the brand. She paused, collected herself, and then said, *"I think I want a Coke right now. You reminded me how much I miss my uncle."* After a mo-ment of awkward silence, the room full of women applauded. Several wiped away tears themselves. Even I was touched. The woman sitting next to her leaned over to give her a hug. This is not some isolated oc-currence. Fully 39 percent of all Americans recall a memory or special experience in their life that involved Coca-Cola.

That's the definition of "connection." That's exactly what Americans are seeking at home, at work, and at play.

Connection isn't just about nostalgia. Some of the strongest connec-tions involve a sense of adventure, creativity, and forward thinking. Take Mac users, for example. They swear by their Macs and swear *at* regular personal computers. They identify as *Mac people,* and they want to identify with *other* Mac people. It's as much about what their com-puter says about them as what it can do for them. Except they don't call their machines computers—they're "Macs." Mac people want you to know they are Mac people. You'll occasionally see the Apple logo on cars or on the backpacks of college kids. You'll never see the Microsoft or Dell logo on public display. It's just not a public statement anyone wants to make. Thousands of people will attend MacWorld, and there are doz-ens of chatrooms exclusively for Mac users. People who own Macs want you to know that they are part of that *community* of people (cool people), just like people with political bumper stickers want you to know where they stand. The word "Mac" is peppered throughout this paragraph because the word itself has become a connective force among a swarm of consumers. This is the very definition of effective branding.

Connection.

Then Apple did for music and photos what they had done for computers, making products that individualized, personalized, and humanized how we live. It started with iTunes, the first customized, user-friendly way to buy music. Then came iPods, which allowed anyone to create his or her own music environment. And then the iPhone, an instant smash because of its groundbreaking new look and futuristic functionality. Before long, Apple stock was soaring as people fell in love with the feeling Apple products gave them. The products looked sleek; we like to feel that way. They were stress-free; we wish we could be, too. They were reliable; who among us doesn't yearn for consistency in life?

But it still didn't end there. All the technology worked in unison, creating a hassle-free connection between human and machine. The technology became smaller and more lightweight, came in different colors, and everything operated at the *speed of life*. And eventually, even the price came down. Except for the period right after the release of the first-generation iPhone, it always worked and never broke. All the key elements of life as we want to live it are represented at the Apple Store:

- more money in our pockets because the products are more cutting-edge and last longer and therefore don't need to be replaced as often
- fewer hassles because the products do exactly what they say they do
- more time on our hands because the products are quick and efficient
- more choices because of constant updates, innovative new features, and new applications
- fewer worries, because the products never break (well, at least updated models) and
- less stress, because the Apple employees take the time to sell you the right product and provide in-store lessons to answer all your questions at your convenience

People are prepared to pay an Apple *premium* because their products satisfy all our other needs. They've even managed to add a human element—the Genius Bar at the Apple retail store—so patrons with the most challenging problems and casual users who just want to talk to a friendly face can get the answers they need. In response, Microsoft is opening stores of its own. One wonders what owners of their products will call themselves. Softies?

We are a wired (or, with the best products, wireless) society, and wouldn't have it any other way. Computers and cell phones are part of our daily routine. Check out these numbers, which are practically universal in the industrial world:

- 88 percent have a cell phone
- 86 percent use a desktop or laptop computer
- 87 percent use e-mail (John McCain just did not understand how out of touch he sounded—or was—when he said he didn't send or receive e-mails)[12]
- More than a quarter of us use a BlackBerry, Palm, or other personal digital device
- Half have broadband or high-speed Internet access (and wireless technology at home is right behind)

Your cell phone might even be keeping your marriage together—fully 70 percent of couples who both own a cell phone contact each other at least once a day to say hello or chat. A quarter say their family is closer today thanks to cell phones and the Internet.[13] And for those of you who are single, this technology has become the primary means for getting dates and building relationships.

We think these technologies have improved our ability to do our jobs and connect us with colleagues, making them a win-win at work and in our personal lives. But there is a downside: It means we work more hours to meet the constant demands of the gadgets, and the added pressure increases our stress levels.

Remember when the cell phone ad first aired in 1997 and featured a harried working mom standing at the kitchen counter stuffing papers into a briefcase as her two children beg her to take them to the beach?

Says Mom, *"Not today, honey. I've got a meeting with a very important client."*

Her little girl looks up at her, pleading, *"Mom, when can I be a client?"*

The child's plea sends an emotional bolt of lightning through Mom.

She spies the cell phone sitting on the table . . . *"Hmmm . . . You have five minutes to get ready for the beach, or I'm going without you."*

Cut to the beach with the happy mom and children frolicking in the sand . . . thanks to her cell phone connection. When that ad first aired, working moms stood up and applauded because it meant the freedom to leave the office. Now they cringe because it represents never being able to get away from the office. Sure, it provides the flexibility women want, but it has come to deny them the freedom they demand. The answer? Turn it off. Just as some families turn off the television during dinnertime, parents should simply turn off their cell phones and Black-Berrys during family time. And if you don't, turn to Chapter Six to learn about the damage it does to your children.

BlackBerrys improve the *speed* of communication, but the devices don't necessarily improve the *quality* of communication. I was at lunch recently with four Wall Street businessmen. They all placed their Black-Berry on top of the table as soon as they sat down. They were courteous enough to put the devices on vibrate mode, but that just meant that the table rattled all through lunch, and no topic of conversation went uninterrupted. How did e-mail become so indispensable that some people actually sleep with the thing at their bedside? It hooked us by tapping into our secret hope that the next message on the BlackBerry will be life-changing or reveal exciting information. It rarely happens, of course. Maybe one out of a hundred messages puts a smile on your face. In reality it's just a tether—an electronic leash. It's a 24/7 device that kills our attention span and thus the quality and thoroughness of our thinking. My employees are required to turn them off at meetings, and that one decision has sharply increased their participation and responsiveness. Client satisfaction isn't far behind. I suggest that any of you whose business and/or employment depend on client or customer service (so, all of you) adopt similar guidelines. As soon as your customers see they are less important than a plastic device, they are going to cease to be your customers.

And when it comes to the intersection of technology and connectedness, which is more important at the workplace: verbal or written communication? That answer is easy. In a high-speed age, the immediacy of responding via BlackBerry, no matter how terse, trumps the importance of speaking and being heard. Here's another question for today's era: Which would be tougher to go without for twenty-four hours, your

WORDS THAT WORK:
THE POWER OF ONE

Consumers are increasingly consolidating their multiple communications devices under one umbrella: cell phone, land line, Internet, even cable. It's *the power of one*—and its potential is unlimited.

Consumers are fed up with the increasing complexity of their communications world. There are too many devices to worry about, too many companies to coordinate with, and too many ways to pass the buck if something goes wrong with one part. Cable guy wants to blame the telephone company for the outage. Internet provider wants to blame the telco guy for your dead Internet.

Business can harness this frustration when they talk about the power of one. One company that coordinates everything in a simple, streamlined process. One device that does it all. One-stop shopping that saves time and hassle.

BlackBerry or your coffee? For many Americans, that's a choice they would not be willing to make. If you are in the technology or communication business, "reliability" is the desired feature, but "connected" is the desired result.

For the wired set, and increasingly for everyone, high-speed Internet access plays an essential role in daily life. Just think about the last time you lost your Internet connection or the electricity went out. You feel naked and powerless, totally disconnected from the world around you. Only a handful of people acknowledge surfing the Web at work for personal content, even though it is well known that website traffic spikes when people first get to work, during lunch hour, and again right before they leave for home. The Internet or television? Which would you rather give up for a day? That's easier to answer. If you're under age thirty, television is just so 1990s.

If customer service matters most to a consumer, they much prefer buying products or services from a local company instead of a national or global corporation. Being located in the neighborhood becomes much more important to the consumer when the purchase is an ongoing relationship, as opposed to a single, one-off item. *"Big enough to deliver . . . small enough to care"* was a slogan we developed for the merger of two major telephone companies. They didn't use it, but it remains exactly what Americans want from their suppliers of modern technology. In fact, any business that can credibly accentuate the local attention angle should use exactly the same approach. Whether you are the president of a local bank, the owner of a regional custom furniture builder, or director of a statewide real-estate brokerage firm, *"Big enough to deliver . . . small enough to care"* will work just as well for you.

GETTING FED

Is orange juice a food or not? Should be a simple question. Comes from *oranges*, picked from *trees*. But an astonishing 38 percent of Americans (including me) think orange juice is *not* food.

One in ten thinks sodas *are* food, and an even higher percentage think potato chips are healthy, provided they're "all-natural."

No wonder Americans consume a lot of *junk*. We're taught in school at an early age about the food pyramid and forced to exercise in sweaty gyms. But those same schools often offer high-calorie soft drinks in vending machines and serve fatty food in the cafeterias, thereby setting up the hypocrisy that dominates our dietary habits for the rest of our lives. More hypocrisy: many schools derive revenue from these high-fat and sugary products, which goes *straight* to athletic programs designed to keep kids fit. Schools privately admit they are as hooked on the money as the kids are on the sweets. Round and round and round we go.

Their parents go to the gym for an hour-long cardio workout, then have two martinis with dinner. Their grocery carts are filled with low-fat foods and a big fat cake from the bakery counter. They whine about paying $3.50 for a gallon of milk and then fork over even more for a ten-ounce gourmet coffee drink. Imported bottled water can be more expensive per gallon than gasoline, and few complain about the high price of that.

Since this is a book about what Americans *really* want, and since Americans *really* want to eat and drink, it's only appropriate to address the consequences. We consume our guilty pleasures, but at least we *admit* we feel guilty about it:

- 61 percent feel guilty about eating fast food
- 64 percent feel bad about eating candy

- 55 percent feel guilty about drinking alcoholic beverages
- 72 percent admit guilt about smoking a cigarette

America is a fast-food nation because we are all about the payoff. It's convenient . . . tastes good . . . and comes cheap. You don't even have to get out of your car to pick up a quick bite. Since the advent of the drive-thru window, you can now have stacks of steaming hot meat lowered into your car in less than sixty seconds—just think how jealous a caveman would be. Fast food is so totally American because it's an embodiment of our ideals, that things should always be better, faster, cheaper, and more convenient. And for moms, it's the quickest and most convenient way to satisfy their children. An astonishing number of people eat fast food several times a month from McDonald's, Wendy's, Taco Bell, Burger King, KFC, and the other chains you see in every community. Six in ten families with children eat at a fast-food restaurant *at least* three times a month.

Yet moms are increasingly wary of fast food. Just because they're buying it for their families doesn't mean they feel good about it. I like to call this feeling they get at the drive-thru window "McTension." There's a moment, maybe only a few seconds, between the time they realize they need to get dinner and the time they order the McNuggets, and in that moment lies the McTension. They know they should dine at home. They know they should cook. But this is fast, it's cheap, it's hot, and everyone likes it. And on top of all of that, they're tired from a long day at work and

WHAT MOMS REALLY WANT: THE POWER TO DECIDE

When we talk about families and food, we're primarily talking about mothers making the decisions. Moms are almost three times more likely than dads to shop for food for the family, and women are significantly more risk averse than men, especially when it comes to a perceived health threat to their children. Men typically defer to women when it comes to the details of mealtime, whether it's in the home or eating out. So if you want to sell a new restaurant, a new cut of meat, a new supermarket—if it can be tasted, chewed, and swallowed, you want to appeal to the women in the household.

having spent the last hour at soccer practice—or at their second job. The McTension wins. These moms are fully aware of the nutritional value of the food and drink their children consume, and they are likely to be cynical about the "facts and figures" put out by fast-food companies. And even what they do "know" is likely to be wrong. But they do it anyway because it's American convenience with a minimum-wage smile.

Quick, how many calories are there in a Big Mac?

It's 590 calories, though moms on average think it's more than 700. So while they claim they want nutritional information about fast food, it only occasionally factors into what they eat or what they feed their children. Two-thirds of Americans say fast food is a personal choice and they don't hold any of the chains responsible for the consequences. Fast food is a fact of life in a majority of households, but moms will still pick and choose among the dozens of options—and what they decide is what their family eats.

McDonald's is still the fast-food king. In business for half a century, McDonald's has more than 30,000 outlets serving 58 million people *each day*. That's almost equal to the population of France. The formula of consistency and uniformity does not endear it to gourmands and health specialists, yet it remains the most popular fast-food restaurant in the country and the world. It is reliable, it is inexpensive, and it provides consistent quality for the price. And if I may, it is affordable even for the most cash-starved families, and can be the only hot food they have during the day. Is it memorable? No, but you can buy lunch for less than five bucks in less than five minutes (unless you're in New York City, where they've also managed to make even fast food slow and expensive). The product is uniquely uniform—a hamburger is a hamburger, exactly 3.5 ounces with a pickle, a sprinkle of onion, and some ketchup and mustard. Each fry is cut from an Idaho russet potato to a precise measure guarded by the company. It tastes exactly the same no matter where you buy it, from Portland to Paris, and from Capetown to Cape Cod.

But what is different, and what American marketers may or may not understand or appreciate, is the difference in attitudes toward McDonald's between upper-middle-class stay-at-home moms who live out in the suburbs and working lower-middle-class moms who live in more urban settings. In one-parent families, the sympathies toward fast food are especially great whereas stay-at-home moms want their children dining at home. They'd rather take the time to shop for and then prepare a home-cooked meal. Harried working-class and single moms have a very different take—a hot meal cooked by someone else that makes their kids happy is exactly what they need at the end of a hard day's work. McDonald's has made a gallant effort to bridge the gap and offer food that is nutritious for children, going as far as to offer "Apple Dippers" for kids, but over the years I have conducted focus groups for various clients addressing the relationships moms have with various foods and beverages and each time the conversation would sound something like this:

Stay-at-Home Mom (SAHM): I want to cook for my kids.

Working-Class Mom (WCM): I don't have the luxury of time to cook dinner. I get home too late and I work too hard.

SAHM: At least take your children to a good restaurant that serves fresh food.

WCM: I can't afford it. At least at McDonald's, I know they get a warm meal and some protein. I watch what they eat, they like the food, and I get a chance to talk to them.

SAHM: My job isn't to give them food they like. It's to make sure they eat the food they should.

WCM: My kids are happy and quiet when we go to McDonald's.

SAHM: When it comes to food, my kids are never happy and quiet.

WCM: Then maybe you should take them to McDonald's once in a while.

I've personally lived this fight. I grew up with it. I have eaten the same McDonald's meal a thousand times—a quarter-pound burger without cheese or onions, large fries, and a diet soda. But only once in my life did I ever bring a McDonald's meal into my parents' home. My mother had cooked fish. It doesn't matter what kind; I hated and still hate anything and everything that swims. So I got in the car, drove to the nearest McDonald's less than two miles away—which I had never been to because McDonald's was not on my mom's approved list of restaurants—and brought a Quarter Pounder back home with me.

The look on my mother's face was half anger, half horror. You'd have thought I brought a crack pipe into the house. With a tone of voice straight out of *The Exorcist*, she spat out, *"How could you bring THAT into this house?"* That's all she said as she stalked out of the room. It insulted her Jewish maternal sensibilities, and it was a complete affront to her cooking. Plus she thought it was bad for me. It hit every wrong note. My father didn't say a word. He, too, would have rather had a Quarter Pounder that evening, but peace in the household was a higher priority for him. I don't want any mothers to put down this book in disgust. It was only her fish dish that I loathed. Her spaghetti with meat sauce was terrific.

When we're feeling good about our checking account balances, we splurge by dining out. It is the single most desired and frequent "luxury" in our daily lives. And when times get tough and we need to tighten our belts, restaurants are the *first* to take the hit. But even under current economic conditions, about half of all adult Americans go out to a restaurant for dinner at least one night a week. However, the choices are changing. People who dine at the most expensive white-tablecloth establishments eat there less frequently, or they order a less expensive entree. And the $125 bottle of fine Bordeaux has given way to a more modest $45 California Syrah, or even more likely, a $6 glass of the off-the-shelf variety. Las Vegas, home of more award-winning chefs and restaurants than any city in America, has been particularly hard hit.

At the other end of the scale, working-class people who saw a mid-level chain like Applebee's or Chili's as a nice evening out are instead eating at home or scaling back to a meal at Denny's, IHOP, or a burger at Wendy's. It's hard to say that any company in the food-service business is doing "well" in this economy (except for McDonald's), but some are doing "less poorly" because Americans are trading down the food cost chain. You can get a double cheeseburger for 99 cents at McDonald's. There's just no way to beat that at the grocery store, especially when you consider what it costs in *time.* And the only thing Americans feel they have less of than money is time. Truth is, if it weren't for the time and the cleanup, we wouldn't mind eating at home. Two-thirds say a good home-cooked meal is more enjoyable than dining out anyway.[14]

One option is the barbecue at home.* Americans are crazy about

---

* For those who enjoy wordplay, in the South, BBQ is a sauce, not a way to cook. They *grill* meat or chicken, they don't BBQ it. Similarly, a Coke is a cola product, not a specific brand, to many Southerners. Conversely, what residents of Philadelphia call a hoagie is called a grinder in Hartford, a hero in New York City, and a sub in most other places (except in New Orleans, where it's called a Po' Boy).

grilling, whether they own a little hibachi or a mammoth 832-square-inch grill with an electric burner and a fridge on the side. Half say they grill a couple times a month, and the hard-core BBQers at least once a week. The barbecue industry has exploded accordingly. You didn't know you needed your own personalized branding iron for the T-bone until some inventive person presented it, most likely in a SkyMall catalog.

Steak and hamburgers are the number-one and -two choices for the grill, followed by chicken. There are some demographic differences. Men are more partial to steaks and sausages, while women lean toward chicken and vegetables. The most fanatical grillers are Baby Boomers and Gen-Xers. And there is a partisan divide, too. Republicans favor steak and hamburgers, while Democrats are happiest with a grilled chicken breast.[15]

To wash it all down, Americans drink an ocean of soda every year—an average of more than 50 *gallons* per person. Put another way, people drink more soda than coffee, milk, and fruit drinks combined.[16] The nanny-state do-gooders may have convinced people to drink more water in recent years (though the environmentalists have attempted to put the kibosh on bottled water because of the millions of indestructible bottles), but millions of people still reach for a soft drink. It's pretty much a guilt-free pleasure for adults. More than 40 percent have *at least* one soda each day.

Words matter when you describe a simple can of soda. As I first wrote in *Words That Work,* out with "carbonation." It sounds too much like man-made chemicals. Moms feel the bubbles aren't a natural phenomenon, so it must be bad for you. So "carbonation" became "**sparkling.**" Sparkling is a feeling. It's natural, and therefore it's appealing.

Taste trumps everything else in choice of a beverage. If it tastes good, people will overlook the lack of nutrients and high calories and price differences. They will *choose* the beverage that they know is less healthy but better-tasting. By the way, moms are more concerned about the ingredients in a *diet* soft drink than in a regular soft drink. "Diet" sounds like the company is adding bad ingredients and chemicals to the soda, not simply deleting calories. Moms were suspicious that the makers must be adding artificial sweeteners so the soda would taste OK when the sugar was removed, right? "Lite" is what worked in Europe. It should be the standard phrase here as well. There is a *lite* version of almost every food on the market. It's time to bring it to beverages.

Here is how people react to various descriptions of the same low-calorie drink:

WHICH OF THE FOLLOWING
DO YOU THINK WOULD TASTE BETTER?

Lite Beverage—45 percent
Low-Calorie Beverage—24 percent
Diet Beverage—21 percent

Words like "refreshing" and "thirst-quenching" encourage people to drink more soda. Thirst-quenching is how you feel while you're drinking your soda. Refreshed is a state of mind—it's how you feel after you've downed your soda. Combined, they are a powerful experience for the consumer. Throw in "ice-cold," and you've got the perfect trifecta of a soft-drink experience.

Once again, it's moms who control the purse strings, and therefore control the beverages. And once again, they feel guilty about letting the kids have soft drinks and frown upon the Britney Spears–type moms who put soda in their toddlers' bottles. Even so, kids drink soda just as regularly as adults do—at least once a day. My focus groups with moms on this topic were fascinating. The women bonded as they related horror stories about their children throwing tantrums because the ads on television made their kids want to drink something of which their moms did not approve. They were annoyed with Corporate America.

Message to beverage companies: if you align yourselves with moms, you'll sell a lot more product to their kids. Both Coke and Pepsi have gone a long way in expanding their beverage portfolios to include water and sports drinks, and both companies have actively embraced socially responsible good-health causes. But if moms don't know all that you do, they'll just assume that you don't do much.

Consider the following statistics from surveys completed over the past few years:

- Three-quarters of Americans are overweight, meaning they weigh more than the recommended weight for their height.
- A full third are obese, meaning they weigh at least 20 percent more than their ideal weight.
- More than one in ten Americans admit to drinking or eating so much that it made them sick. Those younger than thirty were particularly guilty of overindulging—28 percent said they drank until they were sick sometime in the last year, and 21 percent ate until they got sick.

People gorge and binge on food and drink like it's medieval times. A quarter-century ago, a little more than half of us were a little overweight and only 15 percent could be categorized as obese.[17] All-you-can-eat is now a way of life, not just an occasional visit to the buffet line.

There are far more couch potatoes than fitness freaks among us. The fitness clubs and diet programs are multibillion-dollar industries with plenty of room for growth simply because Americans lack personal responsibility and willpower. Even as we gobble another cookie, most people recognize that a sedentary lifestyle is one of the biggest health problems in the country. It is not surprising that more than 80 percent feel guilty about not exercising. What is surprising is how few people actually do anything about it.

It doesn't seem to matter that our political leaders set a good example (Bill Clinton aside). George W. Bush gave up alcohol decades ago and exercised every day, usually on a treadmill, but he often slipped away to a military campus to ride a bike. He methodically chopped away at brush on his Texas ranch, a task that could keep him sweating forever. In addition to being a competitive basketball player, Barack Obama is obsessive about getting to the gym and alternates between cardio workouts and weight training. He is so health conscious (smoking aside) that he could barely hide his revulsion when faced with the parade of deep-fried foods on a stick that appeared on the campaign trail. And California's governor, Arnold Schwarzenegger, had been chairman of the President's Council on Physical Fitness and Sports, and remains a very public proponent of a healthy, active lifestyle.

GETTING FOOD

If Americans worship food, then supermarkets are our cathedrals, and most clergy would envy our frequent attendance. It's a myth that people make just one trip to the supermarket each week. Let's see where you fit:

- Women make up 70 percent of typical food shoppers. Among married couples, women almost always do the majority of the shopping.
- Most people shop for groceries several times a week. In fact, a third of us admit to going to the grocery store five times a week or more, spending more than $20 per trip.
- The average time in a supermarket visit is 25 minutes, though averages in this case are deceiving and the reporting suspect. People claim they spend more time than they actually do, and time in the store is a U-shaped graph, with the vast majority either in and out quickly or lingerers filling up their shopping carts to the brim.
- About 75 percent of us spend more than $100 a week on groceries.
- While we're in the store, we're evenly split on whether getting the lowest price is the most important or getting the highest quality even if it costs more. Moms will pay the additional cost. Seniors will not.

This dynamic shifted slightly when the economy went off the rails. Shoppers began buying cheaper brands. Procter & Gamble saw sales of its low-priced Gain detergent rise 10 percent in the same window as sales slipped for Tide, its market leader. People also turned to store-owned brands, which typically cost considerably less than name brands. Consider Kroger-brand tomato paste versus Hunt's tomato paste. You can see the price difference right on the label, but can you really taste the difference? Probably not.

The timing is just right for a Suave-like advertising campaign on behalf of cheaper store-owned brands all across the retail landscape. Remember the 1970s Suave shampoo ads: *"Suave does what theirs does . . . for a lot less."* That concept, copying the more popular brands in everything but price, turned the shampoo into a billion-dollar brand that now extends to other personal-care products. They refreshed the campaign in 2006 with the new tagline, *"Say yes to beautiful without paying the price,"* which boosted sales 3 percent in just three months.[18]

Even upper-income consumers are cutting back. Information Resources Inc. reported that a third of households earning more than $100,000 started buying more store-labeled goods and 41 percent cut spending on nonessential groceries. More Safeway-brand cereal, less Kellogg's Rice Krispies. I've even seen shoppers in Beverly Hills clipping coupons and walking up and down the aisles with the Sunday circular specials in hand, though the parking lot is still filled with Mercedes and BMWs.

The most significant trend in supermarket shopping over the past decade has been the rise in popularity of genuine organic foods. Not so long ago, pesticides in the fields and chemicals in the stores were embraced as a way to keep food fresher longer. They preserved foods that otherwise would have spoiled, and were therefore accepted and even welcomed by most shoppers. But over time people have come to see certain chemicals in food as unnatural and increasingly unhealthy.

Think about Cheetos for a minute. That neon orange seems like it must have been created by chemicals discovered by the nuclear energy industry. As adults, we know we shouldn't eat food that looks like that, yet more than 60 percent of Cheetos consumers are over the age of eighteen, and they still sell more than $400 million worth of the product per year.[19] Why? Adults don't want to give up all of their kidlike pleasures, and Cheetos reminds them of the simple pleasures of youth. (Message to marketers: repurpose and repackage pleasant childhood memories into mature products and content.) In a 2009 Super Bowl ad, Chester Cheetah, a cartoon character colorful enough for kids but cool enough for adults, encourages a woman to toss a few of her precious Cheetos toward an obnoxious woman talking loudly on the phone ("*I must be on the ugly side of town. Everyone here is, like, really gross*") in the hopes that a flock of pigeons would see this as an open invitation for lunch. Sure enough, the birds attack the loud talker, chaos ensues, and both Chester and the Cheetos consumer smile knowingly. There's only one marketing problem with this ad. Moms who control the food intake for the household don't really want their family eating something that triggers a feeding frenzy among pigeons. A similar ad in the series ends with a Cheetos consumer leaving orange cheese marks on the clothing of another annoying loud talker. The problem once again is with moms who are not likely to want their kids eating foods with color dye that comes off on their hands and ends up on anything they happen to touch. File this under the heading: "What Exactly Were They Thinking?"

Cheetos and similar junk foods won't go away, because they are cheap, tasty, and because American eaters are perfectly willing to espouse the merits of good behavior at the very same moment they are exhibiting bad habits. But there is an emerging alternative market of people who have made a wholesale rejection of unnatural foods in favor of a holistically wholesome diet, and it is here that businesses have the greatest opportunity to create and become part of new eating habits.

Enter organic food, organic farming, and stores like Whole Foods (also known to some as "Whole Paycheck") that charge a lot more than everyone else for "all-natural" food. It's working. Emerging from liberal enclaves like Berkeley, California; Boulder, Colorado; and Burlington, Vermont, into the mainstream, the notion of organic hippie farmers has given way to an extremely profitable and rapidly growing big business. Every major grocery store now carries almost equal amounts of "regular" and organic produce, often in such close proximity that it is confusing to the shopper. Most people don't know, and can't tell, the difference

WHAT (A GROWING PORTION OF) AMERICANS WANT: ORGANIC OR ALL-NATURAL FOOD

The market for organic products, while growing, is not universal. People most likely to buy organics are college-educated, politically left-of-center young adults under age thirty-five who live in the western and Pacific states. For them, organic is more than a food choice. It is a lifestyle decision and sometimes even a political statement.

Conversely, organic still sounds vaguely hippie to older Americans—even those who are health conscious. "All-natural" is preferred among people older than thirty-five, particularly those who live in the South and industrial Midwest. To them, "all-natural" means food that doesn't have a bunch of chemicals in it—and that matters to them more than how the food was grown.

between organic broccoli and broccoli that is traditionally grown. They must trust that the organic grower is adhering to federal rules and regulations that ban use of chemicals on food labeled "organic." Yet even people who *don't* buy organic food think it is safer for the environment and healthier for humans.

The market for organics is lucrative and growing. Sales of organic food and drink have grown from $1 billion in 1990 to a projected $23.6 billion in 2008. While it is still a small slice of overall food sales, it has striking growth potential of more than 20 percent a year.[20]

GETTING TO THE END OF THE DAY

When the workday is finally over, Americans like to socialize—and the most likely social activity at the end of the day is to enjoy a beer.

Think for a minute: Have you ever had a *special beer moment*? As I mentioned earlier in this chapter, most people can remember their first beer—and it is almost universally a positive occasion. In fact, most people can name an occasion within the past year when beer has played a major celebratory role—or at least been present when the celebration took place.

Americans drink a *lot* of beer—more than thirty gallons per person each year. If you subtract the people who don't drink any beer at all, that's, well, even more. The top two beer-drinking states: North Carolina and New Hampshire.[21] My research on beer (strictly professional) has yielded some interesting personal traits of consumers who prefer American-made beers. If moms are the focal point for food, men in their twenties dominate this category. Attitudinally, they believe sharing a beer strengthens friendships and promotes lasting relationships. They love sports—both playing and watching. They create their own style, and they like their women independent and free-spirited. And they're pretty loyal to one brand, preferably made in the USA.

But not all beers—including American beers—are created equal. A Sunday-afternoon beer with friends watching the football games is a very different experience from a Friday-night beer shared over a meal or social occasion. The Sunday-afternoon Bud feels different from the Friday-night Bud. Sure, same bottle, same beer. But the social expectations are different, and so the emotional impact is different. Similarly, the first beer of the evening offers an entirely different experience (and even tastes different) from the last beer before closing time.

Younger, higher socioeconomic drinkers have a strategic plan—they know what drinks they want to try even before they touch their lips to the first one. They're also much more adventurous. Women may start with wine, then move to an apple martini or strawberry daiquiri, and end the evening back with wine. Men will start with a European beer import or an Australian lager and move to a gin and tonic or Jack Daniel's and Coke, and probably end the evening with a Bud Light.

For older, working-class Americans there is less randomness and no adventure. They drink the same thing, at the same speed, month after month, year after year. In fact, the older you are, the more inclined you are to start with an American beer and end with an American beer. I like to call it the ABA, or "American Beer Advantage." But alas, Anheuser-Busch, the largest beer maker in this country, has succumbed to globalization. While your Budweiser and Busch beers are still *made* in the USA, the corporate brewmeister has moved from St. Louis to Brussels (by way of Brazilian financing). In fact, most of the beer sold in America is owned by a handful of giant global conglomerates headquartered elsewhere.

Now, make no mistake: Beer drinkers take their brew process seriously, and once they settle on a beer, they really don't want it to change. At all. That's why Coors loyalists were a little disturbed by the notion of their Coors being brewed anywhere *other* than Golden, Colorado, with

THE SOUND OF BEER

Someday, somebody is going to make a lot of money based on a simple sound—the sound of the clink of a glass or two beer bottles tapped together. It's a toast that connects friends and family personally and emotionally, and makes you appreciate a special moment even more. It's an immediate trigger for celebration. Most important, it makes you want to order another round. Only a few beer ads have shown the toast, and even fewer still have included the sound. An ad built around the clink will sell a lot of beer.

Same with the flip-tab of a can. The sound of air as it escapes the can is the sound of refreshment at hand, whether it's beer or soda. Pop a can and you automatically feel relaxed and recharged even before you taste the liquid.

water from somewhere other than the Rocky Mountains. They'll tell you that beer is not fast food—it can't be brewed in Milwaukee or Latrobe or Johannesburg and taste consistently the same. And consistency in taste is nonnegotiable if you are a beer—or any beverage, for that matter.

Americans drink a lot of beer, and beer drinkers are proud Americans. They applaud the can-do spirit and self-reliance of their countrymen, and think that beer and America go perfectly together:

- 84 percent believe beer is as American as baseball and apple pie. (But hold the apple pie and substitute a hamburger, their favorite food, with a nice cold brew.)
- 83 percent say the Fourth of July is about celebrating our freedom, and a cooler filled with cold beer is part of the celebration.
- 75 percent say making great beer is part of America's heritage.*

GETTING HOME

Ah, free time. A road warrior, you've successfully fought the traffic and arrived home from work. There is never enough time to *enjoy* life. Americans work long hours, and they're proud of their productivity, but they feel shortchanged in leisure time.

The challenge for the Hollywood studios and the entertainment gurus was to find a way to combine the hassle-free nature of television with the entertainment potential of the movie theater. Movie theater attendance had flatlined as an increasing number of people began to choose to watch movies in the comfort of their homes (theaters are enjoying a resurgence in 2009 because it is about the only entertainment we can afford in a recession), and that wasn't good for profitability. Companies like Blockbuster cornered the early market on rentals. Then a California upstart company that understood the changing demands and desires of the movie audience revolutionized the rental business. Netflix ditched the brick-and-mortar stores for an Internet-based ordering system. You order your movies online, they arrive in the mail, and you pop them back in the

---

* An important part of the Budweiser heritage are the Clydesdale horses, which are an instant and lasting image of Anheuser-Busch. Why the horses? To celebrate the end of Prohibition, the first kegs of legally brewed beer were hauled away from the St. Louis brewery aboard a wagon hitched to the great draft horses. Since then, A-B has used those magnificent animals in dozens of award-winning commercials and promotions.

WHAT AMERICANS DO
IN THEIR FREE TIME

Aside from entertaining at home and eating out at restaurants, these are some favorite leisure-time pleasures, according to the U.S. government:

39 percent read books

23 percent go to the beach

22 percent play cards

20 percent play computer games

18 percent go to bars and nightclubs

18 percent play board games

14 percent do crossword puzzles[22]

mail after you watch them. For a flat monthly fee, you get "free shipping" and as many movies as you can watch. Netflix offers 100,000 titles to its 8.4 million subscribers.[23] There are no late fees, no due dates, no race to the store before closing time. Netflix took the movie-rental concept and eliminated all the hassles.

What's next? Eliminate the U.S. Postal Service from the process. It is increasingly easy to download movies from the Web and watch them instantly on your computer. Netflix has 12,000 titles that can be ordered à la carte in this manner, and they cut a deal with TiVo in the fall of 2008 to give TiVo users access to that rental library, combining the convenience of Netflix rentals with the ability to watch your movie on your own television (or computer) screen with the comforts of home.

True, life was simpler just a few decades ago before TiVo and video on demand (VOD), before satellite and cable, when just three networks and a few independent stations were enough to satisfy American entertainment appetites. Now there are hundreds of television channels to choose from, resulting in a painful exodus from the major networks as viewers explore a universe of TV options. More than 80 percent of Americans subscribe to cable or satellite TV. About half of those sign up for premium channels such as HBO or Showtime, where the raciest content is found, as well as a United Nations' worth of international programming. The mandatory transition from analog to digital broadcast in 2009 has opened up a new world for viewers who switched to providers that offer channels they didn't even know existed.

But it's not just what we watch that has changed. It's also how we watch. True, most of us still consume our television the old-fashioned way—in real time with segments separated by commercial breaks that allow us to get food and use the bathroom. But people are increasingly watching programming on their own timetable by using devices like DVRs (TiVo), DVD recordings, and VOD. About a third of homes now have this capability, and it continues to expand as people forgo more exotic escapes in favor of entertainment closer to home. The couch potato has given way to a newly empowered audience who wants the convenience of watching TV when *they* want to, and damn the commercials. This is especially true of people younger than forty, who are fully comfortable with digital technology and have a deep disdain for advertising.

Size is also an issue. One in five Americans owns a television 50 inches *or bigger*. At the opposite extreme, a handful of early adopters are beginning to watch video on the tiniest screen at their fingertips—their cell phones. Only a few million people watch mobile video now, but it will certainly thrive, especially among younger people who rely on their phones for all communication.

We're a little embarrassed about how much time we spend watching TV and browsing the Internet—68 percent feel guilty about watching too much television and 53 percent for spending too much time in front of the computer. For many, they start the day with TV and shut it off only when they turn out the lights. In many homes, TV is like wallpaper.

I know something about what consumers really want from television, having worked for NBC, ABC, Fox, MSNBC, CNBC, FX, and the BBC over the past decade. When I first came on board (to test promos for the NBC fall lineup), the network was trying to prepare itself for the eventual loss of two of its most popular comedies since *Seinfeld*—*Friends* and *Frasier*—and so it had to remake itself, or at least its content, to appeal to a different generation of viewers. But today, most of network comedy is gone or going away. Why? They aren't listening to their viewers. In 1978, all ten most-watched shows in America were thirty-minute sitcoms, led by *Laverne & Shirley*, *Three's Company*, and *Mork & Mindy*—shows still in reruns somewhere. Today, nobody is laughing at what network TV is

WHY AMERICANS DON'T LIKE TV SITCOMS ANYMORE

There's a reason why only one TV comedy in the 2008–09 season—*Two and a Half Men*—ever cracks the top ten most-watched shows in America. It's because the networks have stopped catering to their audiences and started trusting their (unexercised) gut instincts. Having moderated dozens of television focus groups over the years, I have found there's a pattern of desirability that could help someone launch the next *Cheers, Seinfeld,* or *Friends.* Here are the five guidelines for successful sitcom humor:

1. **Hold up a mirror.** Viewers like to see themselves in the comedies they watch. They want shows and characters they can personally relate to. To them, life is a series of amusing experiences that are even funnier when they happen to other people on TV who look and sound a little like themselves (only better) and their friends. They want quirky, but still grounded in reality.
2. **Connect the dots.** Viewers overwhelmingly prefer shows where the story lines are unique, so they can miss an episode and not lose contact with the characters. But they are equally clear that they want the characters to build from episode to episode, with occasional references to past episodes.
3. **Relationships involving conflict.** This is particularly important. Americans aren't looking for sweet, innocent comedy. They want an edge, something a bit dark but still lovable. *The Simpsons* has lasted so long and *Family Guy* was brought back to life because they so perfectly illustrate the graphic humor behind real conflict.
4. **Home is where comedy lives.** People now prefer a home setting for a comedy rather than the office. It's not a rejection of the office environment. It's an embrace of the home and its richness of possibilities. *Everybody Loves Raymond* was a top-20 show for most of its run even though it primarily had only two sets: Ray's home and his parents' home.
5. **Go live.** The spontaneity and pitfalls of live performances, including all the mistakes and outtakes, are a real crowd pleaser. Very few shows have done this because of the cost, but it changes the viewer dynamic from static to active—and so people tune in and stay with the program. *The Drew Carey Show* did live episodes—the only recent show to do this on an annual basis.

showing, and in times like these, Americans really want at least a chuckle. To many of us, cable is the new king of comedy.

TV at its best mirrors the reality of our experience. We learn to cope with the lunacy of life by learning to laugh at it, and that is why we identify with characters on TV who are just a little crazier—but not much—than people we really know.

GOING TO BED

Sexuality is on display everywhere in American culture. Turn on the television, look at a magazine rack in the convenience store, watch movie previews, drive by a billboard—there are half-dressed young bodies everywhere. No wonder Americans are hung up on sex. We live in PG families surrounded by an X-rated world.

Calvin Klein ads show hunky male models wearing low-slung underwear cut down to *there*, with a suggestive smile. *Cosmopolitan* magazine covers scream headlines such as BAD GIRL SEX: 75 TRICKS FOR NIGHTS WHEN YOU WANT TO BE JUST A LITTLE NAUGHTIER. HBO has stripped away long-held inhibitions on the small screen, pelting viewers with equal doses of profanity and fully nude faux sex.

Rare is the opportunity for a pollster to study the sexual habits of Americans above the covers and beneath them. But thanks to *Playboy* magazine, that icon of pinups and sexuality and ribald interviews (remember born-again Jimmy Carter admitting *"I've looked on a lot of women with lust. I've committed adultery in my heart many times"*), I've had this opportunity—several times. As part of my research, I conducted a focus group with eleven Playmates at the Playboy Mansion in Los Angeles about what gorgeous women want in a man. Trust me, it made up for thousands of hours spent on less glamorous research, such as testing hotel toilet amenities and determining whether wallpaper is more desirable than paint.

My editor wanted to remove the box on the following page (*"It's off-putting,"* she wrote), but *Playboy* is uniquely and entirely American and, for better or worse, the magazine and founder Hugh Hefner helped shape the tone and the morals of the 1960s and '70s.* Even today, the bunny icon is universally recognizable globally, alongside Mickey Mouse and the McDonald's Golden Arches. True, the magazine has suffered significant circulation declines as pictures of naked women

---

* My editor also wrote that *Playboy* doesn't resonate with anyone under the age of forty. Little did she know that *Playboy's* most loyal readers are in their twenties. They may not read much else, and they definitely prefer surfing the Web to reading a magazine, but they'll still pick up a copy.

WHAT PLAYBOY PLAYMATES REALLY WANT IN MEN

(and why I'm still single)

So what does it take for a man to get a Playboy Playmate? Not brains, not a sense of humor. It's all material goods. With the cameras rolling, here's what I learned about how Playboy Playmates decide whether a man is *worth* their while.

1. First, they look at his watch, because what a man will spend on a watch is an indication to them of how much money he will spend on a woman. If it's a cheap watch, the gifts to her will be chintzy. If it's expensive, sky's the limit. (Of course, I was wearing a freebie CNN watch that afternoon.)
2. Shoes are second because they reflect how a man will treat a woman. If he gets his shoes shined regularly, it means he'll pamper his woman, too. (I was wearing four-year-old dirty sneakers.)
3. The quality of a man's shirt is third because it indicates his taste for fine things. (I was wearing a blue polo shirt with a beer logo on it.)
4. Finally, the type of car a man drives is an indication of what kind of toys he owns and whether he's fun during the day—and at night. (I was driving a rented turquoise Geo Metro, the dorkiest car since the AMC Pacer.)

became readily available elsewhere, but *Playboy* still occupies a warm spot in most men's hearts. When we've done surveys and identified ourselves as calling from *Playboy, no man has ever hung up.* Ever. In October 2007, I took Americans into their collective bedrooms, figuratively anyway, to talk about their sexual lives. There may be little or no apparent consensus on matters of politics or policy today, but our definitive survey revealed unexpectedly similar sexual proclivities.

Americans are having sex—*lots* of sex—often with more than one partner (and occasionally at the *same time*). Almost half of all adults report having sex at least once a week. *In fact, more people younger than forty have sex once a week than vote for president once every four years.*

Americans start having sex in their teens: 63 percent said they lost their virginity at eighteen years or younger. We consider ourselves to be sexually adventurous. A quarter of us have had just one or two sexual partners in our lives. Forty percent of us acknowledge three to ten partners. And 12 percent admit to more than thirty sex partners in a lifetime.

Nearly a quarter of Americans have taken part in a threesome, so next time you're bored at an office meeting or in line at Starbucks, look around you and try to guess which one out of every four co-workers has engaged in a *ménage à trois*.

A few more tidbits from the boudoir:

- Almost half said they were satisfied with their sex lives. A few more Republicans categorized themselves as *very* satisfied than Democrats did—at least, that's what they tell a pollster.
- 13 percent said they have sex every day or almost every day. A quarter said several times a week. A majority fell into the less frequent window of a few times a month or year.
- Intelligence was the biggest turn-on, followed by sexiness. Far down the scale was beauty.
- Most people consider themselves to be sexually adventurous, but check out this sliding scale of adventurous possibilities: 62 percent have watched pornography with a partner, 40 percent have indulged in sexual role-playing, but only 11 percent have tried S&M.
- One-quarter of all Republicans (25 percent) and a third of all Democrats (35 percent) have had more than ten sexual partners (in their lifetimes, not all at one time).

Some political-sexual notes: Republicans tended to lose their virginity later than Democrats, but once they got the hang of it they were twice as likely to have sex almost every day, even though Democrats think they're a little better in bed than Republicans. In equal numbers, they claim they're sexually adventurous, though Democrats were slightly more likely to watch pornography and play out sexual fantasies in bed.

The taboo against extramarital sex is strong. Almost half said they would definitely not have an affair even if there was a guarantee they wouldn't get caught. Just 20 percent said they might—Democrats a little more likely to say "definitely," and Republicans "probably."

One steamy scenario held bipartisan appeal: having a one-night stand in the Oval Office with a president they found sexually attractive. Twelve percent of women said they would definitely say yes (presumably somewhat passionately, as in *"Yes, Mr. President, YES!"*), and 11 percent said they would "probably" give in to the most powerful leader of the world. At the end of the day, there's something about a man (or woman) who holds the nuclear codes. Or, as Henry Kissinger once said, "Power is the greatest aphrodisiac."

LUNTZ LESSONS

- The morning is about habits. The evening is about choices. And everything else is about getting through the day.
- Focus not on what you are selling but on what people want to buy. The value of your product or service is in the eyes of the buyer, not the seller.
- Pay attention to the changing public mood. "Value" is the definitive attribute for a nation of anxious consumers.
- Take the best of the past and reapply it to the future. The "re" words ("renew," "rebuild," "refresh," etc.) are powerful because they revitalize products, services, and brands for a new generation of users.
- Seek an emotional connection. All the intellectual reasons to buy or use something will have less impact than an appeal from the heart.
- Individualize, personalize, and humanize. People need to see themselves in your products and services. If it appears tailored to someone else, they won't buy.
- "Always," "anywhere," and "everywhere." We live at the speed of life and expect everyone and everything to do the same—without fail.
- Moms are the gateway to the children. Get Mom's permission (or at least her acquiescence) and you have a free pass to reach out to her kids.
- Appeal to all the senses. Everyone knows how to tease the eyes. The great marketers figure out how to trigger a sense of taste, smell, and sound.

2

DON'T STOP UNTIL YOU GET ENOUGH:
The Five Things That Matter Most

Can anybody remember when the times were not hard and money not scarce?

—RALPH WALDO EMERSON

Time is money, especially when you are talking to a lawyer.

—FRANK DANE

So, what matters more to you: more money, fewer hassles, more time, more choices, or no worries? All five of them are important—but one of them matters more than all the rest.

Americans are a mess of contradictions, an amalgamation of angst, driven by what we don't have now and what we want tomorrow. Living, working, playing at breakneck speed from dawn to dusk, we are seekers engaged in a twenty-four-hour quest for balance between home and work, friends and family, the need for money and the desire for free time. Truth is, we want it all.

The American tradition of "living large" worked when we had a competitive advantage over everyone else, when we were the unchallenged global superpower. We bought big houses, big SUVs, big televisions, big speakers, and rang up big credit card bills. Everything was big, and yet we wanted it even bigger.

But as the United States begins to lose some of its swagger, even if only temporarily, everything is starting to get slightly smaller—including our dreams. The specter of economic collapse casts a pall over a people who have rarely known want. In their own lives, the vast majority of Americans are financially worse off than they were a few years ago, and they fear their family income is falling behind the cost of living.

Nationally, Americans are more pessimistic than at any time since pollsters started tracking pessimism—roughly fifty years ago. Consider the following findings from a survey we did in 2008:

- Only 12 percent of Americans think they have a worse quality of life than their parents had when they were their age, yet 44 percent expect their children to have a worse quality of life than them. Conversely, 70 percent think they're better off than their parents, but only 34 percent expect their kids to outdo them.
- Just 34 percent think their children will inherit a better America than what was left to them, while 57 percent think conditions in America will be worse for their children.

This isn't a deterioration of confidence. It's a collapse of confidence—and it has become intergenerational in scope and magnitude. So how do you restore faith in the future? What is the antidote to a toxic quality of life?

My research has led me to five core attitudes and attributes that define what Americans really want. These five attributes will help business leaders understand what drives consumers . . . and what drives consumers crazy. Once you understand what Americans want, you'll be able to deliver. Once you understand more clearly what you really want and can give it the priority it deserves, you'll be able to go out and get it.

All five are interconnected. Because a woman doesn't have enough time, she has less tolerance or capacity for hassles, and she needs more money to ensure greater convenience in her life and fewer worries on her mind. Because a man doesn't have enough money, he can't afford the stuff he wants, so he's got to work longer—and that takes away from his free time to use the stuff he can't afford to buy. Different genders, different agendas, but the same outcome—frustration.

THE FIVE LIFESTYLE ATTRIBUTES THAT REALLY MATTER

(in order of priority)

1. **More money.** No surprise here. Financial success has always been the highest priority for American men, but with the economic downturn, it has leapt to the top among American women as well. And it is not as superficial a wish as it may seem. It's no longer about keeping up with the Joneses; it's just about keeping up, period. For millions of Americans approaching retirement, it's less about more money and more about just getting back to where they once were. For women, money is all about personal security, about having no fears and no worries of the financial kind. Women measure success in life based on personal satisfaction and happiness—and the lack of economic anxiety leads to personal happiness. For men, more money means more freedom, although that does manifest itself in the desire to buy more *stuff*. Men are much more likely than women to measure their success by their accumulation of material goods: house, car, technology, toys—the whole package. And for both, money is more important today than at any time in a long time.

2. **Fewer hassles.** Have you bought a pair of scissors lately? It comes in that shrink-wrapped hard plastic shell that is impossible to open. You basically need a scissors to open your scissors. That's an example of a company that doesn't understand the importance of a hassle-free life. Products that don't perform like they do on television, services that sound much better in the advertisement than they are in reality, technology that breaks—or doesn't work from the get-go—that is the daily grind of annoying, irritating variations on a hassle. And having less of that is now the number two day-to-day priority.

   Hassles might be unavoidable in many areas of life, but that just causes consumers to be all the more choosy about how hassle-free the products they buy can be. It's one area of life they feel they can control. They'll gravitate away from any product they perceive to be more trouble than it's worth. So do *yourself* the favor by doing *them* the favor of making your product easy to access and easy to use.

3. **More time.** This used to be the highest priority for women—and for good reason. From getting the kids up in the morning to paying the bills at night, women shoulder the majority of family responsibilities and household chores, even though the vast majority of women now work outside the home. They have little time for themselves, and they crave it. Money has now surpassed

time as the highest priority for women, but that doesn't make the battle of the clock any easier. I presented this data to Gov. Arnold Schwarzenegger at his home, while seated at his kitchen table. His wife, Maria Shriver, came into the room, so I asked her, "What is more important, more time or money?" She instantly answered, "That's easy. More time." Working-class women and single moms are chasing pennies wherever they can find them. Everyone else is chasing the clock.

4. **More choices.** There is an important distinction between choice and the right to choose. Young people embrace as much choice as possible. Give them fifteen choices of exercise equipment or twenty choices of coffee—the more the merrier. Remember the scene in *Moscow on the Hudson* when Robin Williams, playing a Russian defector, came across an entire supermarket aisle of coffee options? In Soviet-era Moscow, you got one choice—if you were lucky. In an American supermarket, stocked with dozens of varieties of coffee, he was paralyzed by freedom of choice. "Coffee, coffee, coffee!" Williams exclaimed as he contemplated the dizzying array of options. Then he fainted. That was choice on steroids. The writers of the film had it more correct than they could have imagined: The children of immigrants are more likely than any segment of the population to choose more choices as their highest desired attribute in life. Conversely, older people want the right to choose but don't actually want to make the choice. For example: Give them the choice of twenty different doctors or health-care plans, and you've created a situation somewhere between confusion and chaos. To them, too many choices is no choice at all. But for most Americans, denying the right to choose or seeming to limit choice is akin to denying life, liberty, and the pursuit of happiness. Conversely, selling the right to choose or seeming to expand choice is an embrace of the American ethos, and you will find a lot of buyers. As Charlotte from *Sex and the City* so famously proclaimed, "I choose my choice!" It might only have been a line from a TV character's dialogue, but it's also the American ethos.

5. **No worries.** In a time of so much anxiety, Americans have recently begun to seek out an attribute that is very un-American in nature: no worries. Australian in origin and European in tone, "no worries" can mean anything from "Yes, it will get done," to "I will take care of you." It's an expression of confidence that things will turn out right, and it's spoken almost as often as "Have a nice day," only this time the speaker actually means it. A hassle is how long it takes your computer to fire up to a workable stage after you turn it on. A worry is the death of your hard drive. "No worries" is the difference between an inconvenience and a crisis. Or as a certain global shipping giant might tell us, "Relax, it's FedEx."

DOLLARS AND COMMON SENSE

"It was like the running of the bulls."

No, this was not a customer at a pre-Christmas sale at Walmart. Those were the words of Kathryn Finney, describing her experience when she was knocked to the floor at the Saks Fifth Avenue flagship store in New York City by someone lunging for a pair of $535 Manolo Blahnik shoes going for $160. The luxury retailer had been slashing prices to unload excess inventory.[24]

Today, good things really do come in small packages—with small price tags. The human brain processes numbers in the smallest possible increments. We are wired to prefer lots of small bites of the apple rather than big chunks. A power company might offer a plan to provide electricity at $30 a month. They'd be better off advertising the plan as $1 a day—*a dollar a day, folks!*—because Americans prefer the daily option two-to-one over the monthly fee. It's simply this: "one dollar" resonates better in their brains, even though it's literally the same deal. The smaller the amount, the more acceptable it is. Fifty cents a day sounds less expensive to people than $182.50 a year. This factoid is even more important in times like this, when people are living with a one-day-at-a-time mentality.

At the same time, dollar stores and 99-cent stores are on the rise because of the perceived *value* of buying something for just a dollar. A gallon of water. A small tube of toothpaste. A pint-sized bottle of detergent. Ounce for ounce, you might get a better deal at your local supermarket, but Americans are gleeful over the idea of getting a bargain, buying wholesale, cheating "The Man," whoever he or she is. Same principle with the runaway popularity of fast-food "dollar menus." Regardless of whether the $1 cheeseburger is really a bargain, it feels good to pony up just a dollar bill at the register.

The smaller the number, the more acceptable it is to consumers. Part of this psychology is driven by what you *think* the original price was. If you were led to believe the price of a house was originally $600,000 and it was "slashed" to $499,999, then it becomes a *value* even if the initial price was inflated. The definition of value in today's economy is driven not just by an absolute price but in comparison to what others have paid.

Similarly, credibility isn't absolute anymore. It's in the eye of the beholder, only now those eyes are so much more skeptical and cynical. You'll notice that the customer testimonials you see on television increasingly include the name of the person and the city they're from. Why? Unless and until we decide that it's a "real person" and not a paid actor, we won't accept the information—and we assume that actors don't live in Peoria, Illinois; Springfield, Missouri; or anywhere on or near Main Street, America.

In any economic climate, the phrase "guaranteed, or your money back" speaks to the twin consumer obsessions of "hassle-free" and "no worries." Even if you know it will take months to actually get that refund, it's a pledge to the customer that the company has confidence in its product—so she can, too. But ask these same consumers if they truly *believe* the "guaranteed, or your money back" promise, and half will tell you no. "There's always a catch," they'll say—and often they're right. From "re-stocking fees" to "handling fees" to "postage and handling" (what the heck is "handling," anyway—how else are they supposed to get it off the shelf and into your home?), too many companies have been too loose with the "or your money back" claim and have upset too many customers.

We also demand "independent certification" from an unbiased, expert, objective source. The used-car salesman is far less trusted than the person who sells "certified pre-owned vehicles," which is why the so-called used-car lot is rapidly disappearing.

Today, there's a better approach. "We stand behind our..." resonates even more strongly with customers (followed by the money-back guarantee, of course). We found it was the single most powerful endorsement any CEO could give a product. It represents a personal and public commitment by a person of authority that stands head and shoulders above a "promise" or a "pledge." We looked at a dozen tag lines for General Motors—none tested as positively. We've tried it with infomercials. There's nothing stronger. There's depth and meaning that the "money-back guarantee" alone doesn't offer. To consumers, "we stand behind our..." paints a picture of supreme confidence from the supplier and measurable value for the consumer. The consumer thought process is simple: I will purchase this item from the television because the manufacturer has made a personal commitment to me. I will get behind the wheel because the company and its leadership stand behind this car now and for as long as I own it. This is exactly why both GM and Chrysler fought bankruptcy so hard even though bankruptcy was the prudent approach economically; to them it represented a public declaration that the companies didn't stand behind their vehicles and didn't have faith in the future.

That's the reason why Ford made Bill Ford its front man (until he was fired, of course). The great-grandson of founder Henry Ford was featured in a series of ads that connected the auto maker's storied past to its current line of trucks and SUVs. " 'Built Ford Tough' isn't just a slogan. It's what we deliver," Ford declared straight to camera. It is one reason why Ford is in better shape than its two American competitors.*[25]

Credibility and confidence can also be built by leveling the playing field and belittling the competition. We're so desperate to save money that marketers have come to champion the theme "their loss is your gain." A recent example: Marshall's discount stores gloat about buying other companies' overstocks and bankrupt merchandise and then selling them to you at a deep discount. Somebody went bust, and Marshall's lets you benefit from it. We're so damaged as people that we're actually happy when we can score a deal on someone else's mistake or misjudgment of the marketplace. Or how about the *NBC Nightly News with Brian Williams* home foreclosure segment in March 2009 that was pitched to viewers as "one family's tragedy is another family's dream."

Consider the explosion of "Doorbuster" sales during the 2008 holiday season. Inherent in the name itself is the notion that if you line up in the biting cold at three a.m. and bust down the door at six a.m., you can get one of three TVs for a few hundred bucks off. The name is designed to invoke the feeding-frenzy mentality that drives today's über-thrifty shoppers.

They nearly did bust down the door in suburban Long Island in 2008, piling on top of one another in a mad dash to save a few dollars, and a Walmart employee lost his life as a result. Maybe retailers will be a little more careful next year, but you can be sure that the word

---

*   Former Chrysler CEO Lee Iacocca was the first auto maker to adopt this strategy when he brought his company back from the brink three decades ago. He became the face of Chrysler's turnaround, telling buyers, "If you can find a better car, buy it." (Note to Detroit: don't try this campaign in today's anti-American car atmosphere. They will.)

"Doorbuster" will be plastered across even more store ads all the same. The gimmick is just too perfect for our newly depressed economic reality. The adage is actually true: *Nobody* pays retail anymore.

It's the same dynamic in real estate, with whole niche industries growing up around foreclosures, short sales, and bank-owned properties. You can't turn on the television past midnight without seeing a thirty-minute infomercial about how to get a $200,000 home for $50,000 or less—with no mention of the current occupants inside. There are few greater calamities that can happen to any family than to lose their own home; and yet in today's economy, it's hard to begrudge another family for seizing on that misfortunate so they can afford a home.* Buying a nonforeclosure home is *so* 2006. Why pay full price when you can pay half, or even less?

Still, ask Mike Milken, the financier, adviser, investor, and architect of more corporate expansions and start-ups than any living person today, and he'll tell you that in times of great economic stress, "Cash Is King." People (and companies) would do well to sock away any savings. The rule of thumb for families is a minimum of six months of income to cover basic household expenses, and corporations a bit longer to cover operating expenses. But as 2008 ended and 2009 began, it was already too late for the millions of newly unemployed Americans who had little or nothing in the bank to fall back on. Consider the following data from the national "What Americans Really Want . . . Really" December 2008 survey I conducted of 5,900 adults age eighteen and older. Among those currently employed:

And if you lost your job tomorrow, how long would your savings last before you ran out of money?

TOTAL

23%	I Have No Savings
19%	A Month or Less

---

* The most foreclosures and greatest destruction in home value is occurring in Latino communities—the segment of American society who are more likely than anyone else to name home ownership as their definition of achieving the American Dream.

11%	Two Months
12%	Three Months
11%	Six Months
3%	Nine Months
9%	A Year
4%	Two Years
9%	More Than Two Years

Almost one-quarter of all working Americans have absolutely no savings whatsoever, and more than half have just two months or less. Just 35 percent of working Americans have put away what they need to have in these rainy days. With the job market collapsing, millions have already found themselves at the mercy of friends and relatives, while others who never planned for personal economic calamity are struggling day-to-day just to get by. Even in wealthy communities on the California coast, people living out of trailers and mobile homes are littering the landscape. No wonder consumer confidence is at its all-time low. No wonder more Americans than ever think the nation is headed off on the wrong track. No wonder so many people think the future is going to be even worse than the present. With so little saved and so much at stake, can you really blame them?

It is no surprise, then, that the first findings of a landmark new survey by Gallup indicate that the happiest Americans tend to come from the wealthiest areas. The recently launched "Gallup-Healthways Well-Being Index"[26] is a twenty-five-year initiative to track how Americans rate their own level of happiness, health, and access to basic needs. The survey is extensive, analyzing the results of a remarkably comprehensive 350,000 interviews. The questions explore a range of ways to gauge overall satisfaction, such as:

- *Are you satisfied or dissatisfied with your job or the work you do?*
- *Do you feel safe walking alone at night in the city or area where you live?*
- *Did you smile or laugh a lot yesterday?*
- *Did you eat healthy all day yesterday?*

Other questions involved everything from the availability of basic access to clean water and shelter to evaluating your life's progress on a "ladder," from 0 to 10 steps. It is, according to Gallup, "The voice of Americans and the most ambitious effort ever undertaken to measure what people believe constitutes a good life."

Based on this survey, it seems that what constitutes *a* good life is actually *the* good life. The clear trend in the survey is that the happiest, healthiest, and most content communities are those who are most financially secure. Sure, money can't buy you love. But according to these results, it sure can buy you the best quality of life there is to have in America—and happiness as well.

Much to the public's delight and Washington's chagrin, the wise people at Gallup have provided congressional district-by-district findings. Have a look for yourself. Below and on the following page are the top scorers on the Well-Being Index, with first place at the top. Keep in mind that the national median income in America is hovering around $50,000. You'll notice that all but one of the districts is well above that financial threshold—and a majority come from California. Apparently there really is something to this so-called California dreaming:

TOP "WELL-BEING" LOCATIONS

CONGRESSIONAL DISTRICT	REPRESENTATIVE & PARTY	MEDIAN INCOME	ABOUT THE LOCATION
California 14th	Anna Eshoo (D)	$77,985	Between San Francisco and San Jose, including part of Silicon Valley
Georgia 6th	Tom Price (R)	$71,669	Affluent suburbs north of Atlanta
California 48th	John Campbell (R)	$69,663	Portions of Orange County, including Newport Beach and Laguna Beach
Colorado 6th	Mike Coffman (R)	$71,393	Wealthy suburbs south of Denver

CONGRESSIONAL DISTRICT	REPRESENTATIVE & PARTY	MEDIAN INCOME	ABOUT THE LOCATION
New Jersey 11th	Rodney Frelinghuysen (R)	$79,009	Centered in Morris County, a suburb of New York City. Morris County is the sixth wealthiest county in America.
California 50th	Brian Bilbray (R)	$59,813	Suburbs of San Diego
California 30th	Henry Waxman (D)	$60,713	Includes Hollywood, Santa Monica, Beverly Hills, and the surrounding areas
Maryland 8th	Chris Van Hollen (D)	$68,306	Montgomery County, which is an affluent suburb of Washington, DC, and includes Bethesda
California 4th	Dana Rohrabacher (R)	$61,567	Portions of Orange County, including Huntington Beach
California 26th	David Dreier (R)	$68,698	San Gabriel Valley from La Cañada Flintridge to Rancho Cucamonga
California 12th	Jackie Speier (D)	$70,307	Southwestern portion of San Francisco, extending south to San Mateo
California 8th	Nancy Pelosi (D)	$52,322	Most of the City of San Francisco

You have to go all the way down to seventeenth place on the Well-Being Index to find a district with a median income below the national median income. The honor goes to Washington's 7th district, which includes most of Seattle—the same Seattle that was home to the flannel and futility-fueled grunge movement, courtesy of Kurt Cobain and company in the early 1990s. But that was before Starbucks rebranded Seattle as the coffee capital of the country. Perhaps the availability of caffeine on every corner (often two spots per corner, actually) has brightened the city's spirits—if not its skies.

At the other end of the well-being spectrum are some of our country's poorest communities. Whether it's the urban poor or rural poor, it makes no difference. Black or white? Still, no difference. Same goes for north versus south. Poor is poor, and poor equals unhappiness. And through this survey, they are telling us that opportunity and well-being just isn't a possibility for them. To minimize the depressing information, I've cut the list to only the lowest five, with Kentucky's 5th district finishing dead last.

Americans want "the good life" even more than "the American Dream." And they believe—empirically and perceptually—that money is the best path to it. That's why more money ranks as the number one priority ahead of time, choice, no hassles, and no worries.

WORST "WELL-BEING" LOCATIONS

CONGRESSIONAL DISTRICT	REPRESENTATIVE & PARTY	MEDIAN INCOME	ABOUT THE LOCATION
Ohio 17th	Tim Ryan (D)	$36,705	Includes the cities of Kent and Youngstown, a steel city that has struggled in the modern economy
West Virginia 3rd	Nick Rahall (D)	$25,630	Located in the southern part of the state, the district is based in the state's second largest city, Huntington. It is among the poorest rural districts in the United States.
Mississippi 2nd	Bennie Thompson (D)	$26,894	Covers much of western Mississippi and most of the capital city of Jackson. It is the only majority-black district in Mississippi.

CONGRESSIONAL DISTRICT	REPRESENTATIVE & PARTY	MEDIAN INCOME	ABOUT THE LOCATION
New York 16th	José Serrano (D)	$19,000	Includes the urban neighborhoods of Bedford Park, East Tremont, Fordham, University Heights, and others. Yankee Stadium is located within the district. It is a good bet that Yankee salaries are not factored into this despairingly low-median income.
Kentucky 5th	Hal Rogers (R)	$21,915	Eastern rural Kentucky. The district is 95.8% white.

HASSLE-FREE VERSUS NO WORRIES

"No worries" is the absence of fear. It's the European/Australian equivalent of peace of mind, and it has seeped into our language and increasingly into our culture. It means the electric company will keep your power on even after a violent thunderstorm. It means your satellite TV actually goes on when you click the Power button. It means your car engine turns over even when it's two degrees below zero. And in today's economy, it means being able to get your money out of the bank even if that bank has gone bankrupt. No worries is increasing in importance because it tends to involve the more significant things in daily life over which we essentially have no control, but if and when something does go wrong, it takes control over us.

Technology has come to dominate our lives, and we worry daily that for some reason beyond our control, it won't work. Admit it: Every time you turn on your computer, you watch intently as the hard drive goes through the motions to make sure all the vital functions are working. When the welcome screen comes up, you quietly breathe a sigh of relief. People who grew up before the computer age are still slightly distrustful that it will work every time, but younger people are nonchalant about their electronic gadgets. The fact that they never worry about their stuff working—that's the definition of "worry-free."

If "no worries" is really an expression of confidence, "hassle-free" is really an expression of convenience. If no worries is about what we are powerless to fix, hassle-free is about what should have been fixed or prevented long before it came into contact with us—or something we should know how to do but don't. A hassle is trying to make an international call on your cell phone. A worry is losing your phone, and all the vital information in it, when you're in a foreign locale. I have heard dozens of horror stories from people who dropped their cell phone into a puddle of water or a pool or, in one of those embarrassing moments no one wants to admit, a toilet. It's a nightmare to see your electronic lifeline being submerged. Knowing that your data is saved and safe is about "no worries." Waiting fifteen minutes in line to buy a new phone because the store is understaffed and then being put on hold trying to activate the phone—that's a hassle.

There's a lesson here for companies who produce technological products: "Plug-and-play" is more important than ever. Men won't take the time to ask for directions, and they won't take the time to *read* directions either. When they get something new, they toss aside the instruction manual and just try to figure it out. Reading the manual is a hassle to them. They'd rather play with it, force it, jam it, puzzle it out themselves. If you can save the consumer time by making it as easy as possible to use the product, you've got a winner. If they have to actually read the manual, you've just made them furious. Apple has figured this out, and its no-worries, no-hassles products explains why the company is expanding faster than the rest of the tech world. The rest of the industry still doesn't get it.

We demand convenience at home as well as at work. Our daily boundaries are blurred and interconnected. We expect everything to sync with everything else at every moment of the day. One of the biggest complaints about electronics is when they are not compatible. We have different chargers and AC adapters for every gadget in our arsenal: cell phone, BlackBerry, iPod. Is the connector round or square? Is it one prong or two? If you buy a new cell phone, even from the same company, odds are your old charger won't work. This is the opposite of hassle-free, and it costs both time and money.

The ultimate business hassle of the early 1990s was the epic struggle between Apple and PC. At the time, software that worked for one wouldn't work for the other. If you were a typical Mac user and you took a product or service into a PC office environment, you were dead. The computers couldn't talk to each other, because they spoke two distinct languages. The PC-based system eventually won, and Apple was forced to create software that could be read by a PC. But the story doesn't end there. Despite the business/office drawbacks, Mac users refused to give up their machines because a Mac allowed them to do more and do it easier than a PC would. Unlike the PC, the Mac has always been pitched to and designed for the individual user and the creative community. And for the combination of small-business start-ups and college kids who appreciate its versatility, the Mac is back.

Consumers had to endure the two-year heated battle between high-def DVDs and Blu-ray technology, a repeat of the slightly longer struggle between VHS and Beta from thirty years ago. Naming names, Sony is among a handful of particularly annoying companies that aren't interested in making their latest and greatest compatible with existing products. They want to force you to buy *their* gadgets, and *their* accessories, and deal with *their* awful customer service system. In a word, they seek exclusivity. It's an amusing though ultimately annoying premise of entitlement for competitors in a free-market economy. They will fight to the death for supremacy within the market, and consumers be damned. Sure, companies have created more *choices* for more consumers, but they have also created more *hassles* because so few of these products are compatible. You can record audio on one device, but you can't play it on another. You can buy a new digital camera, but you can't look at the images stored on your old camera card. You are forced to buy gadgets to get other gadgets to talk to one another.

This formula of built-in incompatibility and guaranteed obsolescence was fine when consumers were willing to shell out money every year to keep pace with technology, but those days are gone. "Universality" is the name of the game from here forward—easily adaptable products that can be used anywhere by anyone. That's hassle-free technology, and people will pay more for it—up to 20 percent more—as long as they only have to pay once. Moreover, technology companies will need to work backward from the consumer perspective, like Walmart has done, to determine what a customer really wants and then try to produce it.

Hassle-free is as much about what happens when things go wrong as making sure that things always go right. One reason service contracts and extended warranties are so popular among consumers and so profitable for businesses is the desire to be protected. We are

THE POWER OF ONE (II)

Business should take a cue from the telecommunications industry, where companies are increasingly offering consumers the ability to consolidate their multiple communications devices in a single gadget, then pay for multiple services with a single bill.

It's "the power of one" once again, and it offers companies the chance to simplify and streamline their interaction with their customers, while at the same time it gives customers the power to simplify and streamline their technology needs. One company. One technology. One-stop shopping. No hassles. No worries.

Right now, Verizon comes closest with its army of service people standing behind the nerdy tech guy in glasses. It is the most powerful consumer ad campaign in the industry because the message, "Can you hear me now?" and the visual of hundreds of people ready to help says "reliability" from the user's perspective. *"The phone is only as good as the network it's on."* Indeed.

prepared to pay what is, in essence, insurance so we don't get stuck either with a big repair bill or the need to replace the particular item. Now here's the not-so-secret secret, America: It's a total waste of your money. Or at least, it's betting against the odds. In all probability, your washing machine, dryer, stove, refrigerator, television, DVD player— you name it—is not going to break during the life of the service contract. We may not build cars that last, but the technology we import from Asia has a life-span a lot longer than your service agreement. So if you really need peace of mind, go ahead and pay for it. But in these tough economic times, you probably need that money even more. Americans, however, think about this completely backward. They think a bad economy means they have to get the warranty protection because it's a shield against the big, unexpected costs they simply have no savings to cover.

But when a product does break down or a service isn't performed to standard, that's where things get ugly. Ask Americans what really bothers them most about the overall retail experience, and they'll identify one area over all others: customer service. American corporations have failed miserably, and consumers are fed up and ready to fight back.

The most recent example was the initial launch of the iPhone. The battery life was less than advertised, people had trouble getting a signal, and the Web surfing capability wasn't, well, capable. Some people had more trouble than others, but a lot of people had a lot of trouble. Apple had launched the perfect product, a genuine runaway hit. But its consumers couldn't get the help they needed on the Web or via the 1-800 number, and so they angrily flooded the Apple stores. Yet here's an example of a company tapped into what Americans really want. They acknowledged the problems, apologized profusely to the public, and fixed their mistakes. Within months, even technophobes and late adopters were walking into Apple stores willing to take the risk because the product was just so good.

Even if Apple is an exception, customer service in America is almost an oxymoron. In Britain and Germany, there is a high standard of post-purchase service to match high expectations. But in America, people prefer taking out the trash to talking to a customer service representative. And they'd rather have twenty-four-hour customer service assistance that works than a date on Valentine's Day (true facts, courtesy of my polling). There are two aspects of service that drive consumers crazy: first, getting a live (American) voice on the phone; and second, actually getting help from that person. These telephone automated answering systems were created to organize and streamline consumer interaction, as well as replace expensive personnel with inexpensive software and technology. But the cost in consumer irritation is often more than the savings.

The worst telephone automated system I've ever had to deal with is GE's travel department when I worked for NBC and MSNBC (GE is the parent company of NBC). Don't bother to try it now—they've gone through a thorough revamp of the system. But for several years, it went something like this:

If you called at any time other than usual business hours, it had a message that lasted more than a minute scolding you for calling so late/early and attempting to make you feel guilty that the company would be charged an extra fee—ignoring the fact that it was extending your employee cell phone usage, and that too was billed to NBC. If you dared to continue, you pushed "1."

Then the standard message came on telling you that everything you ever wanted to do could be done more easily on their website, which was impossible for anyone in the midst of traveling, because this was before widespread use of wireless Internet access. That message also lasted a minute—probably in the hopes that you would simply hang up and not travel. But if you stayed until the end, it would ask you for your "sign-in number," with more digits than the U.S. national debt. If you got even one digit wrong, the voice scolded you for doing it incorrectly and the system hung up on you with a curt "good-bye," without even giving you the chance to do it correctly.

If you got it right, you still were only 40 percent of the way there. If you happened to call during a holiday period or when bad weather was affecting a section of the country or during the *American Idol* finals, another message would come on saying, "We are experiencing an unusually high level of calls," once again attempting to guilt you into hanging up. But since I have no guilt, I would continue. They'd ask you whether you were part of a group or flying alone (push "1"), whether it was international or domestic (push "2"), and whether it was a new or existing reservation (push "1"). And then, after all this waiting, all these nasty messages, all this phone fingering, would you get a real live person? NO! You'd get the most awful, barely audible hold music that could last as long as ten minutes. No wonder road rage has given way to phone rage as America's number one time-consuming annoyance.

My company has done a fair amount of research into the issues and challenges of customer service because it matters so much to so many people, and because it is so often dysfunctional. There are three attributes Americans really want from customer-service personnel:

First, they want them to be *knowledgeable, well-trained,* and *reliable.*

Second, they want someone who listens as they explain their problem. The combination of head (knowledgeable) and heart (listen to me) tells the customer not only that "you can help me" but "you *want* to help me."

And third, in a word: empathy.

So much of this book is about what's wrong in America that I want to highlight what's right. The best example of good customer service I've experienced is TiVo. Because my business travel keeps me away from home for weeks at a stretch, I always look forward to watching my favorite shows on my own schedule. I don't watch a single commercial;

THE THREE RULES OF AUTOMATED CUSTOMER SERVICE

Companies that insist on automated phone systems to answer consumer questions and complaints need to follow the following three procedures if they want to maintain customer credibility:

1. **Three rings, max.** People *expect* the phone to be picked up just after the third ring. That's the standard set by home answering machines and cell phone voice mail, so people are conditioned to it. Anything longer triggers an immediate negative emotional response and is almost guaranteed to make the call more unpleasant than it would otherwise have been.

2. **Two people, max.** Even more irritating than waiting for the initial telephone pickup is being passed from one representative to another. A company is allowed one transfer. If a generalist transfers you to a specialist, you'll accept that to get the expert advice implied by the word "specialist." But if you're transferred more than once, the customer loses confidence in the company and its ability to figure out what's wrong and *fix it*.

3. **Americans, please.** I don't always agree with what Americans as a whole really want or strongly believe—and this is a good example. People are immediately suspicious when they hear a foreign accent. To them, it's a sign that the help desk has been outsourced to God-knows-where, and it immediately destroys our confidence that the problem will be addressed and resolved. We're finicky— we want our customer assistance to be right here in New Jersey, not New Delhi. That's why entrepreneurial companies like Alpine Access (relying on home-based customer service agents in the United States) are taking market share away from the offshore players in the call center space.

I speed through a thirty-minute show in twenty-two minutes and a sixty-minute show in forty-three minutes. When my TiVo goes down, I am one phone call away from a meltdown. TiVo's customer service is astoundingly good. They speak to you in plain English. They empathize with your problem. They talk you off the ledge. And they know what they're doing. When I get off the phone and my TiVo works again, I'm so happy, I feel like sending them flowers or chocolates. Hassle-free means you can record your favorite TV show. Worry-free means you can actually watch it.

TiVo has mastered the craft of approaching each problem from the customer's perspective. Companies should follow their lead. Rather than approaching the issue from the manufacturer's viewpoint, they should try to put themselves into the heads of the customers. Use the right language to address the customer's anxiety and annoyance. And the best reps can call up your individual service on a computer screen so they're analyzing your particular problem and walking you through a fix based on what you see and experience rather than blindly reciting steps in a manual.

A third of Americans say customer service is worse at major companies than it was five years ago. The underperforming industries need to pay closer attention: Telephone companies, mobile phone companies, and airlines are at the bottom of the heap (though AT & T is considered "best in class"). Restaurants and locally owned stores rate the highest. It's probably because these businesses have the daily obligation to look their customers in the face, smile, and respond to individual needs. The bigger companies like telecoms, airlines, and other underperformers would do well to train their phone service personnel to behave *as if* they had to do the same thing. Customers *know* they have even less leverage when they're dealing on the phone because they feel like just another voice, just another faceless person, just another placeholder in the seemingly infinite waiting line on hold. When you surprise them by treating them like living, breathing human beings, they'll reward you with genuine product loyalty.

"No worries" is not just linked to hassle-free living, and it's far more than a smart gadget. It can also be a state of mind—and at one time in recent history, a state in America.

There was a time when the American Dream meant "California, here I come." Baseball teams, corporate headquarters, and the best and brightest brains headed west to the sun and fun of America's Left Coast for worry-free living. No longer. California now leads the nation in outflow of its residents to other states.[27] The land of no worries has become the state with no future.

One reason is the cost of housing. While some areas of California have plummeted, communities around Silicon Valley and Los Angeles still require sky-high mortgages. Even after the real estate meltdown of 2008, a modest three-bedroom, two-bath house of 2,200 square feet in Palo Alto still sells for between $1.5 million and $2 million. The income it takes to buy such a house—middle-class by size and amenities—is what Obama calls "rich."

In fact, the same is true in many suburban locations, not just in California, but in the Northeast as well. It takes a "rich" income (north of $250,000) to live a middle-class lifestyle if one is still raising children and paying a mortgage. It simply depends on where you live.

Americans aspire to a middle-class lifestyle free from day-to-day worries over doctor bills, car and mortgage payments, and education and vacation costs. (Note: Some in the media elite, like *Forbes* publisher Rich Karlgaard, define this as "upper middle class.") But the income it takes to achieve a "no worries" lifestyle is as divergent as the lifestyle itself. Midtown Manhattanites and those who live in the McMansion suburbs of Washington, DC, and Boston will tell you that a family take-home pay of anything less than $250,000 is simply insufficient to live a worry-free life. Conversely, in Little Rock or Oklahoma City, half that amount would do nicely.

NEVER ENOUGH TIME

When the economy is good, time is the new money, especially for women. Even when the economy is weak, convenience is a precious commodity because it can *buy* time.

I cannot stress or repeat this point enough. Who's responsible for the household in the early morning—waking the children, getting them dressed, feeding them, and getting them out the door? It's women. More precisely, it's Mom. And when the family is home at night, the woman still shoulders 70 percent of family duties—getting dinner on the table, making sure homework is done, and paying the bills. Dad may be the nonexecutive chairman of the family corporation, but Mom is the CEO, the COO, and the CFO. The children are the customers, they are the beneficiaries, and they get the dividends.

Add to this the challenges of health care for her children, perhaps aging parents, too, and—for most—holding down a full-time job outside the home. Yet even though women carry such a heavy load, they still feel guilty about not spending enough time with their children. The truth is, women feel guilty about not spending enough time in so many areas. To understand a woman on her own terms, the level of stress she faces is directly proportional to the lack of time she has on a day-to-day basis. Thanks to decades of habitual television viewing, people now measure time in ten-minute increments—the amount of time between commercials in a typical television show. Any shortcuts or products or services that can shave ten minutes off a task are golden, because they may give her a few precious minutes of "me time."

Bob Evans manufactures family-size packaged entrees like home-style pot roast and chicken to help the harried mom lucky enough to live east of the Mississippi River. One Bob Evans ad depicts a working mom describing her day as a "production" that starts at six a.m. and ends with "Dinner waiting at home. For me to make." After racing through the evening rituals, she sighs and says, "This show's back on at six a.m. tomorrow." But if the packaged dinner saves her ten minutes, God bless Bob Evans. This is a powerful marketing hook for any supermarket or prepackaged food company.

For readers born in the 1960s or before, you may remember the advertisement for Calgon, a soothing bubble bath. "Calgon, take me away," the narrative said, showing a woman relaxing in the tub for a few stolen minutes at the end of a hard day. That commercial went off the air in part because feminists said it was offensive. But when we talk about it to women today, those old enough all remember the tagline and they all appreciate the sentiment because it exactly expresses what they want. They're tired of their kids yelling, their spouse complaining, and every-thing from their boss. They just want to be "taken away" for half an hour—thirty precious minutes for themselves. Calgon is memorable because of what it offered, even though the ads are long gone.

Conversely, remember the 1997 AT&T ad with the mom and her two children described earlier? You can go from Colorado to Cabo and the darn cell phone or BlackBerry signal will follow you everywhere. It's relentless. A convenience morphed into a time-consuming hassle—an electronic leash.

Americans say it's harder to disconnect from work when they are at home and on the weekends; the incessant chirping of e-mail and cell phones is hard to ignore and it eats into their free time and peace of mind. The cliché is true—there isn't enough time in the day. The fed-eral government surveys how people spend their day, hour by hour. (The data is a little skewed because it includes people fifteen years and older, and teens spend far less time working than adults.)

Americans who work full-time clock an average of 7.6 hours a day, further cutting into time for everything else in their lives. Other interesting facts:

- Women put twice as much effort into housework and food preparation than men on any given day.
- Men are more likely to spend time exercising or participating in sports.
- Elderly people log 65 minutes reading and just 20 minutes on the computer. Conversely, teenagers read for just 16 minutes a day and spend 47 minutes on the computer.
- By far the dominant leisure activity is watching television—Americans spend half their leisure time in front of the TV.
- The "2020 Generation," young adults born between 1980 and 1991 (Obama's core constituency), who will be assuming positions of power in politics and the economy around the year 2020, already spend more leisure time on the computer than watching television. This is the first generation since 1960 who hasn't ranked television as their number one free-time activity.

WHAT AMERICANS REALLY DO ON AVERAGE EVERY 24 HOURS[28]

	MEN	WOMEN
Sleeping	8.52 (hrs)	8.63 (hrs)
Leisure & Sports	5.48	4.76
Work	4.52	3.14
Household Chores	1.43	2.22
Eating/Drinking	1.27	1.20
Buying Goods & Services	.63	.92
Caring for Family	.33	.72
Everything Else	1.82	2.41

CHOICE VERSUS THE RIGHT TO CHOOSE

Burger King had it right so many years ago. Remember their jingle?

> *"Hold the pickles, hold the lettuce.*
> *Special orders don't upset us.*
> *All we ask is that you let us serve it your way!"*

It was a silly song, but the language was powerful, and it still resonates today whether we're ordering hamburgers, designing our house,
or determining our health care.

The Burger King example is somewhat frivolous, but it was a brilliant marketing strategy that effectively tapped into our desire to be
thought of as individuals and our resentment toward mass marketing,
mass production, and basically everything en masse. Burger King still
echoes the specialization sentiment, returning to the "Have It Your Way!"
campaign from time to time. By implication, the original ad campaign
was a direct poke at McDonald's, which at the time did everything they
could to deny you any choices. When I was a teenager, if you asked for a
quarter-pounder, *hold the cheese,* it was a "special order" which translated into a public pain in the ass. First, the woman behind the counter
would snarl and ask: "Sir, that's going to take a while, are you willing to
wait?" If you said yes, she'd yell out "special order" so that everyone in
line would know you were holding things up. If you made the mistake of
turning around to apologize to the person behind you, you could feel the
anger from everyone else in line who would gladly cede their right to
choose a Big Mac *right now.* But your special order was standing in his
way (for me, it was always an angry man), as well as everyone behind
him, interrupting the choreographed automation of fast-food success.

After way too many years, McDonald's eventually figured out that
customers come in different shapes and sizes, with different likes and
dislikes, and gave in to choice. Restaurants no longer charge for special
requests, and service personnel are trained to welcome those who wish
to exercise their right to choose exactly what they want.

The ultimate right-to-choose is marketing that gives the customer
a menu of choices and encourages individuality. Acura had a highly
successful ad campaign depicting a husband and wife each building

their own "customized" car by choosing options like color, fabric, and accessories from Acura's website. "That's *my* car," the woman declares as her husband looks on, as though she designed it herself—which, in fact, she did.

Michael Dell created a successful technology company not based on a better computer, but on the right to choose your own components. "Build your own"—very potent words to the consumer.

Beware, however, of choice overload. There is a fine line between choice and too much choice. Some will argue that all this choice is symbolic of American extravagance and is entirely unnecessary. In the 1980s, when British tourists would first experience American cable TV, they were paralyzed. There were so many channels to choose from (at the time they had only four) that they simply couldn't decide. But instead of appreciating the freedom of being able to watch exactly what they wanted rather than what four channels decided they should watch, they complained that it all was "American rubbish" and turned off the tube. Some were actually angry. Undoubtedly a few Americans would agree, but not many. Losing your television signal, even for less than twenty-four hours, can turn a normally sweet suburban family into raving lunatics.

Still, not all choices are created equal. Think about it. Is there really a need for an entire wall of ketchup at the supermarket? It used to be your choice was Hunt's or Heinz. Now you have almost a dozen brands, six different sizes, and there are multiple versions: no-salt, reduced sugar, one carb, organic, hot and spicy—as well as the plain old garden-variety ketchup that most people still reach for. It's no wonder the average trip to the supermarket takes almost ten minutes longer today than it did thirty years ago—even with automated checkout.

WHO WE ARE AS INDIVIDUALS AND FAMILIES

The only safe generalization about Americans today is that how they look is no longer an indication of how they act. You can no longer extrapolate what people think and how they behave just by knowing the demographic group from which they come. Age is a good indicator of whom someone voted for in 2008, but an awful indicator of satisfaction or happiness. Income is a great indicator of what you will buy, but a lousy predictor of whether or not you'll be satisfied with it. Religiosity is a good indication of values and priorities, but it is an imperfect indication of aspirations. Nor can you judge people by whether they smile or frown. You have to judge them by how they think and behave.

As a result, the melting pot of ideas and cultures and ethnicities in our society can be confusing to business. To simplify the study of people and help predict their future behavior based on their current attitudes, I have used dozens of attitudinal, behavioral, and demographic questions to segment Americans into five statistically distinct categories that explain not just who they are, but how they are likely to behave and their view of life around them. This is called a psychographic analysis, and the purpose of this type of segmentation is to offer businesses a greater ability to see the *whole* person beyond their responses to questions on a survey or discussions in a focus group. Which one are you?

- **Relationship People (30%).** The largest segment of the American population, it's also among the youngest. To them, relationships can mean friends, it can mean family, it can mean spouse. They're simply drawn to other people. Their whole idea of the good life is to be with someone all the time. They get their satisfaction out of interacting with other people. They don't care as much about job or career. They are generally satisfied with their life today, but very nervous about tomorrow. They don't save; they spend, and they enjoy spending on other people as much if not more than on themselves. They are all about having a good time with other people. They're cool people to be around because they're engaged and engaging.
- **Spiritual People (25%).** This is the oldest and most female-oriented of the five segments simply because there are so few people in this category in their twenties or thirties. What unites them, in addition to the importance of religion and prayer, are the principles of simplicity and efficiency. They don't need or want to spend money to be happy. They have older cars. They have older TV sets. They don't have TiVo. They don't have satellite radio. They're not just late adopters; they're nonadopters—because *stuff* doesn't matter

to them. If relationship people are the loudest group, spiritual people are the quietest. It's OK for them to be alone, and they tend to do things in their spare time that don't require other people, such as reading and listening to music. They appreciate the outdoors (they're environmentalists) and they have a respect for natural beauty.

- **Health People (18%).** They're younger than average, more male than female, and they're the segment most likely to participate rather than observe. You won't just meet this segment at the gym or on the basketball or tennis court—you'll find them shopping at Whole Foods and having a snack at Jamba Juice. They're similar to the spiritual segment in their desire to be outdoors, but they're parallel to the relationship segment in their desire to be with others. They are the most physically active of all the groups and put a lesser emphasis on career and financial success. They're among the most casual of the segments and are least likely to be found in traditional jacket-and-tie attire.

- **Control People (12%).** These people can be very unpleasant to be around. For them, it's not about money; it's about more time and less hassle. They have everything planned out. Their intensity is similar to the health segment, but while the healthy are engaged in physical activity, control people are engaged in mental or intellectual activity. Control people want to be doing something other than what they're doing. Control people think today sucks, but tomorrow's going to be great. This is the flip side, demographically, of the spiritual segment in that these people are almost exclusively under fifty and more male than female. They're the mirror image in another way: Stuff matters. Their stereo is high-end, their TV screen is *huge*. In fact, everything is bigger—they want the newest and the best of everything. They're willing to spend money, and they work longer hours than the other segments to be able to afford it.

- **Financial Security People (11%).** The fastest-growing segment, these people are *always* unhappy and dissatisfied, and in the current economic mess, they're downright miserable. They judge themselves by how other people judge them. Their reputations mean more to them than they do for any other segment. They're the opposite of self-satisfied; they're almost self-loathing. They have a ton of material goods, but they buy things to make a status statement rather than to enjoy. They tend to be older and wealthier than average, although you'll find plenty of thirtysomethings in this category. They own; they don't rent or lease because they want whatever it is to *belong* to them. They're dissatisfied when they can't have everything they want when they want it. They're the ones who are on the phone complaining if the repairman is five minutes late.

- There's an additional 4 percent that just don't fall neatly into any of these categories.

These attributes and values can be applied to products and services, tailored to appeal to consumers in ways far different from the conventional wisdom. For example, people are interested in technology that helps them simplify and organize their hectic lives in ways that are also meaningful. Think of it this way: They want technology that improves quality of life, not just reorganizes life into blocks of time. For women, that means more time to help them balance family needs with personal needs—and so you'd appeal to the control segment. For men, it means making them more efficient so that they can make more money—an appeal to the financial security segment. In every advertising campaign you mount, you need to aim for one of these segments in addition to any particular demographic targets. If you hit two or more, good for you.

CONCLUSION

The economy may have changed what we do and how we do it, but the basic value system of America can withstand even the sharpest of economic shocks. Sure, we have lost some of our inherent optimism and can-do spirit, but if our political, business, and cultural leaders apply what *they do* to what *we want*, it is possible to revitalize the national mood and put the country back on a more hopeful path. And if individual Americans do a better job of recognizing and prioritizing what really matters in life, our satisfaction and appreciation for all that we have can also be restored.

LUNTZ LESSONS

WHAT AMERICANS REALLY WANT: A CASE STUDY

I was asked by a well-known motivational speaker and life coach to explore the aspirations (and fears) of average Americans and then prioritize what really mattered most. The gender differences were truly striking:

- **Women wanted solutions to help with life's challenges and goals.** Women were more stressed and frustrated at all levels of their life. They had little time to fill the emotional and intellectual gaps in their lives, and they were afraid that time—in the broader sense—was running out for them. In essence, women worried they were *not living up to their full potential.* Throw in a little financial stress, and you've got a good portrait of today's woman. The solutions are products and/or services that help ease her daily burdens *and*, more important, enhance her quality of life. For these women, most technology is a luxury or an intimidating hassle. It is not perceived to be part of the solution.
- **Men want a return on their investment.** Men also shoulder heavy burdens, feeling most keenly the pressure of finances and providing for their families. A few men wanted more time to spend with their families, but they were mostly focused on money. Men were somewhat less concerned about bettering themselves, unless it led to greater financial stability. They wanted the resources to travel, own a bigger home or upgrade, and invest. For them, if there wasn't a financial benefit, it wouldn't be worth the investment.

3

I CAN'T GET NO SATISFACTION:

The Jobs Americans Really Want

If hard work were such a wonderful thing, surely the rich would have kept it all to themselves.

—LANE KIRKLAND,

FORMER PRESIDENT, AFL-CIO

The best way to appreciate your job is to imagine yourself without one.

—OSCAR WILDE

Expert cashiers may not be the most glamorous jobs in America but we all want more of them. Stop making people wait in line to buy stuff. Stop hiring people who can't make change. And stop asking customers, "Can I help you?"

The truth is, people aren't really looking for "help," they're looking for guidance and a personal connection. At a home-improvement store, the employees should ask, "So what challenge can I help you solve today?" At a sports memorabilia store, the employees should ditch the generic question and instead ask, "Who's your favorite sports legend?" If the answer is Muhammad Ali, the employee should immediately take the customer to a signed photo of The Greatest. That question and subsequent effort creates a connection, starts a relationship, and leads to a sale.

But this is not a chapter about customer satisfaction. Rather, it's about employee satisfaction—how to get it, keep it, and deserve it. Once upon a time in America, we worked to live. Now we live to work. Frank Capra idealized the worker in his films and Norman Rockwell in his paintings as a distinctly American hallmark. Work, work, work. Whistle while we work. Taking care of business. All that jazz.

Americans know they work hard—harder than any other work-force on the planet. We take less vacation, work longer hours, and are more committed to our jobs. Right? Wrong! According to a study by the

THE TEN HARDEST-WORKING POPULATIONS

COUNTRY	HOURS PER YEAR	LEGAL ALLOWANCE FOR VACATION*	OFFICIAL HOLIDAYS
South Korea	2,357	10	11
Greece	2,150	20	12
Czech Republic	1,997	20	12
Hungary	1,989	20–30	10
Poland	1,985	20–30	12
Turkey	1,918	14–26	7
Mexico	1,883	8–16	14
Italy	1,800	20–32	12
USA	1,797	None	8
Iceland	1,794	24	12

*(Countries with a range provide more legal days off for older employees and/or those with more years working. The United States has no legal allowance for vacation.)

Organisation for Economic Co-operation and Development (OECD), the United States ranks a distant ninth in hours worked per year. Sure, we may have fewer "official" holidays than other countries and no government-guaranteed vacation time, requiring more actual days at work, but the population of eight countries still work more hours than we do.

Sure, we work harder than the French and their infamous thirty-five-hour work week, and we put in a lot more hours than the Dutch, the Germans, and the Norwegians—all of whom have generous month-long legal holiday allowances. But overall we're not the workaholics we think we are, at least compared to other countries. Nevertheless, America has always been home to a superior *work ethic*. Almost every immigrant who landed on these shores arrived with nothing except his or her desire to work hard as a means to a better life. The American Dream was never to come here to rest. That's what tropical island nations are for. Sure, we complain—everyone does—but America has always been the place for people who want to work hard to get ahead and make a better life for themselves and their families.

But allow me to make a distinction that did not exist in the days of Ellis Island but applies to an increasing number of people today: A majority of Americans don't actually want a *job*. What we want is a *career*. A job is nine to five. A career is 24/7. A job requires you to get up in the morning. A career is something that keeps you up at night. A job means punching a clock. A career means making a difference. Sure, they both describe work, but a job is something you have to do. A career is something you want to do. That's why people who have jobs are often dissatisfied and why people who have careers are much more content.

Work has always been important both for what one does and what it says about oneself. In America, what you do for a living is seen to represent what you've made of your life. Most people came here to work and achieve—or are second- and third-generation American workers who were imbued with that work ethic by their parents. It's our way of life to strive for employment success. So it's only natural that we would measure ourselves against how others are doing in the race to the top.

But something happened on our collective way to the summit. The generation of Americans that came just after the Baby Boom do not share their parents' affinity for work, preferring to prioritize *"quality of life"* (time off, healthcare, benefits, workplace flexibility, etc.) to the more economically based *"standard of living"* (wages and other financial compensation). Whereas their parents would be embarrassed that America was only the ninth most hard-working population, they wear it as a badge of honor—and secretly hope we'll fall out of the top twenty.

And second, the richest kept getting richer, while the middle class flattened and began to shrink. And when the economy turned ugly, so did relations between the haves and have-nots. In a nation that historically and deliberately refused to engage in class warfare, despite the best efforts of some in the political class, the current gap in income and lifestyle has been filled with resentment. The working class feels it is forced to work longer and harder than ever but for no reward. The middle class feels it is paying for the government handouts for those below them and the tax breaks for those above them. And they both resent the already-rich executives who always seem to land on their feet while their former employees land on the unemployment line. Nobody's happy—and you can see this played out every day in workplaces across America.

It is important to ground these perceptions in real numbers, lest we forget the lessons or statistics of recent history. On January 1, 2008, one month into the recession, unemployment stood at 4.9 percent. Now skip ahead eighteen months. Six million jobs were lost between December 2007 and May 2009 (some economists project up to two million additional jobs will disappear by mid-2010), and seven million people have been out of work for fifteen weeks or longer. In fact, the average duration for the unemployed was just over twenty-two weeks—and that too is climbing.[29]

Ugly. Ugly. Ugly. Yet HINTS OF HOPE was the lead headline in the *New York Times* on June 6, 2009. The employment environment had deteriorated so badly in such a short time span that a loss of *just* 345,000 jobs in May 2009, along with a spike in unemployment to 9.4 percent, the highest in almost three decades, was still regarded as an *"unambiguous sign of improvement"* according to the *Times*.[30] If you want to understand the disconnect between America's elites and the rest of us, look no further.

It's hard to identify a time in the postwar era where perceived differences between employer and employee have been as pronounced and as public as they are now. And that's because there has never been a time when job security was a higher priority to more people at the exact same time as more employers were laying off more workers. While the last two decades were marked by a period of relative labor peace, the next decade won't be so serene. With each passing day, more and more employees have come to resent the stock options, end-of-year bonuses, and golden parachutes for senior executives that are paid for with employee layoffs, wage freezes, salary give-backs, and benefit limitations. As company stocks plunge, it's the line workers, not the managers, who are the first to get the boot—and America's workforce demands an explanation.

Not surprisingly, employee trust and confidence in employers is gone. Management can no longer guarantee that employees will have a job from cradle to grave, and employees no longer offer their lifelong loyalty. From Enron to General Motors, from TWA to Lehman Brothers, the social contract between employer and employee has been shattered. It's the breakup of a marriage that has left both sides with broken hearts and lingering bitterness.

As a result, employees are replacing the aspiration of a lifetime of security with the demand for day-to-day security. If a corporation doesn't explain what it's doing, why, and what it all means, it runs the risk of undermining workplace confidence even further. What does the American worker really, really want today? Credible communication and genuine assurance that they're not going to end up like the thousands of workers (including the guy down the block) whose layoffs were announced on the news the night before.* And if you can't deliver that assurance, be prepared for increasing labor unrest.

Companies are operating at the "speed of **now**." The urgency of end-of-month monthly reports, the pressure to turn a profit (or stem the losses) every week, every month, every quarter, every year, has created a tension that you can hear, see, and feel in workplaces all across America. The pressure from management is constant and unrelenting, and it creates anxiety on all sides. There once was a time in postwar suburban America

---

* Senior corporate leaders are not immune to the inhumanity of corporate behavior. The CEO of a well-known dot-com company read about his dismissal in a trade newspaper the day before he received word from the company itself. Even the CEO of General Motors faced personal humiliation when he entered a meeting with government officials thinking he was presenting his corporate restructuring plan only to learn that he was being fired on the spot.

when "opportunity to advance" and "happiness at work" mattered most. No longer. Today, it's "job security"—the knowledge that next week, next month, and next year you'll still be collecting that paycheck. People are actually willing to be miserable for forty hours a week—at least for now— as long as they still have a job. But "job security" doesn't necessarily lend itself to long-term job tenure, and therein lies what employees really want and corporations absolutely need to offer: day-to-day "consistency" and career "predictability." No surprises—except in how few employment environments actually deliver what workers want most.

If you are a business leader, it won't take as much as you might imagine to win back some credibility among your employees. You can start by personalizing your employee relationships. American workers feel more and more like they are just numbers. Can you blame them? Our public dialogue talks about layoffs in terms of big numbers—hundreds, then thousands, and now tens of thousands. Employees think about layoffs in terms of the smallest number possible—one. When Company X lays off a thousand people, it's a one-night story. When Employee Jones loses his job, it leaves a lifelong scar.

Enter the need for empathy. It'll go a long way. Here's an example of the need for some individualized corporate compassion: In 2008, a Fortune 100 retailer asked us to conduct focus groups with their employees to explore issues that were undermining employee satisfaction. We started in Southern California because it is a microcosm of all that is good—and bad—in employee relations, and because it has become such a racially and demographically diverse community. Early in one of the sessions a young man in his mid-twenties spoke up to complain that he had been denied time off to go to his brother's wedding—even though he had made the request well in advance. Apparently this had been a big deal in the store where he worked because others in the group had heard the story, and they all shared his distress. Family events like weddings are important, and I was so surprised that I took his particular case back to the management of the company.

They said he'd only asked for the time off two weeks in advance and because of the late notice, his request had been turned down. Somehow the documentation of his initial request, six weeks early as required, had gotten lost in the corporate bureaucracy. Management insisted he hadn't followed *procedure*. Plus, it was over the Fourth of July weekend, a busy time in the retail sales calendar. Life can't always be predicted six weeks in advance. Weddings and vacations, sure, but not requests for personal time off—particularly when one has children.

It doesn't matter who was right in this particular case. What matters is the disconnect between the company and its employees. Retailers such as Walmart and Target, and supermarkets such as Safeway and Kroger, are financially successful because they can accurately predict and effectively serve consumer demand at a cost that competitors can't match. But if their own employees can't predict whether they will be able to attend a family wedding or a child's soccer game or a family vacation, it sows the seeds of discontent. The company that remembers to take a step back and ask the fundamental question "How well are we understanding and accommodating our employees' most important, personal needs?" will win the loyalty and increased productivity of its employees. This self-review doesn't take a lot of money. It's an investment measured in compassion, not dollars.

Other than holding a job, the key pain point in the American workforce is work-life balance. "I have yet to hear a man ask for advice on how to combine marriage and a career," said Gloria Steinem more than a decade ago. She may have been correct then, but the jury's out today. While men are considerably less likely than women to complain publicly about the lack of "work-life balance," it doesn't mean they don't care. In fact, the greatest reason men turn down managerial promotions at one retail outlet we studied was the stated desire to spend more time at home with family. Still, when faced with the work-life choice, men are more likely to choose work, while women are more likely to choose life. But the best choice to generate employee satisfaction is no choice at all.

Similarly, the lack of day-to-day consistency in management expectations can make the most loyal employee hostile. Random responsibilities, conflicting instructions, multiple supervisors with different measurements of success all contribute to a workplace environment that undermines employee satisfaction and breeds frustration and public expressions of anger. Lack of consistency is one of the most common complaints within the workforce, yet employers often ignore the criticisms or, worse yet, claim that the ever-changing daily requirements is in fact a good illustration of "workplace flexibility." Wrong. There is a clear message here for every manager and supervisor, and it is rooted in the answers to six very simple questions in what I call "The Leading Indicators of Employee Satisfaction/Rejection." Track and address these answers religiously and you won't need to hire another labor relations consultant or fire your human resources manager:

THE LEADING INDICATORS OF EMPLOYEE SATISFACTION/REJECTION

1. **Do I have a job or a career?** By an overwhelming 67 percent to 20 percent, Americans prefer career over a job. If they think they have a career, they're invested in staying with you and your company for the long haul—and they don't want a union getting in the way. If they think they have a job, they're probably looking for one right now. True, people with careers do change employers, but not as frequently.

2. **Does my employer respect me and the work I do?** If the answer is yes, they will feel no pressing reason to leave or join a union. If the answer is no, the perception will be a significant source of irritation not just to those specific employees but to all the employees around them. Importantly, providing ample and well-earned respect can be a more powerful motivational force than increased pay and benefits.

3. **Do I respect what the company does?** Respect is a two-way street. Employees who hold a job for a company that produces products or provides services that the employee doesn't appreciate will lead to a cynical, destructive workplace environment. This is particularly true in the weeks after labor unrest and/or a strike. Companies too often assume that their people are glad to be back at work, not understanding that the resentment that comes with difficult labor conditions will spread and deepen if not acknowledged and addressed.

4. **Do I have some control over my role and responsibilities?** The operative word is "control." Some managers call it empowerment, but that's not a word the average employee would use. One of the strongest pro-union arguments is their perceived ability to wrest control over workplace issues from employers and turn them over to employees. If employees feel they have control already, that's a sure sign of relative contentment. The problem for companies, managers, and employees is that they often see control in a different light. Alignment of perceptions is critical in the current economic climate.

5. **Are the decisions affecting me and my place of work made with some level of reliability, consistency, and predictability?** This is an issue of expectations

versus reality. One of the most powerful words (and concepts) in the English language is "reliability"—we want it not just in our cars and in our televisions but also in our day-to-day work lives. Reliability equals trust. If we feel we can rely on our employer to act in a consistent, predictable manner, we will invest ourselves in our work. If not, we will expect the worst and plan for it.

6. **Will I still be working here three years from now?** That's a time frame beyond the immediate. If the answer is yes, employees have made an investment in the company, and they want and expect to stay.

A considerable amount of survey information in this book is laid out in question-and-answer format, and for good reason. Every major employee initiative should include a written "Q&A" section because that's how employees best internalize and learn the information. We are raised from birth to ask and answer questions—that is the natural learning process for most children and adults. But when there are insufficient answers to too many questions, chaos ensues. In my work for almost two dozen Fortune 100 companies, the single greatest ongoing mistake of management is the failure to answer these day-to-day and career-oriented questions. It's a systemic failure that is costing them both employee loyalty and longevity.

For example, it's not that difficult for employers to figure out whether an employee is in it for the short or long term, or whether they will vote to join a union or fight to remain independent. There are two issues that cause workers to unionize. One is the lack of predictability, consistency, and fairness in the work environment. The other is the lack of balance between work and life. Both cause disequilibrium, leading to a desire to be heard in a strong, unified, protected voice. These are the things that make people deeply unhappy in their jobs, and they will either fight or switch unless and until they get what they want (unless the economy is so bad that people will accept a bad job rather than no job at all).

There's one additional factor that clearly drives the decision whether to stay or go—a plan of action. At a time when the status quo is so upsetting and the desire for change so universal, we have a bias toward action rather than inaction. In fact, "bold action" is the third highest desired priority for business today, just behind "accountability" and "solutions."

Business leaders can and should adopt this lesson from politics. President Obama, in pushing for the passage of his first economic stimulus bill, repeatedly sounded the refrain of the need for bold action. He knew that people wouldn't settle for government doing nothing. And he knew Americans were underwhelmed by the previous attempts to pull the economy up, like tax rebates worth only a few hundred dollars. By declaring that his action was *bold,* he communicated that it was equal to the challenges of the day. With America and its economy seemingly adrift, those who provide clear direction will win loyal followers.

Some readers may complain the word "bold" is meaningless and empty—that there is no real definition with which listeners can identify. In fact, it's exactly the opposite. Bold is in the eyes of the beholder. It is anti–status quo, out of the ordinary, something stronger than change itself. And that is exactly what Americans want from business today. But those words must be followed up by actual measurable deeds that mean something. The worst thing you can do as an employer is to promise what you cannot deliver or preach what you don't practice.

We no longer want incremental change. We explicitly reject products that are "new and improved" because we already know it represents the same old thing with a couple of bells and whistles added. We want something completely different. We buy an iPod to revolutionize our music listening habits—and because they're so easy to use. We buy an iPhone to revolutionize our lives—and because they're cool. We are constantly striving to stay ahead of the curve because we are desperately seeking to live in the future and forget the past. And as for the workplace, we are always seeking better. According to Carl Schramm, president and CEO of the Kauffman Foundation, fifty years ago the average person could be expected to have four employers in his or her lifetime. Today, the average college graduate has eight jobs by the time he or she is thirty. Company loyalty is about as relevant to today's workforce as the VCR and the cassette tape.

And that brings me to the use and abuse of "mission statements" in the workforce. For ten years my firm was paid handsomely to write them for eager clients. No longer. In research we have done over the past few years, we realized that a mission statement to employees is anything but. Employees complained that it was too often put together by outside consultants (like me) who created overarching language that didn't resonate with or relate to the employees they were trying to reach.

A "mission," on the other hand, is the reason why the company exists, why it was created. It explains and illustrates to employees what they do and why they do it. Pepsi's mission is to provide refreshment—very simple but incredibly valuable on a hot summer's day. Disney's mission is to create a world of wonderment for children from one to ninety-two and their success is why every child in America still wants to go to Disney World—and parents are still eager to take them. Las Vegas provides entertainment for adults. These are straightforward missions, and they need to be followed by an equally straightforward commitment from management.

Employees have a simple request for those above them: Say what you mean and do what you say. Fewer than 10 percent of Americans today want a "promise" or "pledge" from management anymore. Fully 80 percent want and demand a "commitment," because it is the life equivalent of putting one's reputation on the line. Particularly in times

WORDS THAT WORK: COMMITMENT

As we face these unprecedented times together, we need to do a better job of communicating the value *of you to you*. And I guarantee you'll see us live up to this Culture of Respect in several ways, including:

Our commitment to offer you encouragement and express our appreciation even in the difficult times

Our commitment to be proactive and future-oriented, focusing more on solutions than problems

Our commitment to focus on what's truly important—proper training, improved communication, better work-life choices, personal growth, and advancement opportunities for all

Our commitment to treat each person as an individual with unique work and life needs and not just an employee number

Our commitment to be straightforward and candid

And our commitment to try to be fair and to explain our decisions, so you're not in the dark and wondering why what's happening is happening of layoffs, employees need to hear that their employer is committed to those who remain. They want to hear you tell them they matter. It's a sad commentary on our world today, but people see a "promise" as being subject to change—good only on the day it's made, at best. But a "commitment" is something lasting. It means there is a Culture of Respect and built-in accountability in good times and bad. A promise is what used-car salesmen make. A commitment is a long-term relationship. The box on page 85 exemplifies what companies need to be saying right now.

American employees want their managers to have skin in the game—to suffer financially or professionally when front-line personnel are suffering. And if you want to do what Americans really want from you, put it in writing and enumerate it. Your employees won't actually read it, and if they do, they will more likely forget it than memorize it. But they want to know it exists. They want to know it's written somewhere so that, if the need arises, there is a standard to which their company can be held.

LUNTZ LESSONS:
The Five Dumbest Things to Say to Your Boss

Employees aren't the only people with gripes in the workforce. Just ask any mid-level manager and they'll tell you how difficult it is to achieve the directives from above while motivating their people below. But while their responsibilities are great, so are the rewards of success. So if your objective is to climb the corporate ladder and someday become or replace your manager, here are the five phrases to avoid at all cost:

1. **"It's not my job."** Of all the things you can say to your manager, none is as likely to provoke lasting anger as the refusal to do a task when asked. It doesn't matter whether it easily fits outside your job description. It doesn't matter if someone else could just as easily do the task. Managers never want to hear *"no"* at the workplace, and they will block your rise if that's what they hear from you.

2. **"I'm not paid for that."** Managers have one primary responsibility: get the job done. For them, employees exist for the specific purpose of accomplishing

whatever senior executives want done at that moment. Anything, or anyone, who makes that purpose more difficult is going to have a tough time come review time.

3. **"I don't know how to do it."** True enough, as too many workplaces fail to offer sufficient job training. But the correct approach for the employee is to ask the manager, *"Can you teach me so I will do it right?"* A good manager won't turn you down.

4. **"I need to leave work early/come into work late."** There's nothing wrong with taking personal time. It's how you inform your manager that matters. *"Can I leave work an hour earlier to pick up my daughter at school?"* is a better approach because it recognizes managerial authority and provides a concrete rationale. Telling is much less effective than asking.

5. **"How do I get a promotion/raise?"** This mistake happens every day and employees don't realize they've made it because it involves just one 3-letter word. Swapping out *"get"* and replacing it with *"earn"* changes the entire dynamic of the request—and improves the nature of the response.

MENTORING VERSUS MANAGEMENT

One of the most powerful solutions for those companies trending toward the "employee rejection" side of the satisfaction scale is an officially sanctioned corporate mentoring program. For the employee, it offers a chance to learn the ropes from someone who's been there and done that. For the employer, it's an opportunity to both teach and train. Sure, mentoring has had its critics, and mentors have been the butt of a lot of jokes.

A mentor is someone with knowledge and hopefully wisdom who can offer life-changing guidance to put people on a positive path within a company. It can't be a supervisor—employees are leery of confiding in them. It must be someone with some unique connection: the same hometown, the same school, a similar hobby—something that forms a bond other than work. Every company should have a mentoring program, and every employee should have a mentor. It is a proven way to promote employee satisfaction.

The reason why corporate mentoring is so important is because midlevel management is so lacking. I have had the opportunity to work for more than a dozen companies with more than 100 different locations

THE SEINFELD DEFINITION OF MENTORING

("The Fatigues," Episode 140,
Broadcast Date 10/31/96)

[George and Jerry are in Jerry's apartment.]

George: I still don't understand this. Abby has a mentor?

Jerry: Yes. And the mentor advises the protégé.

George: Is there any money involved?

Jerry: No.

George: So what's in it for the mentor?

Jerry: Respect, admiration, prestige.

George: Pssh. Would the protégé pick up stuff for the mentor?

Jerry: I suppose if it was on the protégé's way to the mentor, they might.

George: Laundry? Dry cleaning?

Jerry: It's not a valet, it's a protégé.

and workforces that number 100,000 or more, and they all routinely suffer from the same recurring problem: disconnected midlevel workplace management. Let me be clear. This is not about the national headquarters or central office being detached or disengaged. That does happen, but that's not the root cause of employee dissatisfaction. This is about managers who work in the same building, sell the same goods, offer the same services, and eat lunch side by side with those they supervise, yet have no idea what they think, what they want, and what they need out of their workplace environment.

Why? Midlevel managers are too often more adept at managing upward rather than managing down. In plain English, midlevel managers focus too often on delivering for the people above them rather than connecting with the people below—the people actually doing the work. At one major retailer, the employees described their supervisors as "negative," "condescending," "threatening," "inflexible," "aloof," "unable to relate," and "fleeing from problems." Too many midlevel managers are experts at *avoiding* employee contact. They hide in their offices, they hide in the back room, they avoid eye contact that could lead to an actual conversation. Yet few workers blame HQ for setting a bad precedent, preferring to hold local managers responsible.

I have also heard complaints across companies and industries from employees who resented managers who got their promotions from sucking up and held them by sucking up some more. So rather than building a team environment, the promotion process undermines relationships, creates a motivation problem, and only adds to the employer-employee tension.

If the American service industry—retail, restaurants, hospitality, etc.—wants to listen and learn from their employees, their primary focus going forward will be the professionalization of mid-management, for they are the "pain point" for more people in more companies than anything else. They need to be taught how to communicate. They need to be taught how to motivate. Frankly, they need to be taught how to manage—and that training needs to come from above—by management that leads by example. Nothing bothers an employee more than having to train the people ostensibly supervising them. On the flip side, good managers are gold to the company because they act as a magnet to employees, both present and potential. At one Orlando retail establishment, the store manager was so fantastic that people were transferring from the competition just to work for him.

Companies must also guard against midlevel management's arbitrary and capricious application of company policies, which creates dissent and resentment. At one store we polled, three different managers in the same store provided three contradictory directions *on the same day.* Employees also complain that promotions, time off, and assignments are driven more by personal relationships than by work performance. The solution: A "code of conduct" that is publicized and respected by everyone up and down the corporate ladder goes a long way to standardize expectations and minimize grumbling. And build accountability into the code, so that its words yield action. Periodically allow employees to anonymously grade their managers. The "test" shouldn't just be an opportunity for employees to vent. Structure it in such a way that every question measures how well a manager meets an expectation of the company, as set forth in the code. Then, let the managers know they will be graded *against* their fellow managers. Reward the best performers, and focus your retraining efforts on those who bring up the rear.

In an era when we want to be heard and understood, what we have is, in the words of Strother Martin in the movie *Cool Hand Luke,* "a failure to communicate." You can swap companies and industries, but the situation is almost always the same. I'd gather focus groups and ask everyone what they like most and least about their jobs. First I'd ask the employees what the managers would say, and they got it wrong. Then I'd ask the managers what the workers would say, and they got it wrong, too. Employees didn't know what the managers thought of their day-to-day responsibilities, and managers didn't know what employees wanted and needed from their workplace environment. Worse yet, both sides got indignant when I suggested they had no sense of what was going through each other's minds.

Communication is vital. Don't overwhelm employees with a constant barrage. Too many numbers is not a good thing, and employees aren't asking to learn about every business decision. But they *want* to be in the loop. So keep these simple rules in mind:

- More conversation with employees is better than less.
- More relevant information about day-to-day employee responsibilities is better than less.
- More training is better than less.
- And above all, avoid surprises. Nobody likes to be caught off guard, whether it's good news or bad. The earlier you can provide insight and context to a change in situation, the better the relationship with your employees will be. When challenges aren't communicated until they become real problems, you generate stress and animosity.
- Listen, listen, listen.

WORKPLACE WORDS THAT WORK

"Here's where we got it wrong, what we've learned from our mistake(s), how we plan to correct it, and how we're going to do it correctly in the future. We all want to be smarter and do things better. It's our commitment to you—to listen, to learn, and then to lead."

More than compensation or benefits, Americans really want job satisfaction, training, and communication—and they are listening attentively to any sign of job instability. In fact, they're listening to everything you say. They want to be acknowledged and appreciated. They want to be more than cogs in a massive machine. They want to be thanked for a job well done, to feel valued as employees, and to know that what they do matters. And studies have consistently shown that satisfied employees have better output and make fewer mistakes than those who are dissatisfied.

Managers, take note. Here are the four ways you can demonstrate respect for your employees:

RESPECT AND REWARD: WHAT EMPLOYEES WANT MOST

1. "Appreciation" means you thank someone individually for good work. I've heard horror stories where employees have gone weeks or even months without a verbal "thank you" from supervisors. The simple effort of uttering two single-syllable words—and meaning it—costs nothing, but is worth so much.

2. "Recognition" means you thank someone publicly in front of others. As the workplace becomes more technologically advanced, the human touch becomes that much more important. Companies are increasingly measuring output statistically, by computer. They've got statistics for everything—output per minute, output per customer, profit per sales, sales per customer—all designed to measure productivity accurately. But by focusing on the statistics, companies have removed the humanity from a human workforce. It should go without saying that people want to be treated as human beings. Unfortunately, it goes without doing.

3. "Individual identification" means you provide specific feedback about performance on an ongoing basis. It is not enough to conduct an annual evaluation; by then you're talking about ancient history. Former New York mayor Ed Koch used to walk down the street yelling out to passersby, "How'm I doing?" He really meant it, and so do employees when they ask for a personal evaluation.

4. "Daily celebration" means there should be an employee of the day *every* day. Managers must celebrate small successes along the way to achieving the big picture. By acknowledging individual and team successes on a daily basis, and encouraging a little friendly competition, you ensure that employees will become connected to the corporate mission over the long term.

Companies like Lowe's have been successful because they created a customer-centered culture. The customers know it and the employees know it. They all talk about the importance of customer service and they are 100 percent committed to it. It's one reason why they have weathered the economic times better than their competition, and that's why they're still opening stores at a time when Home Depot is closing theirs.

But when you focus on the customer component *only*, you lose your employees. The workers start to wonder, "Why don't they treat *me* the way I treat my customers?" When a customer complains and the store manager always takes the customer's side, it builds resentment among employees who feel their loyalty has been taken for granted. Retail establishments that embrace "the customer is always right and the employees are always wrong" philosophy in a dispute risk alienating the very people they need to deliver the customer service they want. A dual approach to respect leads to a much happier work environment. In plain language, corporations should treat their employees the way they want their employees to treat their customers. It's a corporate twist on the Golden Rule: "Do Unto Others as You Would Have Them Do Unto You."

Sounds elementary, and maybe it is. The rules that create a cooperative playground environment will also contribute to a satisfied and productive Fortune 100 company. But just because it's *elementary* doesn't mean it's *easy*. If it were, company after company wouldn't have to hire *my* company to help them relearn the Golden Rule.

Do not underestimate the power of *pride*. Do not make the mistake of assuming that your employees only care about their personal satisfaction, security, and pay. *Do* trust that most employees have an inherent desire for the company to do well and take pride in their work, and use that pride to increase the collective strength of your business.

In our work for a major national retailer, we learned how important it was to demonstrate a competitive advantage. Showing you're on the winning team makes all the team members want to be a part of that success. Performance numbers favorably comparing my client to their primary competitor were celebrated among managers and employees alike. The employees took genuine pride in outperforming the opposition. No matter their individual complaints about their own work environment, they joined together to emphasize and celebrate their own store's advantage whenever the comparison was raised. Remember, everyone wants to work for the best—so give employees the statistics to back it up.

THE RISE OF ENTREPRENEURSHIP AND THE NEW AMERICAN DREAM

The single greatest change in workplace attitudes over the past fifty years is the slow shift from "opportunity" to "security." The employee of today wants the protection of the safety net more than the thrill of shooting for the stars. It means workers will be more likely to play by the rules and less likely to rock the boat. It also means we will not find the greatest experimentation and innovation in companies that exist today. We'll find it in companies being born tomorrow.

One of the dumbest things I have done in my professional career involved strolling around the campus of Columbia University while on a cell phone, engaged in a shouting match with CNBC economist Larry Kudlow on his weekend radio show. Live. He was noticeably peeved when I suggested businesses should stop advocating for "capitalism" and instead replace that phrase with "the free-market system." I argued that "capitalism" had become the equivalent of a four-letter word, that Americans believed capitalists were corrupt and that they represent unfair competition.

"I'm a capitalist!" Kudlow bellowed. "Capitalism is what built America." Fair enough, but in today's world, "capitalists" frighten people, and "capitalism" is shorthand for CEOs taking tens of millions of dollars on the same day their pens wipe out 10,000 jobs. Americans think capitalists are all about profit and nothing else—victory at any cost—getting ahead without caring about those left behind.

Americans have discarded that model.

What they want instead are entrepreneurs. Entrepreneurs are innovative, involve others, and achieve. Unlike the "greed is good" motto of Gordon Gekko and some hedge fund managers and venture capitalists, entrepreneurs are seen by Americans as business innovators and wealth creators. In fact, by better than a 3 to 1 ratio, Americans now trust entrepreneurs more than successful CEOs. There are two aspects of entrepreneurs that make their pursuits so heroic to so many people— passion and inspiration. We appreciate Bill Gates for helping to create the information age and Michael Dell for putting computers into every home. We are grateful that Steve Jobs allowed us to combine all aspects of our lives into a single portable gadget, and we admire Warren Buffett for financing the next great technological breakthrough. We even love the scientist who tries hundreds of different formulas ("the one-in-a-thousand fluke" wrote the *Times* of London in 1996) before he hits on what he is looking for—the heart drug that morphed into Viagra. What's not to love? The experimental drug that was supposed to open up your arteries if you're having a heart attack instead opens the blood flow to another important organ! The search and experimentation, the trial and error, benefiting from failure, sharing success—it's what makes entrepreneurs among the most valued occupations in America today.

In a landmark survey my firm conducted in September 2008 for the Kauffman Foundation, the leading entrepreneurial think tank in America, it's hard to tell which has become the stronger emotion: respect for entrepreneurs or hatred toward CEOs. As the question below clearly illustrates, building something from scratch now is held in higher esteem than rising to the top of the corporate ladder.

Hypothetically, if you had to choose, would you prefer to be? . . .

TOTAL

80%   The Owner of a Successful Small Business You Started
      That Employs 100 People

14%   The CEO of a Fortune 500 Company That Employs
      More Than 10,000 People

6%   Don't Know/Refused

Take a moment to rethink the survey results above. It might be easy to chalk the staggering 80–14 spread as a reaction to the obvious CEO excesses of recent years. But think about what exactly this 80 percent of Americans would choose—and exactly what they would willingly forgo. The small-business owner, even if she (female-owned small businesses are among the fastest-growing components of the shrinking economy) is successful, isn't making bonuses totaling tens of millions. She has no golden parachute, unless her business is providing skydiving lessons. She has to look her employees straight in the eye when it comes time to lay them off rather than just issuing a corporate edict. She has endured a lifetime of sleepless nights, tossing and turning about whether the business really was going to make it and whether she was going to let her employees down.

Americans realize that there is far greater risk in investing your own time, your own money, and your own heart into starting a small business—and it's even harder to make it a successful one. And these risks made by small-business owners are all in search of far less financial reward than their CEO counterparts. But the noneconomic benefits that come with pride and achievement still drive that 80 percent to reject the millions that come with being a captain of industry. They'd rather pilot their own ship.

So, how to equip a generation of Americans for successes in entrepreneurship? Forget about MBAs. Most business schools teach you how to be successful in a big corporation rather than how to start your own company. But starting something from scratch and nurturing it as it grows is where our country has always been at its strongest and most innovative. Returning to the Kauffman survey, vast majorities of adults believe American students should learn about entrepreneurship in high school and college.

- 81 percent say universities and high schools should actively develop entrepreneurial skills in students.
- 77 percent say the state and federal governments should encourage entrepreneurs.
- 70 percent say the success and health of our economy depend on it.

Fostering a spirit of innovation among the younger generation is a surefire way to create the next wave of new ideas—and the jobs that will follow. But don't call the coursework "economics." This isn't the study of theory. It's the study of real life. It's not Econ 101, but Building a Business 101. Throughout the course, let the theme be how free markets reward innovation and entrepreneurial hard work.

Think about it. We teach government, civics, and American history, and that's why Americans grow up believing that democracy is the best form of government. Liberals, conservatives, and almost everyone schooled in this country agree—and we certainly don't agree on much. The theme in American government courses is usually that *freedom* is good because it allows us to pursue happiness and achieve for ourselves.

So why don't we teach the value of *free markets,* the backbone of U.S. global strength? Imagine if classes in free markets were mandatory, like math and history and language. Our children would be bursting with ideas about how to turn their dreams into businesses.

Even in this sad economy, the yearning to "work for yourself" is strong and growing even stronger. Some 70 percent of full-time employees have considered starting their own business.

Every year 600,000 people start a new business, and upward of 45 million Americans run their own business today.

These entrepreneurs are drivers of the economy. They invent and innovate. Nearly all the private-sector jobs created each year come from companies less than five years old, according to research by the Kauffman Foundation.

FedEx, Apple, Microsoft—they are among the most respected companies in America. Yes, they are now corporate giants, but they started out in our lifetime as a gleam in someone's eye and grew into financial stalwarts thanks to CEOs with visions greater than the status quo.

Most people know a successful entrepreneur. Or, more likely, they are familiar with a small business—a friend who opened a restaurant, a relative who owns a convenience store. Entrepreneurs are driven by wants and desires shared by millions of Americans: to control what they do, to earn and keep more money, to be in charge of their hours, and to be their own boss. They love the profiles of success stories like Walt Disney (old) and Bill Gates (new). It is the story of America—to start with nothing and build a success, to have a brilliant idea and bring it to life.

So if we really want the things that can only be achieved through entrepreneurial behavior, why have so few Americans given up their day jobs and become 24/7 entrepreneurs? Three words: fear of failure—or in their own words, the fear of "losing it all." The entrepreneurial decision making involves a simple cost-benefit analysis: Are the rewards associated with going out on your own *worth* the potential loss? Statistics indicate that more than half of Americans are afraid to fail or to be labeled a failure. This is especially true in a climate where savings are limited, credit is hard to get, and customers even harder to get.

But failure has a positive aspect, too. According to our 2008 Kauffman survey, overwhelming majorities of Americans believe:

- Most *successful* people have failed at some point in their lives (95 percent).
- It's better to have *tried and failed* than never to have tried (92 percent).
- One thing that sets the United States apart from the rest of the world is its *entrepreneurial spirit* (86 percent).

What do you consider to be a safer path to financial security?

TOTAL

46%	Working for Myself
36%	Working for an American Corporation
18%	Don't Know/Refused

Americans already *think* like entrepreneurs. Almost half say they've had a specific idea for an entrepreneurial venture in the past year or see opportunities in the economy for such ideas. But they're unsure how to proceed—only 35 percent would know where to go for help. Think about it: We live in the most economically free country on the globe, yet only one person in three knows how to get help to get started in business. If even half of them launched those ideas, imagine the positive impact on the economy.

Just ask Michael Dell, Ben and Jerry, and Jeff Bezos.

As a college student, Dell had a simple concept in 1984: Sell directly to the consumer. Now his Austin-based company is the number-one provider of PCs in the United States, and he runs his *own* Fortune 500 company.

Ben Cohen and Jerry Greenfield took a $5 correspondence course in ice-cream making and opened their first shop in Vermont in 1978. They turned a $12,000 investment into a $300 million company (which they sold to Unilever in 2000, at which point many of its pro-worker policies were eliminated).

Jeff Bezos started Amazon.com on three tables at his home in 1994 after deciding that bookselling would be more efficient on the Internet. His plan, which he typed up while his wife drove their car from Texas to Seattle, led him to a net worth of more than $3 billion and *Time* magazine's Man of the Year in 1999.

T. Boone Pickens told a 2007 high school graduating class, including his grandson, of his boom-and-bust years and how he'd learned as much from failing as from succeeding. Approaching eighty, Pickens said he'd trade places with any eighteen-year-old graduate just for another shot at life's promise. Not content to sit on the sidelines, Pickens last year jumped feet first into a self-funded wind power venture.

Ask America's youth, as we did, what impressed them the most about these famous entrepreneurs and they'll answer you with wonder: "They started with nothing." Young people *think* differently. They're wired to follow their dreams. They want to stand out in the crowd. By and large, they are unencumbered by debt and willing to take a chance. Why *not* be an entrepreneur? Six in ten college students say they've had a specific idea. The biggest obstacle holding them back is "I don't know how to get started." What do they *really* want? The information to help them get started and the chance to succeed.

Young or old, the single biggest obstacle to entrepreneurship is . . . money. Even the fear of not having a regular paycheck pales in comparison to lack of startup cash. For the most part, potential businesspeople have no idea what loans might be available to them or how to obtain them. And for those who did have a general sense, many simply thought the money wouldn't be available to them.

Our advice to Kauffman stands for the business community too: Americans want to be excited about their jobs. They want a sense of passion and control in what they do and how they do it.

Control over their lives is the number-one motivation for people to start their own business—even more than earning and keeping more money. In a risk-averse era, ownership of one's future is a compelling selling point. It is brave to open a new business during a downward economic spiral. But compare the alternative: sitting at a desk in a New York City high-rise, waiting for the "Can you come into my office?" call from HR to fall on you like a ton of bricks. Or if you already lost your job, isn't it better to create your own job than to wait for Washington and Wall Street to make you a new one?

With ownership comes control, and with control comes freedom, security, and peace of mind. So how can government help? There is bipartisan support for state and federal governments to promote and nurture entrepreneurs—though the means are certainly different. Democrats want the government to actively facilitate entrepreneurship while Republicans want the government to do less—less paid in taxes, less regulation, less litigation. The message to the politicians is equally clear: "Great ideas shouldn't require mountains of paperwork to put into action." Red tape should be shelved in favor of encouraging breakthrough ideas that may shape this century. Lawmakers need to be reminded that today's big entrepreneurial ventures started out small and grew *despite* bureaucracy and regulation, not because of it. And they should be cheerleaders for genuine workplace freedom, whether it be the factory floor, the office cubicle, or the brand-new start-up:

- The freedom to choose when, where, and how to work
- The freedom to try and fail and try again
- The freedom to follow your dreams wherever they take you
- The freedom to live your own life on your own terms

Sound like the American Dream? It should.

US VERSUS THEM

Americans are a competitive bunch. When it comes to competing on the international trade front, we want to *win*. Just like a Yankees–Red Sox game, the only acceptable economic outcome is a crushing victory. But what happens when the definition of victory is not so clear, the rules of the game keep changing, and even the players themselves are poorly defined?

Support for a "Buy American" campaign to reward American companies who hire American workers still surpasses 70 percent—and is much higher among people age fifty and older. Americans really want to help their brethren weather the financial storm. But frankly, we don't know what an American company is anymore. You tell me which company is more American and/or more important to our economy:

Company A assembles 80 percent of its products in the United States, employs more Americans than most American-based companies, but is foreign-owned and foreign-controlled. The CEO can't even speak conversational English, yet his company donates millions to communities all across America. They pay good American wages, though the profits are taken out of the country and most of their taxes are paid elsewhere.

Or . . .

Company B is owned and headquartered right here in America, but it currently assembles 70 percent of its products in foreign countries. While it reinvests its profits here at home and pays American taxes—a lot of them—it continues to shift thousands of American jobs to foreign locations.

Both companies clearly add value to the American economy, but we dislike Company A because it's foreign, and we dislike Company B because it is creating foreign jobs at the expense of American workers. We absolutely deplore the "outsourcing" of American jobs to foreign countries, and we are equally angry when a foreign company buys an American brand. Global economics, like life itself, has become messy, and you can't tell the good guys from the bad guys without a scorecard—or *The Wall Street Journal*.

Americans have come to accept a certain level of economic confusion, but they don't like it when they don't know who to root for. It's easier just to assume that everyone's a bad player—which they do.

Let's take a specific example. Consider Honda, which made its debut in the United States in 1979 when it opened its first plant. Its investment in American workers has steadily grown along with its car sales. In 1997, Honda spent $6.4 billion in parts and materials bought in the USA. A decade later, Honda says the total is $17.1 billion, spread across 520 suppliers in 34 states. That translates into tens of thousands of jobs, in addition to the 25,000 directly employed at Honda plants.[31] Same with Toyota, which now directly employs more than 43,000 people at its 11 factories in the United States. So the two Japanese auto giants alone employ some 68,000 people in America, and they're still growing—as are BMW, Mercedes, and almost every other foreign-owned auto manufacturer.

So which is more American—GM, which assembles tens of thousands of its vehicles in the Far East, or Toyota, which assembles tens of thousands of its vehicles here?

True, the Detroit chieftains like to point out that what is at stake is not just the workers who built the cars and trucks. There are three million auto-related jobs across the nation, at dealerships, repair shops, parts, wholesale, and manufacturing. And it's clear that no one wants to see the end of American automotive manufacturing. But Americans vote with their paychecks, not their hopes and wishes. Toyota has surpassed GM as the top auto seller in the USA. We value the jobs, but we value a good car even more.

While this is a book about what Americans really want, it is equally important to point out what Americans really hate. We value good old-fashioned American common sense. We hate extravagance—particularly when we're stuck with the tab. When taking the short hop from Wall Street meetings to Washington, DC, to ask Congress for $25 billion in funds to stave off bankruptcy, the CEOs of the Big Three American car companies—one would assume—would either take the Metroliner (at a cost of roughly $250 for first class or $150 for business class) or the Delta or US Air shuttle at $300 a ticket. Not these guys. All three chose to arrive on their corporate private jets—individually—rather than ride with the public . . . at a combined cost of $28,000.* A subsequent ABC News investigation revealed that the top three automakers have together spent "several hundred million dollars" to "buy, maintain, and operate a fleet of top-of-the-line private jets for their top executives." In this case, the "us" are 300 million Americans, and the "them" are three very out-of-touch CEOs.

Another example of the "us versus them" division I learned the hard way. For a guy who makes his living by wooing corporate chieftains, my overt bluntness and unedited candor often get me into trouble and occasionally cause me to lose a client. Back in 1997, I was in Senate Majority

---

* What they should have done is organize a caravan to Washington, DC, of 1,000 workers in 1,000 American-made vehicles, all decked out in American flags.

Leader Trent Lott's ornate Capitol Hill office waiting for a meeting when the Washington representative from UPS stepped over to introduce himself. UPS was in the midst of losing a major national strike, and so I took the opportunity to jump all over this guy for the company's failure to communicate. I told the guy quite emphatically that his company was not only ineffective in its antistrike efforts, but that it had single-handedly revitalized the labor movement in America. I then pointed to two specific problems with management's communication: their apparent insensitivity to their workforce and the strategic brilliance of the union in putting a woman out front as its primary spokesperson.

The female spokesperson humanized what the striking workers were going through in a way that a man could not. First, her gender was an immediate attention grabber because it went against the expectations of both a truck driver and a union official. Second, she would describe in great detail the day-to-day life of a UPS worker and the challenges and skills it took to be a truck driver. And only then would she make an appeal for public support of the striking drivers. She succeeded because people could empathize with her portrayal of the overworked, underpaid worker and why she was on strike.

UPS was seemingly insensitive to all this, and I complained rather loudly to the Washington UPS rep that he should tell his CEO to get his act together (I actually used a more scatological term) and stop making the business community look so "pathetic" with such an anemic response to the union. He looked at me with visible embarrassment and said, "Tell him yourself," at which point a well-dressed, soft-spoken gentleman sitting behind him stood up, extended his hand, and introduced himself as James Kelly, the CEO of UPS. He probably thought I was somewhere between a vagrant and a nut. I hadn't shaved that day. My hair was uncombed. My polo shirt was lightly stained and heavily wrinkled, and he probably noted that I looked worse than a UPS deliveryman at the end of a brutal shift through driving rain. My outburst forever ended any hope of landing UPS as a client, but the points I made were valid.

The 1997 UPS-Teamster strike ended in one of the clearest defeats for business and victories for labor in modern times. By 2 to 1 margins, most polls had the public siding with the strikers. As Arthur Shostak, a nationally recognized labor expert, summarized in a *Business Wire* press release at the time:

Not since 1981 when the White House fired 11,400 air traffic controllers has a labor-management showdown so captured public attention, inconvenienced so many, involved so many workers, and so tested labor's mettle. . . . The union made a creative effort to win public support, something the air traffic controllers ineptly sought only after the fact. The Teamsters held press conferences and public rallies before and during the strike. . . . UPS Chair James Kelly complained the union had a "media blitz ready to go." This time, the union succeeded in linking its case to issues the whole country could identify with. The union sought a raise for part-timers and an option to go full-time, bargaining demands that resonated with all Americans who felt victimized by "take-it-or-leave-it" terms of employment.

Most companies do a far better job understanding their employees—what they think, how they feel, and what they need. FedEx is a good example. Fred Smith is a bona fide genius who has run FedEx since its inception in 1973. Today, it has $38 billion in revenue and the ability to move 7 million packages around the world on a daily basis. The company works just as hard to understand its workforce as it does its customers—and communicates to them just as frequently. Most companies justify what they've already done; FedEx tells their employees what they're going to do *next*. That way, they get midcourse corrections based on feedback from the workforce as well as greater buy-in. Unlike many Fortune 500 companies, FedEx employees are proud of the company they work for, and a surprising number can recite from memory the company's motto, affectionately known as the Purple Promise: "I Will Make Every FedEx Experience Outstanding."

FedEx correctly believes its strong relationship with its employees gives it a leg up on the competition in today's cut-rate, cutthroat business environment. They're right. There is no "us versus them" culture at FedEx. It's all "we."

Not all companies share a commitment to listen, understand, and communicate—and that's when I get a chance to see the internal damage up close. I was brought in by a Fortune 100 company to conduct an "instant response" focus group to learn about and help resolve an increasingly "us versus them" culture in one of their divisions. The effort took me to a Northeastern city, corporate headquarters and ground zero for what one executive politely described as "the troubles." Passions were running deep. Managers warned their subordinates not to participate, in the focus group. Three dozen workers ignored the animosity from the top and showed up anyway—four more than were actually invited. Several came from out-of-state. One person drove seven hours from West Virginia. They were so angry that I could hear the four-letter words being spit out in the adjacent waiting room. The four female participants each could have broken my arm. Even before it began, I knew it would be the focus group from hell.

And it only got worse. The focus group room was much too small for thirty-six people, and I found myself backed up and leaning against the one-way mirror—on the other side of which the division CEO and his direct reports were watching. People had clearly come to vent, and I was their victim. One guy stood up (the only time in more than a thousand focus groups that anyone had ever stood up) and said he wanted to push me right through the glass, he was so mad. "They lied to me," he kept saying about the company he had worked for and represented for more than a decade. "They lied to me. They're all a bunch of f—ing liars." People were leaning forward, poking their fingers in my face from the second and third row, all yelling. It was the "us versus them" mentality times a hundred—and I clearly wasn't one of "us." They wanted to scare the hell out of me. They wanted me to feel the anger they felt. They wanted me to feel it physically.

Well, it worked.

I tried to take charge of the room again and again. At one point I suggested they "calm down and relax," which drove them right to their emotional breaking point. They had been told this again and again, year after year, by their managers—and nothing had ever changed. Once again the threats started, and I could hear through the window suggestions by one of the observers that they should come "rescue" me.

What I did not hear was any comment at all from the division CEO. Not a word. Nothing. Even after I had restored order and took a moment to slip away from the focus group and into the observation room, the division CEO was still silent. He had nothing to say. Nobody would look me in the eye—and they wouldn't look at him, either. For years he had told his managers that they didn't have a problem, that everything was fine, that everything was cool (though he told his team to bring his car around to the back to ensure that none of the disgruntled workers would see him). At that moment, everyone realized what he had refused to acknowledge: The "us versus them" mentality had taken control—and it was too late to fix it. The focus group session that looked like it might cost me a shove through a plate-glass window ended up costing him his job and his career. He was prematurely "retired," and a new team was brought in to clean up the mess.

Sadly, pictures like this one have been painted across the business landscape. It is unlikely that CEOs will ever reclaim a broad-based level of trust, confidence, and respect. The American public was discouraged by their conduct during the "greed is good" years, but we've been devastated by their behavior and abuses in more recent times—and the scars won't heal easily.

The alternative? Start locally. Your business, even if you're Fortune 100, can't carry the water for our national confidence problem. But you *can* and *must* start with your own people. Let your managers rebuild shattered confidence one relationship at a time. Let your executives prove—with their paychecks, because that is the root problem—that *your* company isn't like *those* companies. Turn "us versus them" from "employee versus employer" to "our business is your business." How powerful it would be if your employees had real reason to believe that your company was an exception . . . a role model . . . a sanctuary from the excesses, abuses, and unfairness that are rampant everywhere else. Their loyalty will lead to your productivity—and that is truly what Americans really want . . . really.

Yes, ethics really do matter—and not just to employees. As the ranking from a Fall 2008 poll of full-time employees clearly indicates, it is the highest priority for all Americans.

The solution to another "us versus them" dilemma was found by an unlikely source. Several years ago, U.S. Steel and the United Steelworkers did an unusual thing. The company was steadily losing ground to foreign competition, and that meant a smaller and weaker union. But instead of glaring across the table at each other, they decided to collaborate to try to communicate the value of American manufacturing and the factory worker to the rest of the world. Strange bedfellows indeed—sworn enemies cooperating for the betterment of everyone. I presented my research findings separately to the industry executives and to the

THE 10 ATTRIBUTES PEOPLE WANT MOST IN A COMPANY
(Ranked in Order of Preference)

1. Establishes and Demands High Levels of Ethical Business Practices
2. Has a Corporate Governance System That Ensures Accountability and Protects the Interests of Shareholders, Employees, and All Other Stakeholders
3. Consistently Exceeds Customer Expectations for Delivering Quality Products and Services
4. Creates a Positive Work Environment and a Culture of Respect for All Employees
5. Is Active in Trying to Solve Economic and Technical Challenges Facing America Now and in the Future
6. Takes Major Steps to Protect the Environment
7. Makes a Positive Impact on Communities Where It Operates
8. Actively Invites Input and Feedback from Employees, Customers, and the Community
9. Is a Good Company in Which to Invest
10. Supports Economically, Ethnically, Regionally, and Gender Diverse Employees and Suppliers

union executives (cooperation only goes so far). The industry execs were a breeze. The union was not.

The union leadership was a physically intimidating bunch. Their average weight was well over two hundred pounds, and one could immediately see why. Breakfast was vats of scrambled eggs, hash browns, bacon—and no one was shy about having seconds. The sheer volume of protein consumed was shocking. Picture breakfast with the Sopranos just before a big hit.

Leo Gerard, union chief, introduced me. His introduction was short, but far from sweet: "Everyone here should know Frank Luntz. He's done a lot of damage, elected a lot of bad people. He's responsible for a lot of bad things. You have a lot of explaining to do. The floor is yours."

Huh? In my entire life I've never been introduced as though I had committed war crimes. I looked around the room—tough, lifelong union organizers to my left, right, and straight ahead. But if someone comes at you with such raw animosity, the best you can do is go right back at 'em.

I challenged him right off the bat, and we went at it for two and a half hours.

I told the union leadership that they were their own worst enemy, that their language was out of the 1970s rather than the twenty-first century, and that their tactics were alienating rather than embracing. This meeting, I said, felt and looked like a business meeting from 1973. Gerard and his deputies weren't used to people challenging them. They loved it. For every shot they took at me, I threw one back. By the time we were done, they wanted to hire me to work against the company that had paid half the bill. (I turned them down.)

Back to the alliance. Our goal was communicating the value of the manufacturing workforce to an American public wanting to protect their jobs but not fully understanding why.

Their cause was worthy. The challenges were daunting. People simply don't understand what "manufacturing" means. They don't understand that manufacturing was the great innovation that built the twentieth century, and they surely don't understand its relevance in the new century. To make matters worse, they view manufacturing jobs in a very poor light. They think it's mindless "dirty work" that requires minimal thinking and a lot of physical labor. They picture factories that are more like yesterday's Rust Belt than the state-of-the-art facilities of today. That is the largest hurdle they needed to overcome.

There is a bright spot: When it's put in the proper context, people do understand and appreciate the importance of manufacturing to the economy. From nanotechnology to robotics to lasers, we are at the cusp of incredible advances in manufacturing, at a pace never before seen in history. The problem is, when people think of nanotechnology, they think of Silicon Valley where many of these ideas were born. They do not think through to the next step, where the new idea is manufactured. You can have the best idea on the planet, but if it can't be built, it's just an idea. When people think of robotics, they think of what they can do, not how they are made. And lasers more often suggest new technology rather than new manufacturing. Sure, Americans regard technology and manufacturing at par (89 percent compared to 88 percent) in terms of the importance to the economy overall. Moreover, we do not believe the Information Age and the Industrial Age are mutually exclusive. On the contrary, the public values the synergy. But almost three-quarters of

Americans (72 percent) think we're losing the manufacturing battle even as we're winning the technological war.

Now, as the old saying goes, "Your windshield is larger than your rearview mirror." That is, you should spend more time looking ahead than at what's behind you. It's true of manufacturing as well. We encouraged steel not to dwell on the past and to focus instead on the future. Step one is to stop referring to their facilities as "factories." It is an early twentieth-century word associated with unskilled workers and physical labor. Instead, it is essential that they talk about "high-tech facilities" that employ "highly skilled workers" who operate "state-of-the-art computers" and other sophisticated equipment to make "cutting-edge products" that are sold worldwide.

Step two is to teach Americans about the need for free and fair trade. If China heavily subsidizes its industries to make its products less expensive in U.S. stores, is that fair? *No!* If they flood U.S. markets with cheap products to gain market share, is that fair? *No!* And if China then makes American-made products too expensive for their people to buy, is that fair? Again, *No!* It's one reason why Walmart has dropped off most "most admired" lists—because people see that their business practices may lead to lower prices but that they also lead to less employment for (and unfair treatment of) American workers. The best international trade environment is one where "everyone benefits" and where "everyone follows the rules."

Step three is to demand accountability, not only from the offending countries but also from U.S. political leaders vested with the authority and responsibility to demand strict adherence to trade laws. This is not about "protectionism"; it's about "accountability." No cheating. We want—demand—that our elected representatives fight for American workers at least as hard as they fight for their jobs every two, four, or six years.

And step four is the national security component. If companies can link national security with the need for a vibrant manufacturing base, Americans are thumbs-up—88 percent want equipment for the U.S. military to be manufactured in America by American companies. They don't want to be held hostage to foreign companies in this critical area. The same holds true for other products deemed "critical" to the economy. Americans are simply uncomfortable relying on other nations for our economic security. We want to rely . . . on *us*, not on *them.*

PEOPLE, NOT NUMBERS

Some Americans love to work, and we all love the *idea* that we love to work. It's the legacy of the Protestant work ethic on which this country was founded.

We pride ourselves on our productivity. We work to produce foodstuffs to feed the world. We produce technologies that push and transform the world. We create small businesses that create more jobs. Two-thirds think most people can get ahead *if they're willing to work hard.*[32]

But we grow anxious when we don't feel valuable or valued. Business must learn the language that tells each and every employee that he or she matters. Americans think they're worth every penny of their wages (and more). Too many employers talk about employees in terms of capital assets and lines on a ledger sheet. Wrong. First and foremost, they are people. As the Elephant Man pled to anyone who would listen, "I am not an animal. I am a human being." A similar plea can be heard by service workers across America every day.

In 2003, after heated exchanges between management and the unions, grocery workers went on strike against Albertsons and Vons stores in Southern California. As a result, Ralphs, the largest of the food chains, locked out its union employees—in essence putting them on strike as well. And right from day one, the strike was nothing short of a disaster for employees, all three employers, and for millions of customers as well.

The strike itself began on October 11, 2003, and lasted an unprecedented 141 days. My mission was to learn how to make things right for the employees going forward.

What I heard from that initial post-strike focus group is seared into my professional psyche as much as the strike itself had been seared into their souls. These workers were permanently scarred. Never again would they trust any company to do the right thing. Never again would they trust their union to do right by them. Never again would they believe there is a sense of compassion or caring from Corporate America. The pain and fear they faced for 141 days will live with them for the rest of their lives.

We held that session in Beverly Hills, in the modern office building that is home to Castle Rock Entertainment and other Hollywood-related businesses. We brought in freshly baked croissants and fresh-cut fruit. Workers carpooled from their neighborhoods, which were very different from the affluence of Rodeo Drive. Our creature comforts were welcome, but did little to alleviate the pain in the room.

Their stories came tumbling out. One woman knew a striker who had killed himself because he couldn't support his family. Most knew people whose families broke up. Several people lost their cars, one person lost his home. It was financially and emotionally devastating. Everyone had a hardship story. But to my surprise, I didn't hear much anger. I didn't even hear a sense of resignation. What I heard is the worst emotion of all: surrender. These people had given up. To them, the American Dream was dead—killed by a company that locked them out and a union that would not settle.

At the end, I couldn't speak. I couldn't do a proper debriefing. To borrow the words of President Clinton, I felt their pain. There was only one supermarket manager present behind the one-way mirror. He, too, couldn't speak. We just looked at each other in silence. I finally said, "I'm sorry," and I left the room.

It was a classic failure to communicate. The strike didn't have to be

WORDS THAT WORK

The Road to Rebuilding Corporate Credibility

Restoring faith and confidence in Corporate America will require **change** and **action, commitment** and **vigilance, time** and **patience.** But it must happen. Now it is time to pick up the pace.

The following six words summarize what Americans really want most in their employers and those who employ more than 100 million Americans:

- **Change** in the way things are run in the workplace
- **Action** rather than just words
- **Commitment** to actually get it done
- **Vigilance** to ensure that the old ways never return
- **Time** to adjust to the ongoing economic transformation
- **Patience** with our people as they learn and adapt

so devastating. The eventual agreement was no better than the first offer. The union could have settled much earlier and avoided so much
pain and suffering. The intervening months destroyed the morale of
the workforce—and the profitability of the company. It also chased away
some customers who found new places to shop and chose not to return
after the strike ended. Everyone lost. [33]

Only one question remains: Can Corporate America deliver?

Companies can attract and retain better people by addressing
the needs of employees *as people*. Companies that monetize employees
rather than appreciate them and measure compensation instead of satisfaction will eventually pay the price for thinking of their employees as
numbers, not people. The ranking that follows is from the Fall 2008
poll measuring what Americans really want and expect from Big Business.

The 20 Attributes That Best Describe a Good Corporate Citizen
(in rank order)

1   Accountable

2   Responsible

3   Quality

4   Employee-Focused

5   Environmentally Friendly

6   Reliable

7   Efficient

8   Innovative

9   Consumer-Friendly

10   Community-Focused

11   Transparent

12   Solution-Oriented

13   Fair

14   A Leader

15   Green

16   Common Sense

17   Affordable

18   A Role Model

19   Diverse

20   Caring

A WORD ABOUT THE BIG BOSS

Blue-collar crime and white-collar crime shouldn't have different punishments. It's very important for the average person to know that the judicial system will treat serious crime by white-collar criminals just as seriously as we treat crime by blue-collar criminals.

                                                    —FRANKLIN RAINES

Those lofty words by Mr. Raines, the once highly respected chairman of Fannie Mae, were spoken less than three years before he was forced to take "early retirement" as a result of investigations by the SEC and by the Office of Federal Housing Enterprise Oversight. He had been paid $90 million in salary, options, and bonuses during his six years as chairman of the organization (in 2003 alone, his compensation was more than $20 million) at a time when Fannie was overstating its earnings by more than $6 billion. The collapse of Fannie Mae two years later didn't hurt Raines much—his legal settlement, in his words, was "consistent with my acceptance of accountability as the leader of Fannie Mae," and it allowed him to keep most of his ill-gotten gains. Raines had also used his position as a public official to secure a below-market-rate loan at Countrywide Financial under the category "FOA—Friends of Angelo" appropriately named after then-CEO Angelo Mozilo. Raines got rich, and the American taxpayer is left to pick up the pieces.

And he is not alone. Consider this: The average CEO of a Fortune 500 company made more money in the calendar year 2007 than the average American makes in a lifetime. How out of whack is CEO pay? That same year, the S&P 500 chief executives averaged $10.5 million in total compensation. That is *344 times* the pay of the typical American worker.[34] The furor about CEO compensation may never die down, because most Americans cannot relate to multimillion-dollar salaries topped by annual bonuses that can reach into the tens of millions. Throw in some unethical or criminal behavior on the part of a few, and all of a sudden the vast majority of honest CEOs are lumped in with the bad boys—and girls. No wonder Americans don't have much trust and confidence in Corporate America today and *really* don't like Fortune 500 CEOs. From the survey:

Generally speaking, how much trust and confidence do you have in Corporate America today?

TOTAL

1%	A Great Deal
14%	A Good Amount
39%	A Fair Amount
38%	Only a Little
9%	None at All

Generally speaking, how much trust and confidence do you have in Fortune 500 CEOs?

TOTAL

1%	A Great Deal
10%	A Good Amount
31%	A Fair Amount
41%	Only a Little
17%	None at All

Scandals in the corporate boardroom are not the main source of credibility problems; it is CEO compensation. Most Americans believe that most CEOs are overpaid, and that it is disproportionate to the performance of the company. Asked which made them more angry at CEOs:

- 61 percent said CEOs earning millions of dollars while shareholders are losing money and employees are being laid off.
- 34 percent said corporate scandals involving CEOs who committed crimes and were involved in illegal activities.

Let's take a step back and think about this 61–34 split. Americans have a strong respect for the law. Much of our long-term political stability is attributable to our acceptance of the importance of the rule of law. There is nothing illegal about making millions in bonuses while laying off employees (at least, not until President Obama conditioned bailout money on reduced executive compensation). But criminal corporate scandals quite clearly *are* illegal. Still, Americans are angrier with the legal excesses than the illegal criminal activity. Why? Americans realize that there is a higher moral code that governs us all than the legal code that punishes only certain behaviors. So business leaders, please remember: Just because you *can* does not mean you *should*.

In one microcosm, the food service industry employs more than 9 million nonmanagement workers. Their average pay is $18,877 per year. Their CEOs earn an average of $6.7 million.[35]

But Americans do believe in pleasure as well as punishment. People want CEOs to suffer financially when the stock price of a company fails (64 percent) and when they lay off their own employees (52 percent). If the company is doing well, let the good times roll: 60 percent said CEOs deserve to make a lot of money.

Americans want to think of CEOs as a "chief *ethics* officer," not just chief executive officer. To the public, actions speak louder than words, and ethics and accountability should be a daily practice, not just a corporate motto or creed. When things go wrong, the public prefers that companies rein in abuses in-house, with greater shareholder oversight. Similarly, half wanted greater checks and balances between the CEO, chairman of the board, and the board of directors to ensure greater accountability and transparency.

This is a long way of saying Americans demand real accountability, the kind of accountability that results in the forfeit of ill-gotten gains. They want business to pay a price because *they* are paying the price. Auction off the executives' fancy houses. Sell their boats. Force them to make the humiliating perp walk—it's like a balm to the masses. Remember the collapse of Enron? More than 5,500 people lost their jobs and their retirement funds after top executives defrauded the energy company out of millions. When police escort a suspect into a squad car, they typically guide the perp's head as he ducks into the car door. In the case of Jeffrey Skilling, that didn't happen. Thanks to an unhelpful federal agent, he banged his head squarely into the door frame. People cheered when they saw that video in one of my focus groups. They knew they shouldn't, but they secretly thought, "For this one minute, he's feeling the same pain that I am." Anything that strips the guilty CEO of public respect and replaces it with public humiliation will have the support of the public. They believe that if the miscreant executives are punished, and the punishment is public and lasting, it'll stand as an example and prevent other businesses from doing the same.

And that includes jail time. Enron's chief executive officer Jeffrey Skilling went to prison. His boss, Kenneth Lay, died before he could be locked up, igniting outrage from shareholders who felt they'd been "cheated" out of seeing him sent away. For victims of Bernie Madoff, prison isn't enough to repay a lifetime of wages lost to corruption. Tyco chief Dennis Kozlowski is behind bars. WorldCom founder Bernard J. Ebbers is in prison for effectively the rest of his life. These people bilked their companies out of millions of dollars, and put thousands out of work when the companies collapsed. There are dozens of open criminal investigations emanating from the Wall Street crash. The public wants even more. Retirement funds lost *trillions* in value, generating a hang-'em-high attitude among average people with little hope of recovery. The only people who will make their money back are the defense lawyers, but if at least a few of the corporate chieftains are made to pay, it makes the financial loss slightly more bearable.

What would you like to see a CEO do to inspire more trust and confidence?
(top five answers)

TOTAL

46%   Institute a More Efficient and More Effective Way to Do Business

17%   Be More Engaged and Active with Employees

10%   Assemble a Strong Management Team

8%   Be Engaged and Active with Customers

5%   Be Engaged and Active in the Community

CONCLUSION

The American people believe Washington was caught napping while corporate leaders were raiding the cookie jar, and nothing any politician or CEO says will convince them otherwise. Speeches, conferences, and annual reports have limited value in explaining what the workplace of tomorrow will look like. There is a better approach to demonstrating that Corporate America is headed in the right direction:

LUNTZ LESSONS

Imagine spending 141 days with no job, no paycheck, no place to go, and nothing to do except wait for your union and your company to stop fighting and start negotiating. That's what happened to tens of thousands of supermarket employees in Southern California in 2003. The ten lessons for employee-employer relations (notice *"employee"* comes first) are derived from focus group conversations with thousands of employees over the past decade. They have told me, often with resigned hopelessness, what they so desperately wanted to hear from their management and their shop stewards before, during, and after a contract negotiation—and they apply in all work environments:

1. **The Number One priority: information.** More is better than less. Details are better than generalities. Comprehensive is better than simplistic. Long-term is better than immediate. Employees want to know the facts—all the facts—and they will reward those who provide them in easy-to-understand bites and punish those who deny them the truth. Summarize the material for those who want to read less, but provide the fine print for those who want to know more. Lawyers be damned; put it in writing.

2. **Say what you mean and mean what you say.** Nothing irritates employees more than management or labor communicating to them in terms that are so obviously meant to hedge, straddle, confuse, or ignite. The workplace is neither the Wharton School nor the union hall. Being calm and direct is a much smarter long-term approach than being inflammatory or circumspect.

3. **Set the context. Explain why.** The biggest mistake companies make is to assume that employees understand the condition of the company, the marketplace, and the long-term outlook of the economy. The biggest mistake unions make is to assume that employees are only concerned about their own situation and don't care about what happens to their employer. Both are wrong. If you want your decisions to sit well with your people, you have to tell them exactly where they stand.

4. **Communicate everywhere.** Employees don't stop talking about the workplace when they leave the workplace. They talk to each other on the Web and they talk to their families and friends at home. Management and unions should strive to provide websites that are chock full of information and shouldn't shy away from sending e-mails if the information is sufficiently important. They will definitely be read.

5. **Communication delayed is communication denied.** Employees are susceptible to rumors and exaggeration, and silence will be interpreted as guilt.

Companies need to provide answers to individual employee job-related questions within 24 hours, and 48 hours for corporate policy questions. In times of contract negotiation, a 24-hour telephone hotline is a welcome addition to the communication arsenal.

6. **Explaining for now. Training for tomorrow.** The most common request among employees, often asked with exasperation, is to be taught how to do more, and how to do it better. They directly link job training to their ability to turn that job into a rewarding career. Even if the job is to stock shelves or answer phones, most Americans want to do it well so that they can move up. Companies shouldn't just talk about best practices. They should teach it, unions should demand it, and managers should enable it.

7. **Link customer satisfaction with employee satisfaction.** One of the great disappointments for workers is the seeming disconnect between customer satisfaction and employee reward. Employees want bonuses, merit pay, and performance pay directly linked to how well they serve customers and colleagues.

8. **Don't tell employees that you are *"fair."*** Fairness is in the eyes of the beholder. Employees do not like and do not appreciate either management or unions telling them what to think. It is a far better approach to provide the information and invite employees to make conclusions for themselves.

9. **No one wins in a strike. Not the company. Not the customers. Not the employees. No one.** This is a truism, and in the current economic distress, it is factually true as well. Aggressive efforts by unions to make it easier to organize by attacking employers have not been well received by those they wish to represent. Now is not the time to drive a spike between employers and employees. Now is the time for cooperation, not confrontation.

10. **These lessons can't be a strategy. They have to be a culture.** It is not enough to adopt these lessons just before contract time. It has to be a core component of employee-employer relations 365 days of the year.

4

THE BUCK STOPS HERE:
What We Really Want from Government

I ran for president because I thought we needed big changes. I do think in Washington it's a little bit like American Idol, *except everybody is Simon Cowell.*

—BARACK OBAMA ON *THE TONIGHT SHOW*

Author's note:

The material in this chapter is based on more than 75 instant response dial sessions conducted in 2008–09 with over 2,000 Americans face-to-face, as well as two dozen nationwide polls over the course of the 2008 election and the first six months of the Obama presidency. Some readers may disagree with some of the conclusions, but the text reflects the genuine opinions of the American people.

Enough! In a single word, gently nestled within a speech universally hailed as one of the most powerful indictments articulated against the status quo, Barack Obama captured all the frustration, all the anxiety, and all the anger the American people feel toward *their* government and *their* leaders. The night he accepted the Democratic nomination, Barack Obama captured the inner rage and public outcry for change.

Enough! It is unequivocal. Enough! It cannot be misinterpreted. Enough! It defined exactly why the American people turned to him and

A LESSON IN AMERICAN CIVICS

Americans' indignation toward Washington is indeed understandable . . .

- More young people think UFOs exist than think Social Security will exist when they retire.
- More people would rather have their wallet or purse stolen than be audited by the IRS.

But their opinion is not always indeed informed. . . .

- More people can name the Three Stooges than three justices on the Supreme Court (and they've been dead for decades—the Stooges, that is).
- Fewer than half of all Americans can name all three branches of government.

away from the policies that had essentially guided America for a quarter century. And on Election Day 2008, from one end of Pennsylvania Avenue to the other, the public rejected representatives of the status quo and turned to a new voice and vision. When asked to explain the election on Fox News in the earliest hours of the morning, I summarized it in as few words as I could:

Never in modern times have so many promised so much and delivered so little.

In a single sentence, that's what Americans believe about their government. They find it corrupt, lazy, out-of-touch, and riddled with lobbyist influence and special-interest power. Ask any Americans anywhere, and they'll tell you what Washington has done *to* them—not *for* them. The universality of hostility is staggering. It doesn't matter whether they're the beneficiary of student aid loans or Social Security, whether they get Section 8 housing or subsidized small-business loans. While all segments of society still believe in the principles of democracy, there is barely a sliver of American society with a positive outlook toward "government." After pork barrel blowouts and Wall Street bailouts, who can blame them?

It has taken America more than 230 years to get this uniformly fed up. It will take a while for them to get over it.

ANGER AND ACCOUNTABILITY

This is the only chapter in this book that addresses more of what Americans *don't* want rather than the positive approach—and for good reason. Americans are more focused today on what's *missing* in their government and in leaders than the benefits they derive from democracy.

The single greatest strategic imperative for people in politics, business, the media, or popular culture is to recognize the anger in America and, as a result, demonstrate genuine, measurable accountability in what they do and how they do it. Acknowledge the mood, and then demand accountability as the solution. I've been asking the classic question riffing off the movie *Network* since I worked for Ross Perot in 1992: "Are you mad as hell and not going to take it anymore?" In that notable year of anger, 31 percent agreed, and more than half of them cast their ballots for Perot. On January 1, 2009, 72 percent said they were "mad as hell." Scary indeed.

The list of complaints is endless—and certainly justifiable. Americans have seen politicians govern without accountability and spend money with abandon while we fall further into personal, national, and generational debt. Ordinary people feel that hard work isn't enough to get ahead in today's America—and they think Washington barely works at all. If you live in a row house in the shadow of the Capitol dome, you

WHAT AMERICANS *REALLY DON'T* WANT "WHAT MAKES YOU ANGRIEST ABOUT WASHINGTON?"
(top two choices combined)

The politicians are out of touch (53 percent).

They're beholden to lobbyists and special interests (43 percent).

The negative attacks in political campaigns (27 percent).

Extreme viewpoints (23 percent).

Nothing ever gets done in Washington (22 percent).

know the heightened police presence is about protecting the politicians who live there Tuesday through Thursday, not the people who live there every day of the week.

Not all of Washington is disconnected, negligent, and corrupt. Thanks to a news media legitimately focused on uprooting government corruption but disinterested in promoting success stories, there are plenty of false examples. Too much of our information about government is based on faulty perceptions, misinformation, and half-truths that are spread like viruses on the Web to promote and exaggerate an "us versus them" mentality. Many of us believe (inaccurately) that members of Congress have private jets and stretch limos at a time when we're carpooling and lining up for mass transit. They don't. In fact, it is almost impossible for a House member, other than the Speaker of the House, to fly privately. The "all-expenses-paid vacations" are in fact "CODELS," an acronym for congressional delegations, designed to allow members to travel abroad to meet with and learn from leaders across the globe. Others think congressional leaders have chauffeur-driven vehicles. Nope—those cars are part of the highly trained Capitol Hill security force required by law after 9/11. Some perceive that our Washington representatives are paid millions from our hard-earned tax dollars (the actual annual salary in 2008 was $169,300) when we're struggling just to keep our middle-class jobs. And many think members of Congress are being wined and dined at chic French restaurants by lobbyists and special-interest groups. If they are, they may be breaking the law. The fact is, they're not.

Nevertheless, Americans see all the spending and the burgeoning tax code as a direct consequence of this perceived illicit behavior. Our tax code typifies how out of touch Washington politicians seem to be. Americans believe it is nothing more than a legislative playground where lobbyists and congressmen frolic together, scheming to benefit at the expense of others. More loopholes for them, less clarity for us. More revenue for Washington, more regulation and burdensome red tape for small businesses. It's like an annual bailout from Washington to the accounting industry. The more complex the code, the more billable hours the accountants get to rack up.

And it certainly doesn't help instill trust and confidence when the Secretary of the Treasury—the man with ultimate oversight over the IRS—admits he did not pay his correct share of taxes for years. And when the initial Obama nominee for Health and Human Services Secretary did in fact have a chauffeur-driven vehicle that he never reported to the IRS.

Add to that the Chairman of the House Ways and Means Committee, who actually writes the tax legislation for you and me but doesn't pay his taxes, either.

And add to that a half dozen appointments to sub-cabinet positions who had to withdraw their nominations in embarrassment because they, too, had "*tax problems.*"

And on . . . and on . . . and on.

In the wake of a campaign premised on change, these revelations were more than just embarrassing for President Obama. They represented the first red flag for Americans that for all the change Obama represented *himself,* Washington might be too big and too broken for one person to fix.

Now, if you're from Washington, pay attention. We're fearful when we pay our taxes that we got it wrong, that we made a mistake. It's a genuine source of irritation and anxiety for millions of Americans every year. April 15 has become a date people dread more than a root canal. More of us would rather be mugged than audited by the IRS (5 percent say there's no difference). So we reluctantly pay someone in some company to prepare our taxes for us and pray to God that the person got it right. One day a politician is going to become incredibly popular nationwide by championing a tax code that is *simple, easy,* and *fair.*

But it's not just the tax code that angers Americans. It's not even the amount of taxes. It's how *(ir)responsibly* those tax dollars are spent that matters most. When voters respond to political promises to reduce their taxes, it's not necessarily because they want to keep more money in their own pockets. It is primarily because they want to prevent the government from wasting their hard-earned dollars any more than they already have. Most people don't begrudge paying taxes, as long as it is a *fair* amount and it's invested wisely.

In a survey we conducted for the U.S. Chamber of Commerce in 2006, people set the value of fair taxes at about 25 percent. Anything more is considered abusive. And even if the average total tax rate were pegged right at that 25 percent threshold (we can dream, can't we?), the way Washington spends that money, and where it spends it, can still tick people off. They will punish politicians if the money they busted their butts to make is spent on programs riddled with waste, fraud, abuse, and mismanagement.

Americans can deal with taxes—and with adversity—if they believe "we're all in this together" and *everyone* is working to fix the problem. But that's not the perception. The public is drowning in higher health-care costs, higher energy costs, and a higher cost of living, yet not only does Washington refuse to throw us a life preserver, they've attached a lead anchor to our feet and they are pushing our heads underwater at the same time. What makes Americans really angry is less about the detachment of Washington from day-to-day life and more about the perception that Washington is actually benefiting from our hardship.

Here's a key point: It matters less that Americans are mad as hell. What matters *more* is that they're not going to take it anymore. Americans have hit a tipping point with Washington and, moreover, its political parties. Today's Americans know too much . . . care too much . . . and are too connected to one another via Facebook, MySpace, YouTube, or even simple e-mail and mass media to tolerate politics as usual from Washington. They care about accountability even more than ideology (i.e., party) because at least accountability will eventually lead to some sort of action. Ideology, on the other hand, has become the politicians' favorite tool for doing nothing in the name of "doing what's right."

The easiest example of what Americans will now refuse to tolerate is pork-barrel spending. (Quick language quiz: What makes people angrier? Pork barrel spending, earmarks, or set-asides? They're all names for the same thing—wasteful spending. But it is the phrase "pork barrel spending" that makes people groan loudest.) Lawmakers like to argue that one man's pork is another's jobs program back home. But let's give the taxpayers some credit; they know a heist when they see one. For example, $640 toilet seats, $436 hammers, and the infamous Bridge to Nowhere. These are all vivid visuals. People can *picture* them, and they're disgusted by that kind of waste at *their* expense.

More than almost any member of Congress in recent history, former Alaska senator Ted Stevens personified wasteful Washington spending. His ultimate political demise is our best example of how voters are mad as hell about Washington politics-as-usual and, more important, aren't going to take it anymore. Though he was indicted midyear on corruption charges, Republican voters made Stevens their nominee after a tough primary battle. He was convicted in October 2008 on seven separate

A WORD TO AMERICA'S LEADERS: HOW TO DEFLECT ANGER AND DEMONSTRATE ACCOUNTABILITY

1. **A video record.** Nothing is more powerful than demonstrating that what you said is what you've done, and nothing proves it more effectively than seeing your words on screen just as you said them (include the date and location on the footage), and then the result of those words. The more your constituents see this evidence, the more likely they are to see you as committed to accountability.

2. **Let the voters speak *first*.** The best way to get the anger out in the open is to give voters the chance to articulate what makes them angry at the outset of any public gathering, and then use your time to respond. It is better to have voter anger expressed at the beginning of your presentation than at the end.

3. **Vote NO on additional compensation.** There's nothing that makes voters angrier than watching the people they elected vote themselves a pay increase. Politicians who refuse the cost-of-living adjustment and tie their decision to the lack of a balanced budget or to the inability to give our soldiers a pay increase or to the principle of "shared sacrifice" are usually rewarded with reelection.

4. **Zero tolerance for ethical lapses.** A major reason why Republicans lost control of Congress in 2006 was the willingness to justify or overlook the criminal activity of some of its own members. Accountability requires adherence to consistency and law over party loyalty every time.

5. **"Say what you mean and mean what you say."** Of all the candidate attributes, this one best reflects a sense of accountability to voters.

counts for abusing his position of power and illegally accepting gifts of value. He didn't apologize. He didn't resign. About a week later, his name was still on the ballot for reelection to the Senate. He lost that election, becoming the longest-serving senator in American history ever to be booted from office. His conviction was vacated in 2009 by the U.S. Attorney General because of serious prosecutorial misconduct, but it was too late to save the man responsible for more pork for less people than any person in Senate history.

To fully appreciate the significance of Stevens's rise and fall, it's important to offer a little history. Ted Stevens was elected in 1968 (the same year as Richard Nixon's election and Johnny Cash's show at Folsom Prison). The last time his home state of Alaska voted for a Democrat for president was Lyndon Johnson in 1964. Before 2008, Alaska hadn't voted for the Democratic candidate for Senate in almost thirty years. Stevens quickly became a local icon for bringing home the bacon from distant Washington, DC. Due to his budgetary dexterity, he rose to chair the Senate Appropriations Committee for eight years. Due to his seniority, he was the President Pro Tempore of the United States Senate for four years, which put him third in line for presidential succession. This is a Washington résumé even a Kennedy would envy—and it was from the state farthest away from the nation's capital. Alaskans directly benefitted from his rise to power. It's hard to blame them for reelecting him over and over again. Their state was a better place to live as a result of his influence.

But even Alaskans believe their senators have a responsibility to the nation, not just their home state. He went too far—even by Washington standards, and even for the constituents he benefitted. He (temporarily) secured the funds to build the Gravina Island Bridge, a structure nearly as long as the Golden Gate Bridge and taller than the Brooklyn Bridge, at a projected cost of $398 million. The bridge would link the island's fifty residents (that is not a misprint) to the nearby Ketchikan International Airport. But you probably know the project by a different name: the Bridge to Nowhere—the most infamous pork project in a generation. As a result of the bridge's offensive price tag and Senator Stevens's adamant refusal to abandon the project, the Bridge to Nowhere became the poster child for Washington (and therefore Republican) waste. When efforts were made to reallocate the funds for rebuilding a hurricane-ravaged New Orleans, Stevens took to the Senate floor and threatened to resign, thereby guaranteeing national attention and voter ridicule.

But it wasn't enough to purchase and gift-wrap the single most effective talking point for use against Republicans nationwide in 2006. In 2008, Alaskans turned their own breadwinning senator out of office. Why? Because, in the words of Barack Obama, enough *really was* enough. Stevens had accepted business deals and renovation work on his Alaska home at below-market rates and was convicted in a court of law for it. In the end, his personal greed ruined his own career at a time when he should have been taking his final victory lap. Perhaps it is poetic justice that he was convicted not in Alaska but in Washington, where he gamed the system professionally for decades *legally*, only to be brought down for accepting personal gratuities *illegally*. His political kingdom was built on a foundation of pork. But those times are ending in America.

And that's the fundamental point with accountability that voters understand but government officials don't: When something important that should go right ends up very wrong, someone must be punished. I've spent the last few pages talking about accountability without offering a definition—and for good reason. Just as Supreme Court Justice Potter Stewart once refused to define hard-core pornography and obscenity but still noted, "I know it when I see it," the definition of accountability lies in the eyes of the beholder. More often than not, it involves some sort of punishment inflicted on the perpetrator. From the public's perspective, it's "You hurt us, so we get to hurt you back." But there is a positive component as well, best defined as "saying what you mean and meaning what you say." Politicians who make specific pledges of achievement and then go out and accomplish them are held in high esteem primarily because it happens so rarely.

Accountability also evokes a sense of "take-charge" leadership in times of crisis. Take note of how Americans remember their leaders from the most trying moment in our recent history, the attacks the morning of September 11, 2001. New York mayor Rudy Giuliani didn't become "America's Mayor" until he leapt to action that morning. In fact, he wasn't all that popular among his own constituents at the time. But he became the epitome of accountability in the days and weeks after the terrorist attacks.

By comparison, President Bush will be remembered, at least by Democrats, for reading "My Pet Goat" to a class of schoolkids and then spending much of September 11 on *Air Force One*. At a time when Americans needed to know their government was still in control, their Commander in Chief was invisible—and did not emerge until a brief address to the nation that night. Today, we are told that President Bush had no choice; security protocols were in effect that necessitated remaining in the air and out of sight. True enough, and to his credit, President Bush would later give his security people fits when he visited the site of the attack, grabbing the bullhorn to declare his defiance against the attackers. That gesture will be remembered as the greatest show of strength in his presidency, but it seemed late when compared to Mayor Giuliani's response on the actual day of the attack.

Security protocols certainly didn't square with Mayor Giuliani's run *toward* the smoke and fire of the World Trade Center. Risk be damned, he did it anyway. His city was in flames. His people were in fear. He knew his place was at the scene. Why? Because it was his job. He simply had to be on-site doing anything and everything he could to restore order, reduce anxiety, and begin the rebuilding process. That is what the City of New York had elected him to do. It was his job. Simple as that.

Politicians, take note. You call yourselves "public servants" all the time. Americans believe that firefighters and policemen are the *real* public servants. September 11 reminded those of us who may have forgotten how much they sacrifice. We believe these men and women are the real public servants because they measure up to the standard of accountability we set for them—every day—without complaint or question. No matter how dirty they get (real dirt, not Oh-I-need-to-dry-clean-my-thousand-dollar-suit ketchup stains). No matter how little they get paid. In fact, we *honor* them for their low pay because it means they truly chose their career as a service. We *know* you politicians like to be honored; the rest of America is seeing their salaries reduced, so why not voluntarily take a pay cut?

Americans expect the same standard of you as of these first responders. When Mayor Giuliani acted *the same way as the real public servants,* he became a hero. He didn't just want to hear the facts. He wanted to see them, assess them, and then act. His character commanded that he do the job he was elected to do regardless of the danger. It was his job. That's take-charge accountability. Not surprisingly, he joined the short list of the most respected political figures in America—an honor that lasted until it was tarnished by an ill-conceived and poorly executed presidential campaign in 2008.

Like many of the best elected officials in American history, Mayor Giuliani through his leadership inspired private acts of responsibility and courage. We know government can't do it all, nor should it, but Americans do expect it to lead the way—or get out of the way. It's no surprise, then, that private boat owners organized themselves and rescued

100,000 people off the island of Manhattan that day. Food, water, and other supplies flooded the city within hours, long before federal aid arrived. Volunteer police, fire, and medical aid arrived from a thousand miles away, ready to work. People came to help, and Rudy was there to put them to work. Like the local councilman who gets you an answer about when your street's potholes are going to be filled, Mayor Giuliani showed people he was ready to respond to the problem of that day—and so they responded to him.

This is accountability as defined by the American people: Listen first, then act. Communicate always. Accept responsibility. And in times of crisis, it's just a bigger problem with the same approach—everyone working together.

If the response to 9/11 is what Americans want most from government, the response to Hurricane Katrina is what Americans fear the most. The uncoordinated, bungled response to that disaster shattered public confidence and public trust because there was no accountability—anywhere. Government at every level had let down the people of Louisiana in 2005—and much of the ravaged Lower Ninth Ward still remains an empty wasteland years later. There were plenty of excuses and finger-pointing to go around. The most common excuse was that since the city of New Orleans and the state of Louisiana were known by "everyone" to be corrupt and incapable of governing, Washington should not have waited and instead should have immediately stepped in to fill the vacuum. Imagine that. The perception of local government corruption and incompetence in one of America's major cities and states was so great that most people simply assumed Washington—a thousand miles away—should and would come to the rescue. Yet it didn't happen—for days—and in this age of twenty-four-hour eyewitness news, the fabric of this country appeared to rip apart right before our eyes.

No one took responsibility for the buses that were stranded in floodwater, for the thousands of people left behind to seek shelter on their rooftops, for sick people abandoned in hospitals, for decaying bodies left exposed on the streets, for communications systems that took weeks to restore, and for the lawlessness that erupted even as water cascaded over the levees. FEMA was absent for days. The mayor, the governor, and the president continue to blame one another for the chaos and neglect. In New York in 2001, people kept the faith because the mayor showed them the way. In New Orleans in 2005,* faith in government and in the occupant of the White House blew away in the winds of Katrina.

And now, with Katrina-like conditions in our economy, we are witnessing the collapse of whatever confidence the government still held. The CBS/*New York Times* "right direction/wrong track" gauge of the public mood, already slipping as 2008 began, plummeted to record lows by the end of the year. Just days before the November election, only 7 percent of Americans thought the country was headed in the right direction, while an incredible 89 percent felt things "had pretty seriously gotten off on the wrong track." Everyone—Republican, Democrat, Independent— felt America was going to hell politically, economically, and socially, and they were being dragged down with it. What a unanimous, devastating indictment on the government's handling of the economy . . . and the war . . . and Katrina . . . and health care . . . and everything else. And the three reasons why people turned thumbs-down on their country all begin with "W": Washington, Wall Street, and W. himself.

It took a new president, a 2,000-point surge in the Dow Jones, and a visually successful presidential tour across the globe to begin to turn public perceptions in the Spring of 2009—but one has to question whether the long-term universal optimism will ever return.

In his farewell speech to America in 1961, President Dwight Eisenhower warned Americans about the dangers of the industrial-military complex (he put the words in reverse order). Fair enough, but now we have an equally scary complex to worry about between Washington and Wall Street. They have pampered and protected each other at the expense of the rest of America. Both McCain and Obama's campaigns were flush with Wall Street cash, and both presidential candidates dutifully endorsed the government bailout that made some CEOs rich and saved the jobs of many others. But the infusion of cash didn't stop the markets from tanking, housing prices from crashing, or companies from laying off more than 500,000 workers a week—week after week after week. People with good credit still couldn't get loans, and those with bad credit watched as their homes went into foreclosure.

The prime reason the public was and remains opposed to the financial bailout of Wall Street is because they don't see an end to it—and they

---

* A number of newspaper editorials even called on Giuliani to take on the role of Disaster Czar in New Orleans. He politely refused.

don't envision anything in it for themselves. And they were right. After the bank bailout came Detroit . . . and then the trillion-dollar stimulus . . . and then more money for AIG . . . and then the foreclosure bailout . . . and then still more money for AIG . . . and then the biggest proposed budget ever . . . the Chrysler bankruptcy bailout . . . and then the GM bailout . . . and then . . . and then . . . and then. The small tax cuts (that averaged ten dollars a paycheck) and government benefit increases that were built into a few of the bills weren't enough to bail anyone out of their personal distress. It was, to borrow a line from J.R.R. Tolkien, like butter scraped over too much bread.

During Financial Bailout I, the bailout to begin all bailouts, the politicians wondered out loud whether the $700 billion allocated to save the economy was enough, but the American people had a different set of questions:

- What's my share?
- How much do I get?
- Will any of this money trickle down to people like me who need it most?

Wake up, Washington. These are fair questions. Why aren't you answering?

Think tanks, pressure groups, and even the media assume the majority of Americans take an ideological approach to government. They don't. People relate to government based on their own personal relationship with it. For example, the reason why African Americans have voted Democratic for decades is because Washington integrated their schools, their businesses, and their lives against the wishes of those demanding "states' rights." True, there were a handful of Democratic segregationist governors led by George Wallace who rebelled and said no to integration. But black voters have forgotten them, and instead remember the efforts of JFK and LBJ to right two centuries of wrongs. And since then, the Democrats have taken a very active, activist national approach to government, while Republicans have been on the side of state and local control. So it only makes sense that African Americans back the party that is more vocal about intervening on their side of the equation. The legacy of Lincoln isn't relevant anymore to a population fighting for equal pay, and neither is the legacy of Wallace.

Today, the defining battle is over the government's role in providing economic security. Traditionally, if you receive more in government benefits than you pay in taxes, you're much more likely to be pro-government than if you're among the unlucky ones who pay more than they get. In one sense that's ideological, but the ideology stems from a cost-benefit analysis. But when the stock market sheds 4,000 points in a single year, and then keeps on falling, everyone is a net loser. Everyone is hurting now, and everyone is seeking help. Americans see the value of their homes—likely their single biggest asset—shrinking. When they open their 401(k) statements—the heart of their retirement—they shudder. (Some have taken to calling them 201(k)s.) The average family net worth dropped 25 percent in the past two years and 9 percent in the last quarter of 2008 alone—the biggest quarterly drop since the Great Depression. And whom did they blame? The three W's (Washington, Wall Street, and W.).

This is why it was so baffling when John McCain suspended his campaign on September 27, two days before his first debate, during the height of the economic crisis to rush back to Washington seemingly to defend the unpopular president and support his even-more-unpopular Wall Street bailout plan. In that fateful forty-eight-hour period he was undermining the underpinnings of his own campaign by voting for, in the minds of the American people, "wasteful government spending" for "Wall Street fat cats" paid for by "hardworking, middle-class taxpayers." On that day, by his own hand, McCain doomed a campaign that was already sputtering.

What he could have done, what Americans actually wanted him to say at the time, is a simple declarative: "No bailout—not now, not ever. We will find a better way to right the economy." He should have declared, "I didn't come to Washington to work for Wall Street. I work for Main Street. It's time for the corporate con men to do some time for costing us some dime." This would have made him a hero to tens of millions of hardworking, middle-class voters who resented their hard-earned tax dollars going to fund the retirement packages of the Billionaire Boys Club.

But he didn't. For two decades, John McCain studiously built a reputation of righteous indignation toward Corporate America coupled with insistence on accountability to his colleagues that made him a hero well beyond his political base. Yet with one ill-conceived decision, McCain seemed to place himself squarely on the side of Wall Street and Washington—and in the embrace of the most unpopular president in

WHAT AMERICANS *REALLY* WANT
"IN THESE CHALLENGING ECONOMIC
TIMES, WOULD YOU RATHER HAVE
CONGRESS COMMIT TO . . ."
(top two answers combined)

Ending wasteful government spending	62%
No new taxes	41%
Balancing the budget	34%
Protecting the value of home ownership	23%
A freeze in current government spending	21%
A cut of 5 pennies per dollar in government agencies and spending	14%

modern history. McCain undermined his crusade against wasteful spending and lost his "I am not George Bush" argument simultaneously. His polling numbers fell as a result.

While this chapter is about government, I can't leave the discussion of the economic situation quite yet. In focus groups throughout the fall election campaign and into 2009, the toughest, hardest-hit communities all had the same question: "When will it end?" They knew the CEOs who made the mistakes that created the crisis were being rewarded. They knew the Wall Street guys were still collecting (or trying to collect) multimillion-dollar bonuses. They knew the corporate leaders were still attending lavish retreats as though nothing had happened and were still spending millions on naming rights to sports stadiums. And it was— and is—all bought and paid for by the government in Washington and, by extension, us.

Unbelievable? Let me repeat: With taxpayer dollars in their pockets, some big corporations are still moving ahead with the frivolity of putting their tainted name in big, bold letters on athletic facilities.

- Citibank is paying the New York Mets $400 million over two decades to name the new stadium Citi Field.

- AIG (beneficiary of two bailouts and counting) is paying Manchester United $125 million to have its logo appear on the British soccer team jerseys.
- Bank of America has a $140 million deal with the Carolina Panthers to put its name on the team's football arena.

Ask Americans if they think this is a good way to spend public taxpayer dollars. You don't need me to answer—you know it already—and neither Washington nor Wall Street will even ask, because they don't want to know. Maybe we should simply put a U.S. Treasury seal on each stadium and name them all People's Park. After all, you paid for it. And George W. Bush has accomplished what Ronald Reagan, Newt Gingrich, and two generations of Republicans failed to do: He has *proven* beyond a doubt that Washington doesn't work.

OBAMA-NATION

Motive and intent are at the core of how we evaluate the goodness of people, companies, and institutions.

Perhaps President Obama's greatest advantage is that the overwhelming majority of Americans continue to trust his motives and intentions. Americans believe that he is the right man, at the right time, for a monumental task. In other words, he oozes *credibility*—a stark change from the previous administration. He has confidence in his ideals and the people have confidence in him.

It is this inherent confidence in *his* inherent confidence that will continue to buoy his approval ratings long into his administration, even if Americans grow more concerned about his policies on a line-by-line, issue-by-issue basis. Ultimately, Americans will judge him by his results, not just intentions. But considering the difficult circumstances surrounding his entry to office, they are willing to bank on his personal attributes and give him the benefit of the doubt for a long while still.

Unfortunately, others in Washington, Democrats and Republicans alike, enjoy no such confidence. If they wish to restore their credibility, at a minimum, government should follow the Hippocratic Oath: "First, do no harm."

It should abide by the same rules and regulations, by the same laws, which the average American has to live. Congress was once nicknamed "The Plantation" for its infamous refusal to play by the same rules that they legislate for the rest of us. They don't abide by the same labor laws or the same criminal statutes. They have better benefits and privileges. And taxpayers foot the bill—their bill.

The John McCain of 2000 understood this, and it was reflected in his campaign speeches and even the name of his campaign bus: The Straight Talk Express. The John McCain of 2008 had more difficulty articulating an anti-Washington message, though the old McCain did seep through on rare occasions. It's unfortunate for McCain that his anti-Washington approach had peaked in 2000, when hostility toward the government was relatively low. If the 2000 McCain had run in 2008, when hostility toward Washington was at Watergate proportions, we might have had an entirely different electoral story.

Still, McCain had his moments. A true-life joke told at the Republican debate in Orlando on October 21, 2007, earned him the highest evaluation of any GOP presidential candidate at any debate during the primaries. He was running a distant fourth in some polls. His campaign was out of money, and most of his staff had been let go. The media focus was on Rudy Giuliani, Fred Thompson, and Mitt Romney as they were all battling for the spotlight. Mike Huckabee, a debate pro, was gaining. McCain, too ideologically timid and tired for many Republican debate viewers, was fading. And then one response broadcast live on Fox News to millions of Republicans nationally permanently changed the dynamic of the presidential race.

I have fought against out-of-control and disgraceful spending that's been going on, and I have saved the American people as much as $2 billion at one stroke. In case you missed it, a few days ago Senator Clinton tried to spend $1 million on the Woodstock Concert Museum. Now, my friends, I wasn't there. I'm sure it was a cultural and pharmaceutical event. I was tied up at the time.

People laughed, they applauded, and then they gave him a standing ovation that went on and on and on. A Republican media operative on CNN that night said it was McCain's last hurrah. It turned out to be his rebirth. It was exactly what Republicans wanted to hear.

As for the rest of the country, ask Americans who know their twentieth-century history (a small fraction of the overall population) and they'll tell you they want the courage of FDR, the plain talk of Harry Truman, the optimism of Ronald Reagan, the youthful vigor of John Kennedy, and the transcendent ability of Barack Obama.

It is the Obama phenomenon I want to address. You picked up this book because you want to know what the American people really want. So even if you are one of the 46 percent of America's voters who did not support him in 2008, there is something to learn from the 53 percent of Americans who did—and how arguably the least qualified nominee in a century could overcome the long odds in a primary and general election and come to reflect what a majority of the country was so desperately seeking.

Let's start with the statistics. More than 130 million Americans voted, the most ever, with the highest turnout percentage since 1968. They handed Obama a larger share of the popular vote than any Democrat since Lyndon Johnson in 1964 and expanded the comfortable Democratic majorities in the U.S. House and Senate. It was both an endorsement of Obama's campaign promise of change and a repudiation of the last eight years of Republican rule. People who wanted change voted for Obama by a stunning 89 percent to 9 percent over McCain. They also wanted a president who was in touch with people like themselves. It surely didn't help McCain's image that he couldn't operate a BlackBerry and didn't know what a fist-bump was.

Obama redefined American politics. His opening statement from the January 31, 2008, Democratic presidential debate in Hollywood set a positive tone for his campaign and changed the course of history:

I don't think the choice is between black and white or it's about gender or religion. I don't think it's about young or old. I think what is at stake right now is whether we are looking backward or we are looking forward. I think it is the past versus the future.

Obama's message wasn't just about change or hope. It was about restoring confidence in tomorrow. Republicans ridiculed him at their national convention, declaring, "Change is not a destination, just as hope is not a strategy." Sure enough, but they offered no real alternative. In a time of great economic anxiety and distrust in the institutions of power, change and hope are certainly better than nothing. It was this emotional framing of a standard political message that would expand Obama's appeal well beyond the traditional Democratic base. Standing next to him, it instantly placed Hillary Rodham Clinton as frozen in the past, much as her smile was frozen on her face.

It wasn't just the message, or even the messenger, that was the most striking element of the 2008 campaign. It was the crowds. Most campaign rallies draw hundreds of people. Presidential events leading up to the election often draw in the thousands. But never in American history has a candidate hosted events with tens of thousands of participants on a daily basis. It was proof that despite the cynicism, despite the despair, despite the anger, the American people *want* to believe in Washington again. They don't relish their current role as malcontents. On the campaign trail, then-Senator Obama's presence, promise, and potential gave them reason to believe that there was a reason to hope.

When an unprecedented 30,000 people from all walks of life came in December 2007 to see Obama and his new friend Oprah Winfrey at an outdoor rally in South Carolina, it was clear that Obama was not the typical candidate and this was not going to be the typical campaign. Hillary Clinton had a substantial twenty-point lead in the national polls, but it was Obama who was packing them in. The bar went a little higher just prior to the April Democratic primary when 35,000 people showed up at Independence Park in Philadelphia to hear him speak. Clinton's crowds were a third the size, yet she soundly defeated him because her voters were older—in one of the oldest states in America—and therefore more likely to go to the polls. In May, he attracted an audience of 75,000 in Portland, Oregon, and by the time of the Democratic convention, more than 80,000 piled into Invesco Field in Denver at Mile High Stadium to hear him accept the nomination. But even that wasn't the most attended event of the campaign. Obama cracked the 100,000 attendance barrier in St. Louis on October 18 and then shattered it a week later in 39-degree rain back again in Denver (McCain was drawing 5,000 to 10,000 on his own during the same week). And that doesn't even include the 200,000 who came to watch Obama speak in Berlin, Germany—almost none of whom could actually cast a vote in the U.S. election. It was easier to get a ticket to a Bruce Springsteen concert than to see Barack Obama up close.

As of this writing, Obama-mania hasn't subsided. Snagging Spring-steen tickets remains easier than snagging a government job in the Obama administration. For the first time since John F. Kennedy deliv-ered the call to "ask not what your country can do for you—ask what you can do for your country," it is cool to work for the government. Yes, people hated the federal government on November 4, 2008. They still do, but now they want to own it, control it, and be in the middle of it. There were more than one million job seekers for the nearly eight thousand—"plum"—White House political appointee positions as listed in the "United States Government Policy and Supporting Positions" manual—otherwise known as "the Plum Book." Compare that to the 44,000 job seekers in the Bush transition and 125,000 for the Clinton transition. Now people see Washington as Obama, and Obama as Wash-ington, and everybody under age thirty wants to work for him and with him. And the people just keep on coming. More than two million strong descended on Washington to attend the inaugural festivities— the biggest crowd in DC history and more than two times greater than any previous inauguration. They thronged to Washington, a city they hate, to see the new president they adored. Obama's inauguration was JFK's inaugural and Martin Luther King Jr.'s "I Have a Dream" speech all rolled up into one big celebration. Some came to see history and then left. But a significant portion came to stay and help write history's next chapter.

It may have seemed chaotic for those who attended these overflow-ing events, but for the Obama team, these events weren't random gath-erings. They were staged with the precision of a military invasion. The visual backdrop is a powerful message in politics. Ronald Reagan un-derstood the power of the picture. He was always surrounded by Amer-ican flags, a star-spangled red-white-and-blue visual that became an essential part of his message of rebirth and patriotism. Bill Clinton un-derstood it too. It was easier to say "I feel your pain" when there are people around you, so he put people in his backdrops, becoming a mes-senger for the portrait of humanity standing behind and around him.

Obama's team realized early on that their candidate was becoming the antidote for those who had lost faith in the political system, but that for him to succeed, the visual put out to America had to be a visual of the entire country rather than any one special-interest bloc. It wasn't about a few individuals. It was about mass numbers, making the most of those massive crowds as a symbol of his viability and promise. The photographs and television shots showed a sea of people, all shapes and sizes, ages and colors, chanting his name with a gleam in their eye. There were no crowd-control handlers like you saw at other candidate events. He didn't need them. The enthusiasm was genuine. Those giant crowds spoke as loudly as the candidate they came to support. I'd ask people at these rallies why it mattered that so many people attended his events and they all said the same thing: "There's someone like me here." People want to belong. They want to be embraced, even if it's by ten thousand strangers. Rather than being intimidating, those throngs were *affirming.* You could stand in the biggest mass of humanity of your life and marvel, "All these people think the way I do; they're just like me."

This was a time for the likes of Peggy Noonan and Ted Sorensen, the masters of soaring rhetoric for Ronald Reagan and John Kennedy. The Obama team was right to reject the James Carville, Karl Rove, Lee Atwater school of tough operational tactics. They correctly read the lay of the land early on: Why trade body blows when your fighter has a knockout punch? Ignore the calls for ideological trench warfare by Keith Olbermann, Arianna Huffington, and MoveOn.org and instead offer a more uplifting alternative. Let the innards of the campaign microtarget swing voters within swing areas of swing states.* But let the candidate swing for the fences. Republicans had to depend on high-tech data-mining and segmentation analysis because they had no overarching message. Obama had transcendent abilities, and he marshaled them perfectly. He offered a message connected to the heart, not the gut. His campaign of mass e-mails, mass rallies, and mass advertising was to the Bush era approach of politics what World War II was to World War I. Good-bye trench warfare, hello tanks and nuclear weapons.

Perhaps the most stunning result of 2008 was the Republican loss of the political center. The decline of highly overt partisanship has been an acknowledged phenomenon for several decades, requiring both parties to woo those in the middle. In the past ten presidential elections, the party that captured Independents captured the White House. Since 1968, Republicans had won the middle in seven of ten elections. But in

* Thanks to the ability to overlay neighborhood census data, polling data, an endless array of consumer data, and even online behavior, it is now possible and increasingly affordable for campaigns to send an individually tailored phone, mail, or e-mail message to a specific person in a specific household, in a specific neighborhood.

2008, Obama beat McCain by almost 10 percent among Independents—and Democrats all across the country came close to matching his electoral success in state and local races as well.

This is not a disintegration of the Right. America is still a center-right nation. But Independents no longer see the Republicans as the center of America; they only see them as on the Right. It is always dangerous to take a single election and extrapolate for a generation. With every action comes a reaction, and just when it seems one party is down for the count (see Democrats, 2004), it comes roaring back. Still, 2008 is notable not just for the election of the first black president of the United States, but because it exiled Republicans to the wilderness of minority status for the foreseeable future.

I once worked with another agent of change—Newt Gingrich. He turned the U.S. House of Representatives on its head, seizing control from the Democrats after forty unbroken years of unchallenged power. Say what you will about Gingrich (and people do); he deserves credit for delivering a majority and maintaining it against all odds, and he deserves a second look today.

Long before anybody took Obama's candidacy seriously, Gingrich and I spent a fair amount of time talking about swing voters. Our discussions in the summer of 2007 predated ObamaNation, but we could both see it coming, even if it was just a small dot on the horizon at the time. Voters knew what was wrong, but wanted to hear from someone, anyone, how to make it right. They remembered how things used to be, but wanted to know how things could be in the future. They heard the word "change," but they wanted to know when and where. It's déjà vu to look back today at the memo I wrote for Gingrich in August 2007.

> To the ears of independent voters, the political language and presentations of today sound just like everything they've heard and come to reject for the last decade. They don't hear much in terms of innovation plans or ideas, and so they're even angrier than back in 1992–1994. Frankly, they've lost hope—and hope is what you must give these voters if you want to win them back.

That document could just as easily have been written for the Obama campaign team. They understood the psychological condition of America better than any of his competitors, and "change" was just what the doctor ordered.

The lesson about what Americans really want is this: They want us pundits on TV to stop referring to them as red-staters or blue-staters. They want their leaders to listen, understand, and accommodate their individual needs again. Stop painting with a red or blue brush wide enough to blot out a state; start styling with the tip of a person-sized purple pen.

Here's a news flash from November 4: All the young people who gave their hearts to Obama are not leaving the political process. They're here to stay. This election was a gateway to get involved in the world around them, and they aren't going to close the door behind them.

Now, it is true that adults born between 1946 and 1964, the Baby Boomers, made up the single biggest slice of the electorate—37 percent, which gave them twice the clout of their children.* But unlike their middle-aged parents, who were evenly divided between Obama and McCain, the Gen-Y and Millennial kids had a clearly defined point of view. Eighteen percent of voters were eighteen to twenty-nine years old, just one percentage point more than in 2004. But look at it another way:

- Nearly a quarter of Obama's voters were under thirty—a first in modern politics.
- Two-thirds of voters under thirty cast their ballot for Obama—also a first.
- Fully 70 percent of first-time voters were Obama voters—again a first.[36]

No matter how you slice it, the youth numbers represent an encouraging picture of generational engagement now and in the future. Surveys we did for Declare Yourself, a nationwide organization devoted to registering and energizing the youth vote, all indicate an even greater level of participation in politics and civic activities. These young people are listening. They stood up. They have been counted. And guess what?

---

* In 2006, when the first Boomers turned sixty, the U.S. Census compiled a collection of notable facts and figures. For example, the most popular names for boys and girls in 1946 were James and Mary. Today, James has fallen to seventeenth, and Mary doesn't even finish in the top fifty. (The names Americans most want for their children today: Jacob and Emily.) In 1947, just 5 percent of adults had earned a bachelor's degree. Today, fully one-third of adults are college graduates.

They will hold politicians and companies to a different standard. Politicians will be challenged to speak clearly, in plain English, about what they believe, and they will be required to talk about the impact of their policies on the future, not just the present.

What applies to politicians is equally relevant to Corporate America. Companies will also need to act in a more socially responsible manner if they want to earn this new generation's respect and, more important, their business. For example, today's twentysomethings want natural, organic, healthy products. They want to know who makes those products and whether their workers are treated with respect and dignity. Wake up, Corporate America. It's not just about shareholders anymore, it's about community.

In such an unstable world, America's youth have realigned their priorities. They would much rather have government institutions that are accountable. They demand that companies be responsible rather than profitable, offer products that are reliable rather than luxurious, and provide us with energy that is sustainable and not just affordable. "Consistency" and "predictability" appeal to them more too—even more than "risk" and "reward." They're not asking for the world to be handed to them; they just want it to remain in one piece, peacefully.

If you really want to understand the minds of today's political youth, pay attention to where these new voters get their information about politics. Fox News, CNN, and MSNBC all had record years. Stephen Colbert and Jon Stewart, the comedians who provide political "news" on Comedy Central, saw their audience grow by almost 50 percent from four years ago.[37] Tina Fey's drop-dead caricature of McCain's running mate, Sarah Palin, gave NBC's *Saturday Night Live* an autumn to remember and its best ratings in a decade. What we've seen in the past few years is an actual shift in the mind-sets of many young Americans. Being political has become palatable thanks to more fragmented media outlets and pop culture injections into usually dry political content. More than ever, politics is starting to bring young people together to talk about ideas, issues, and candidates in ways they wouldn't have dreamed of doing even a decade ago. Their shared experiences with the follies and foibles of the people in power give them a narrative about American political culture to debate and discuss.

However, for all that television has done to reshape the story of American politics for young Americans, the real lessons of 2008 can be found on the Internet. In fact, the Internet is now the most powerful communication vehicle among young voters. More young people got their information about politics online than from traditional outlets. The Huffington Post quadrupled its number of unique visitors during the election season, and other blogs like RealClearPolitics became almost as famous as the candidates they were covering. Government may have failed to provide the desired level of accountability, but thanks to the Internet, everyone can play the role of fact-checker and political communicator.

And while it is certainly encouraging that today's youth are more engaged and informed than in recent memory, the problem is that Congress is not wired to send or receive vital information through this still relatively new medium—a source of friction particularly among younger voters. Senator John McCain isn't the only Washingtonian who doesn't send or receive e-mails via BlackBerry. Congress still relies heavily on traditional media to communicate in a one-way, outward fashion with the public—television, radio, newspapers, direct mail, and newsletters. They've adapted slowly to online communication, ignoring or simply not understanding that politically engaged citizens are using websites, blogs, e-mail, text messages, and databases to mobilize fellow thinkers. One study for the Institute for Democracy, Politics and the Internet coined the term "poli-fluentials" for politically active Internet users. They were far more likely to watch a political video online, use a search engine to research an issue or a candidate, sign an online petition, send an e-mail orchestrated by an interest group, or sign up for e-mail updates from a candidate or party.[38]

Even among *all* adults, the Internet is critical to their information-gathering. A quarter of Americans turn to a senator's or representative's own website to find out his or her position on an issue, and 22 percent rely on the website of a trusted organization. Another 18 percent use a general Web search.[39] Contrast that with the percentage who use traditional media to gather the same information, which has now fallen into the single digits. For those who want to know, the Internet is becoming the standard, not the standby. It's not an emerging technology. It's the new status quo.

The 2008 election was also the breakout year for "viral" politics. Videos about the campaign and the people running for office drew millions of viewers on YouTube from people seeking a mash-up of information and entertainment. There were real clips of Hillary Clinton singing the national anthem completely off-key and Joe Biden making a derogatory remark about Indians working at convenience stores. But the magic of YouTube was in the entertainment/political videos. The sexually provocative "Obama Girl" who pined about her crush on the Illinois Democrat was viewed more than 11 million times. (By comparison, only 2.6 million viewed the "McCain Girl" alternative, which was even less than the 2.9 million who clicked on the "Giuliani Girl" video.) By Inauguration Day 2009, 15 million people had viewed will.i.am's "We Are the Ones" tribute to Barack Obama—the most for any political video ever. At the Super Bowl, I asked will.i.am whether he ever expected to be a central figure in the presidential campaign. "I never set out to do something political," he told me. "I'm not political. I wanted to make a social statement. It was others who saw it as political." For the first time, the political elites didn't matter. The combination of video and viral marketing allows individual citizens to communicate in ways that were once limited to the professionals—and the best communications now have the power to influence history.*

Americans want coverage of our democracy itself to be more democratized. We have seen the explosion in sales of home-based video-editing equipment to produce content that expresses personal views about political issues. Most of it you'll never see. But the aggregating, cooperative, global nature of the Web almost guarantees that the truly interesting, unique, or even entertaining content will work its way up the YouTube ranks and potentially take on a life of its own. The desire to be *noticed* or even to make a difference will spur a generation of young people to invest real thought, creativity, and time into producing these homegrown videos and podcasts. We had *thought* real choice and variety in the public dialogue had finally arrived with the advent of cable news competition. But now, with all the content on the Web . . . how narrow do the mediums of CNN, MSNBC, and Fox News look to you?

---

* The Web also offers unprecedented fund-raising opportunities. Howard Dean gave birth to Web-based organizational politics, and Barack Obama brought the practice to maturity, but it was Ron Paul who set the all-time record for online fund-raising in a single 24-hour period. On December 16, 2007, in events across the country commemorating the Boston Tea Party, his campaign raised a spectacular $6 million from more than 30,000 Web donors, half of whom donated to Paul for the first time.

Social networking as a political tool—pioneered by Meetup.com in 2004—also became a critical framework in 2008 for discourse among young people. Not only did the campaigns have pages on Facebook and MySpace, but young users created their own networks to build support for candidates, raise money, and bug their friends to register and vote. Twittering morphed into a message-alert system overwhelmingly dominated by Obama backers who would text-message bursts of information to one another and to an ever-expanding circle of users simultaneously. It worked so well that today, even stodgy Republicans are using it. In early 2009, Karl Rove was named the most influential Twitterer in Washington. And even John McCain who, as previously noted, was once a borderline Luddite, tweets.

There are many politicians reading this book who have resisted the trend toward online social networking like Facebook and Twitter. Maybe some of you have joined to keep tabs on your kids. Nevertheless, the lesson is this: Once *Washington insiders* start to embrace a technological trend, either follow or fall painfully behind. The speed of life has accelerated to the point that you need to put more of your personal self into the public realm. Connectivity is king.

What 2008 proved is that the power of the Internet in politics has no limits. Interestingly, this modern technology has returned America to some of its roots of political discourse. The Internet has restored the ability of those seeking office to speak to us in long form, much like the Lincoln-Douglas debates 150 years ago. Newspapers of the day reprinted the texts of those debates in full (with some, but limited, editorializing), allowing voters to comment and decide on their own—the original participatory journalism. Of course, newspapers 150 years ago also carried commercial advertisements on the front page. The point is, the Internet has loosened the hold on information and participation that the traditional news media have had on the American public since the advent of television news and the "sound-bite" culture. For all its flaws, the Internet has leveled the information playing field when it comes to getting information out there, wherever "out there" is. Candidates have more ways to put out unfiltered messages than ever before, and voters have more ways to be heard, all thanks to the Internet.

The Internet also allows a much wider variety of viewpoints to flourish. Bloggers, think tanks, and researchers can disseminate their product widely at low or no cost. The result is that the marketplace of ideas—essential for a free society—is more heavily populated now than ever. Anyone with an idea anywhere in the country can share it with everyone, anywhere, in seconds. You don't have to be a great writer, or even a good one for that matter. You don't have to be on the staff of a newspaper or TV news show. You just have to have a computer, an Internet connection, and an opinion. The world is your audience; you just have to find someone to listen.

But there is a problem with the Internet, with cable news, and with how Americans consume information that does not bode well for the future. For decades, our political mission was to be *informed*. Today, we'd much rather just be *affirmed*. In years past, we actively sought the opinions of a variety of news sources—or one news source that was ostensibly unbiased—to ensure that we had a well-balanced outlook. Today, we seek out news sources that confirm what we already believe and reject what we dislike. If you don't believe me, take this test. If Fox News is your primary source of information on politics, I bet you voted for John McCain, and if MSNBC is where you go for news, you voted for Barack Obama. Instead of trying to capture all perspectives, we are increasingly choosing to be experts on a single worldview: our own. We are losing the common experience and set of facts that the media is supposed to provide, and then we wonder why we can't even agree on events, on facts, on anything. It is also why public discourse in America has become so angry and bitter. Maybe it's because the shouting heads on TV actually do represent the people shouting at home.

Another new Internet twist: Over the course of his campaign, Obama collected the e-mail addresses of 13 million supporters. That makes "ObamaNation" the most powerful special-interest group in the country. Only AARP has more members (40 million), but many of them are not computer literate or have no desire to be actively engaged. I call the online Obama supporters ObamaNation because they are more connected and devoted to a person than to any other cause or community.

The ramifications of ObamaNation are immeasurable. With the stroke of a computer key, this national grassroots army of 13 million can be activated and deployed on any issue. It creates immense potential for political interaction, geotargeting, and rapid-response fund-raising. Three million of the 13 million donated to the Obama campaign at least once. And with every engagement of a supporter, the Obama camp learns, records, and saves ever more information about each individual slice in this ever-expanding pie. It's a new form of proactive governing, waiting to be tapped for policy concerns as well as political campaigns. And it's free. The Republicans are more than four years and ten million e-mails behind.

THE GOVERNMENT AMERICA REALLY WANTS

Regardless of what some campaign professional might want us to think, the government is not just one person. It is 513,000 elected officials across the country, at every level. More than eight in ten Americans say the change needed to get America back on track is so big, it requires far more than just the presidency to change it. They want change at their city council, their county commissions, their school boards, their state legislatures and, yes, in Washington, too.

The number one thing people want from government is *accountability*. They want elected officials to be responsible with their tax dollars and to apply common sense to the decisions they make. They want Washington to instill responsibility, reform, and common sense to Wall Street. They want government spending to be as efficient as they strive to be with their household budget. And they want those officials

WHAT AMERICANS *REALLY* WANT: "WHEN YOU THINK OF GOVERNMENT, WHICH OF THE FOLLOWING IS NEEDED MOST?"

(top two answers combined)

Accountability	50%
Common Sense	36%
Change	32%
Responsibility	29%
Reform	27%
A Balanced Approach	23%

to answer to the people they serve. The Congressional Management Foundation studied the communication between Congress and the public in depth prior to the 2008 election. Their findings are instructive both for those who may run for office and the voters who will elect them:

- 44 percent of Americans contacted a member of Congress in the past five years—much higher than ever before.
- 43 percent used the Internet to contact Congress—more than twice those who used the mail or telephone.
- 84 percent had been prodded to do so by an interest group. (Note to activists: Congressional offices are deeply skeptical of these orchestrated campaigns.)
- People were unhappy with the response they got. Two-thirds said they got a reply back, and half were dissatisfied with it.[40]

Do not underestimate their passion. People who actually take the initiative to contact Congress almost unanimously (91 percent) do so because they care deeply about an issue, even if an interest group gave them the impetus to do so. I have now surveyed and/or conducted focus groups in all fifty states. I have heard firsthand what Americans want from their elected representatives—and what makes them angry. If you've ever dreamed of a career in politics, tear out pages 155 and 156 and carry them with you.

One reason for the horrific disconnect between the elected and those they serve is the language they use. Politicians routinely mangle their words when communicating with the public, assuming what they know is shared with the people they represent. For example, many in Washington call for "tort reform." The problem is, to the average American, a tort(e) is a French pastry. It would have been better and more effective to label it "lawsuit abuse reform." People understand lawsuits and outrageous judgments. They get what abuse is. Calling it "tort reform" is about as useful to the average American as calling it "éclair reform"— do I get angry about it or eat it with coffee?

In 2007 I devoted an entire book to the topic of clean, clear language: *Words That Work: It's Not What You Say, It's What People Hear.* It is essential that the Obama Administration and the loyal Republican opposition commit publicly to educating the population about the genuine economic challenges and security threats to the country while using language that is designed to inform rather than just proselytize. In plain English, they need to speak in plain English. Here's a perfect example of what *not* to do, direct from Section 8 of the federal banking bailout legislation proposed by the White House in September 2008 and rejected by Congress:

> *Decisions by the Secretary pursuant to the authority of this Act are non-reviewable and committed to agency discretion, and may not be reviewed by any court of law or any administrative agency.*

In plain English, it says,

> *Decisions by the Secretary regarding the bailout are final and cannot be challenged.*

There are two problems here. First, apparently the White House and the Treasury Secretary hadn't received the need-for-accountability memo. The American people would have been outraged if they had known that all power would rest in the hands of one man and decisions were final. Maybe that's why this provision was deeply buried in the fine print.

Second, and even more important, the public has a right to know—and demands to exercise that right—when it comes to issues affecting their economic and personal security. Bureaucratic and legislative legalese denies the public the ability to know what their government is doing, and therefore undermines their ability to provide feedback. It will take a Herculean effort to restore credibility to Washington, and clean, clear language is a good first step.

I don't want to rehash the examples from *Words That Work* in this book, but there are three notable examples since its publication that helped doom President Bush's popularity and undermine support for congressional Republicans.

Late in 2006, the White House and the Pentagon began explaining the change in tactics in Iraq as a "surge." The problem was, when people heard the word, they immediately thought "escalation," which immediately conjured up images of Vietnam, which immediately led to despair and a sense of defeat. It was a horrible word that doomed initial support for an eventually successful policy. They would have been much better off if they had talked about a "candid assessment" and a "strategic resource realignment." It is more clinical and more technical, and it suggests applying wisdom and analytics to a military challenge rather than simply throwing more troops into harm's way.

Another example was the phrase "warrantless eavesdropping," a term admittedly used more often by the media and those hostile to the policy. For several years, the public accepted as a matter of course the need for the government to listen in and track the conversations of people it suspected could be connected to international terrorism. In fact, support for the PATRIOT Act held between 60 and 70 percent for Bush's entire first term and well into his second four years. But rather than framing it as "electronic intercepts" as they did in the early days, they started to call it "warrantless eavesdropping." There are two problems here as well. First, people think "eavesdropping" is what you do when you're listening to the people in the hotel room next to you, or you deliberately overhear a conversation in the lunchroom. Second, the word "warrantless" is often confused with "unwarranted," meaning the effort or action wasn't justified. Put them together and you watch support for the program plummet. Some politicians started calling it "wiretapping," but while that generated slightly fewer negative perceptions, it still reminded people of *The Sopranos*. The best language, "electronic intercepts," earns the most public support because it sounds high-tech and it suggests thwarting dangerous criminal activity.

But the worst linguistic blunder from Republicans was the Wall Street bailout. The $700 billion plan to shore up the financial industry was the purest example of mismanaged communications in years. It could have been a "rescue plan," as some in the administration tried to call it. It could have been a "recovery plan," as Barack Obama opined. I suggested a "financial assistance plan" to friends on Capitol Hill. But no, congressional supporters and opponents labeled it a Wall Street *bailout*, and things quickly escalated into a clash between Wall Street and Main Street. Well, Main Street would not go gently into the good night. Coming just weeks before the elections, congressional offices were buffeted by livid callers irate that their tax dollars would go to the perpetrators of the economic collapse rather than the victims. (The language I confidentially recommended to people opposed to the bailout: "America shouldn't punish success and reward failure.") Angry calls to House members ran against the first bailout vote at a rate of more than twenty to one (the only people calling in support of the plan were stockbrokers and members of the Chamber of Commerce). By the second vote, the ratio had narrowed—now four to one against. By Election Day, it was clear that the establishment-backed plan had failed to stop the slide—and the majority of voters had cemented their opposition to it.

Some politicians have an instinctive bond with people, and they can transcend the hostility Americans feel toward the generic politician. I attended a town hall meeting in Ohio sponsored by two then-congressmen: John Kasich and Christopher Shays. I saw Shays turn and control an entire room in an instant with a demeanor and language that would melt even Nancy Pelosi's heart.

The issue was an emotional one—Medicare spending. The Republicans were trying to argue for a smaller increase over the coming years, and Democrats were portraying it as a cut. This was an interesting case of political language and guerrilla tactics—and it's exceedingly tough to explain even now. Here goes:

Fact: in 1995, the government was spending $4,800 per person for Medicare. By 2002, it was scheduled to grow to $7,100 per person based on previous federal budget allocations.

Fact: Newt Gingrich, then Speaker of the House, wanted to try to move Medicare into the black by setting the future price point at $6,700 rather than $7,100—but still well above the $4,800 baseline and above the inflation rate.

So, is that an increase in spending or a cut in spending?

When asked, the public supported "slowing the increase in Medicare spending" by a five to three ratio, but they opposed "cutting Medicare spending" by almost three to one.

This was one case where the issue definition determines the public response. Gingrich called it "slowing the increase," even using hand gestures to show how $6,700 was more than $4,800. Didn't matter. Democrats called it a "cut," their language stuck, and they eventually won the argument. This is not just about semantics; the government was going to increase Medicare beyond the rate of inflation—in real dollars—yet seniors everywhere thought their health care was about to be slashed.

Back to Shays. At this political event, there were about two hundred people sitting theater-style in a large auditorium about two-thirds filled.

In the back row was a severely disabled woman in a wheelchair seeking recognition. Her physical handicaps suggested she would give the lawmakers a hard time on the issue—and she was determined to do so. Kasich called on her, knowing it would jumpstart the discussion. But her speech was affected by her disabilities and she had a hard time getting out the words she intended. The room was silent, all eyes watching her intently, only adding to the pressure. She got very emotional, froze, and stopped speaking. Shays got out of his seat at the front of the room, walked to the back of the auditorium where she was sitting, got down on his knees beside her wheelchair, and put his hand on top of her hand.

"It's OK. Take your time," he said. She got even more emotional. "Take your time and tell us what we need to know," he said. Her voice steadied and she told her story. Any reduction in Medicare spending was a "cut" to someone in her position. It wasn't just semantics; it was her life, her quality of life. When she finished and Shays went back to his seat, the audience applauded. They were applauding not just her story but his empathy.

Footnote: Shays was the last House Republican in New England. He hung on for years as his GOP neighbors and colleagues lost their seats, one by one. He even won in 2006 when Democrats regained control of Congress and got rid of all the other New England Republicans. But Shays lost his Connecticut seat in 2008, when Obama won his district by 30 percentage points. No congressman can survive a thirty-point headwind, not even one as good as Chris Shays.

So far I've been hard on elected officials for not understanding or appreciating the expectations of the people who put them in office. It's appropriate. This is a book about what Americans want, and Americans want Washington to be called out for what it's done—and what it's failed to do. But as Mick Jagger sang more than three decades ago, *"You can't always get what you want. But if you try sometimes, you just might find, you get what you need."* And what Americans *need* right now are leaders who lead.

I know many members of Congress and elected officials. I have seen good behavior and bad. One political client invited me to a private dinner to meet his mistress, knowing how much I liked his estranged wife. I have seen a congressman so drunk that he hit his daughter in the face with a rolled-up newspaper at an inaugural ball. When I was working for Ross Perot as he weighed a presidential bid in 1992, he openly denied he had a pollster. I had to fudge facts, saying I was the "director of research." My mother was indignant. My father thought it was funny that Perot was twisting me like a pretzel.

On the good side of the ledger, I have seen a Texas lawmaker weep as he recalled the details of a devastating tornado, a year after the fact. I watched Jack Kingston, a Georgia congressman, get his hands dirty in the parking lot at a baseball stadium to fix a flat tire for people he didn't know. Former Senator Bob Graham of Florida faithfully pulled shifts alongside workaday Floridians throughout his career, spending more than four hundred days as an auto mechanic, a waiter, a farmhand, and even Santa Claus for a Kiwanis Club in Little Havana. He wanted to know how all Floridians lived, not just those who attended his fund-raisers. It wasn't always easy work, but it was always important.

There is a perception that Congress is filled with lawyers and businessmen. It is largely true. But it is also filled with farmers and teachers. I wish people could have been there, as I was, when Sen. Chuck Grassley of Iowa and Sen. Lauch Faircloth of North Carolina, both *farmers,* talked passionately about pigs and corn. Grassley, a corn farmer, was articulating the hardship of not getting fair market value for his corn. Faircloth, a hog farmer, was unhappy about the price of corn he needed to feed his animals. They *understood* life as lived by their constituents because they *lived* that life. Their conversation was not theoretical, it was real. There is power in that. You know the phrase "salt of the earth"? Grassley and Faircloth defined it. They truly understood how Middle America lives.

The same is true with Reps. Brian Bilbray and Dana Rohrabacher. They're surfers (San Diego and Orange County beaches). Perhaps not an essential skill for a congressman, but their surfing provides a rare glimpse into the real people that they are—and the people they represent.

And to this day, they've never sold out.

I know some of these people have resisted the temptation to become creatures of Washington. They may work *in* Washington, but they will never be *of* it. And yet many of their constituents will always assume they're out of touch. To an extent, it's true. The life of a congressman simply can never mirror that of a nurse, teacher, or cashier. It's only the best officials who can recognize this disconnect and make the right decisions *in spite* of it.

The public should know the flipside of the coin. Members of Congress have to keep two different homes, one in Washington and one in their home district or state, forcing them to live split lives. They're constantly flying back and forth. They have to raise money if they want to keep their job. They rarely have a private moment for their families. Even when they're with their kids and spouse, the lawmakers have to be "on," accepting the interruptions and always responding to constituents. Divorce and dysfunctional families are more rampant on Capitol Hill than interns nursing dollar-bill-beer hangovers. The truth is, what we expect and demand from our elected officials cannot be performed by an extraordinary human being, let alone an average one. We expect them to be Superman and Superwoman. And even when they are, we despise them because they are inexorably a symbol of Washington and everything that's wrong with it.

Here is the point: Americans really want accountability. Just remember that true accountability cuts both ways. It must require consequences for failure, but it should also reward success. Americans today are blessed with more tools for tracking our elected officials' actions than ever before. Use them. Watch those who represent you closely. Hold them accountable for the things they do and the people they are. Just keep an open mind while you do, and if you happen to catch your representatives in the act of doing their job the right way, reward them for it at the polls.

During the presidential primary debate season in early 2008, I flew to Orlando to listen to swing voters from a swing state. This was nine months before the Wall Street meltdown, yet the mood about the economy was already dour. My first provocative question to this focus group gathered at a hotel just outside Disney World: Is the middle class getting screwed? All twenty-six hands went up. Every one of them claimed they were middle-class, and every one of them said they were getting screwed by Washington.

One man summed it up for everyone: "I want to believe these politicians. I want to have faith in them. Instead, I feel like I just found out there's no Santa Claus, there's no Easter Bunny, and there's no Mickey Mouse. And you know what? That sucks."

If only the political kingdom were as simple as the Magic Kingdom.

LUNTZ LESSONS

THE TEN THINGS AMERICANS
REALLY WANT FROM THEIR
ELECTED OFFICIALS

1. **Be genuine in everything you say.** When asked what attribute matters most in an elected official, "someone who says what they mean and means what they say" has finished first in almost every survey for a decade. We want to know what you really think. That also means fewer prepared remarks and more off-the-cuff presentations. Voters want to see your eyes and know that the words are truly yours.

2. **Be genuine in everything you do.** Put an end to the flag photos and the posed pictures with constituents. Keep it natural and keep it real. Voters want to see you hard at work, not mugging for the cameras. However much time you're investing in constituent service today, increase it.

3. **Bring back the gerund.** WorkING, fightING, pushING, demandING, etc. "Ing" is the most active-sounding, energetic form of any word. It tells voters you're working on their behalf right NOW. Elections are a reflection of the past, but more important a referendum on the future. If you can't show voters you've been doING anything, they won't have a reason to return you to office.

4. **Create and publicize a "getting things done" checklist.** The public has a right to know what you've done, why you did it, and what it means to them. By learning what you've already accomplished, the public has a good sense of what you are likely to do in the future. They want to see a record—proof that they can believe what you promise. They will read it and then decide whether you deserve to be reelected. Make that decision easier for them, and more beneficial for you, by giving them a list they can touch, see, and think about when it comes time to vote.

5. **Ask people what they think—and listen to their answers.** The single most effective way for an elected official to connect to a constituent isn't to respond to their question, it's to ask them a question and then listen carefully to the response. The late Sen. John Heinz of Pennsylvania was fabulously wealthy and had little concept of how his rural constituents actually lived, but he created a constant feedback loop with them with his newsletter surveys. Anyone who responded would promptly get the results . . . and another survey. It became his connection to Pennsylvanians. (In his final poll, "He listens to us" was his number one attribute in the eyes of the voters.)

6. **Acknowledge the frustration and empathize with it.** A simple "I know how you feel," followed by "I feel the same way," and ending with "I get it," is required to overcome the perception of distance from the day-to-day concerns of the average American.

7. **Individualize, personalize, and humanize.** Yes, today's challenges are complicated and proposed policies are not always clear-cut. But that's why it's imperative that you *individualize* your communication so that voters see how it applies to the average person, *personalize* your communication so that they see how it applies to them, and *humanize* your communication so that it appeals to the heart, not just the head.

8. **Admit a mistake.** Most politicians hate this advice, and a fair number reject it, but voters want to know that you're humble and human (the human part they question at times). Acknowledging that you got something wrong and then explaining what you learned and how the public benefitted in the end goes a long way in removing the tarnished image that afflicts most politicians. Not admitting a mistake shows that you are either out of touch or have false pride—neither of which voters will tolerate. President Bush waited until his last two weeks in office to admit he made a mistake. President Obama admitted it within the first two months. Take a look at their respective approval ratings next time your pride prevents your candor.

9. **Show a passion for your work and a connection to the people you represent.** Gone are the days when we wanted professional, cerebral people like Adlai Stevenson, Daniel Patrick Moynihan, and Henry Hyde representing us. Today, we want to see and feel the commitment. We don't want people who think for us. We want people who fight for us.

10. **Say "Thank you."** It's simple. Voters, like everyone else, want to know you appreciate them. Remember, they underwrite your paycheck. Give them a reason not to regret it.

5

GOD HELP US:
What We Really Want from Religion

The problem with writing about religion is that you run the risk of offending sincerely religious people, and then they come after you with machetes.

—**DAVE BARRY**

What do we really want from God? Fully 92 percent of Americans believe that God exists, but the answer to this question is hardly as universal. In fact, there may be as many answers to the question as there are Americans who believe in God.[41]

Even though the world sees America as monolithically Christian and thoroughly devout, we are increasingly fractured when it comes to what we believe about belief. In "Christian America" there are wide swaths of the population who would swell with pride if called an "evangelical," while just as many would hurl it against another as an insult. Millions of Americans are *freaked out* by the very notion of being "born again," while roughly eighty million Americans insist it is the only path to salvation. And it is because of this variety of different perspectives that simplifying what we really want from God to something neat and tidy is going to be very messy.

This chapter won't—*can't*—boil it down to a few simple conclusions about "the American public," though something you'll read here will probably make your blood boil. But it will help you take a step back and just observe the nature of our religious dialogue (or lack thereof) and understand it from a perspective that might be different from your own.

Let's start with the easy part. Americans do agree on the generalities of religion. The overwhelming majority of Americans see God as a source of strength and a standard for good. Our nation was born of a search for religious freedom, and the United States is still one of the most churchgoing, God-fearing nations in the world. Fully 84 percent of Americans identify with a specific church and/or religion.[42] We attend houses of worship for spiritual growth and moral guidance. We attend for a sense of community, and we attend to stay grounded or to be inspired. We attend for a sense of community. And we attend to worship God.

Yet there is a continuing tension between how much we want *from* God and how much of our personal life should be *for* God. On one end of the spectrum (let's call it the right, for simplicity's sake) are those who'd like you to call them "people of faith." Borrowing from C. S. Lewis, they'll tell you that the real question is not "What are we to make of God, but what is He to make of us?" What true believers want from God is governance over most corners of life. Slightly more than a third of America falls into this category.*

In the middle are those Americans who'd be most comfortable being called "spiritual." Christmas Christians and High Holidays Jews, they make of God what they find through experience. What they want is guidance on a personal level, but would kindly ask that a wall of separation between church and state be maintained. About half of America would describe themselves this way.

And on the left, politically and religiously, are the remaining 10 percent or so who reject either the notion of God or organized religion, or both. To them, the question is not why God created man but why did man create God—and why are people sending their hard-earned dollars to people on television just because they ask.

In the introduction of this book, I mentioned how America is more vegetable stew than melting pot. Nowhere is that more evident than in religion. There are many distinct ingredients that make up our collective national religiosity, and this mix simmers at a constant boil. We are far and away the most religiously diverse nation in the world. Regionally, there is an assumption that the South is more religious—

---

*   The atheists on the right call themselves "libertarians" rather than "conservatives."

earning the name Bible Belt. In fact, some of the most passionately religious people live in the Midwest, in states such as Kansas, Missouri, Iowa, and Indiana—all north of the Mason-Dixon line. And unlike Southern fundamentalists who are less likely to pry, Midwesterners are more likely to ask you whether you are "a believer" and then engage you in religious discussion if they think you have made a "special commitment to Christ" that they, too, have made.

But more and more, the differences aren't regional, or just about religion versus religion or denomination versus denomination. Stay within even the same denomination of a Christian church, and the black version is going to be very different from the white version. In 2000, I visited two churches in Memphis. One white, one black. People in both churches were praying to the same God. They believed in the same Holy Trinity. There the similarities ended. The white church parishioners were quiet, reserved, subdued. The black church community was loud and proud and overtly embraced their religion. It's part of their day-to-day life. They talk about it, sing about it, and even dance about it. And they wanted to share it all with me. I remember visiting a similar black church a few years earlier and being hugged by a short, plump black woman with a bright purple hat who was actually jumping up and down, made joyous by my presence and interest. Religion was a physical experience in her church. In some mainline white Protestant churches, you shake hands with your neighbor and murmur "peace be with you" or "good morning." In this church, you spend three minutes in conversation with your neighbor. They genuinely want to welcome you and tell you that not only does God love you, but they do too.

So, what to make of the diversity of belief and practice? A good start would be to have an honest dialogue about it. Unfortunately, the one thing Americans hate to talk about the most is religion—or, more precisely, *someone else's* religion.

I was raised with the admonition from my parents that everything was acceptable in polite public conversation except religion and politics. On the political front, half of America doesn't vote in nonpresidential years, and almost half of those who do vote are unhappy with the outcome, so I can appreciate that directive. But almost all of America has a deep connection to religion—and almost everyone believes in God.

And yet for many, religiosity is in the eyes of the beholder. It's like the classic George Carlin bit about being in your car speeding down the highway. Anyone driving faster than you is a maniac or dangerous. Anyone driving slower is an idiot or a moron. Apply that to religion. Anyone more religious than you is a zealot. Anyone less religious than you is godless. Think about it.

The Pew Forum on Religion & Public Life conducted an exhaustive study of religion in 2007, and their findings clearly demonstrate that we are a nation of faith—at least those who are Baby Boomers and older. Gen-Xers are less religious than their parents, and Gen-Y even less so. Now consider the following about America as a whole:

WHAT AMERICANS BELIEVE[43]

- 92 percent believe in God or a universal spirit. Evangelicals, Mormons, Jehovah's Witnesses, and black church members are most certain in their belief.
- 82 percent of Americans say religion is an important part of their lives.
- 74 percent believe in life after death, and the same number believe there is a heaven as an eternal reward. (Fewer think there is a hell.)
- 72 percent attend religious services a few times a year or more.
- 60 percent believe God is a person with whom they can have a relationship rather than an impersonal force.
- 58 percent say they pray once a day or several times a day. Most of these say they receive a definite answer to a specific prayer request.
- 39 percent are weekly churchgoers.
- Only 10 percent say God never answers their prayers.

In general, people who have God in their lives are happier, healthier, and more content compared to nonbelievers and nonpractitioners. They are more likely to be happily married and more likely to spend time with their children. They are more likely to do volunteer work and less likely to engage in antisocial activities. They are better adjusted and closer to family and friends. Every type of positive pathology that we believe is good for the human condition has a direct correlation with religious activity.

Harris Interactive and MBA students from Brigham Young University developed a "happiness index"[44] based on a list of questions such as positive relationships with friends and family members, worry about work and finances, and spiritual beliefs. There are a few areas where there is no distinction between religious and nonreligious Americans: They worry equally about finances, wish they had more enjoyable hobbies, and feel their voices aren't heard in national politics. But for the most part, the results were conclusive: The happiest people were those who described themselves as very religious and those who pray or study religion every day. Religious people worry less about their health and are less frustrated with work. At the very bottom of the happiness index were people who said they were not religious at all. The angriest people are atheists and agnostics—and they fill most of the seats at comedian Bill Maher's performances.

Believing in something greater than yourself, something more important than human existence, causes you to think differently and behave differently. It is not a coincidence that a majority of criminals hold no religious beliefs or that one of the most important steps in breaking a drug or alcohol addiction is the reemergence of faith. Without faith, we are more likely to act in a selfish, self-centered, destructive manner. Conversely, faith validates and empowers respect for the human condition and is the glue that holds society together.

What differentiates Americans from other nations of faith is that the relationship between God and man is not just personal—it is national and fundamental to our American way of life. Without being endowed by a Creator, those inalienable rights provided in the Declaration of Independence that are the hallmark of our society just don't hold up.

While many Americans are shy about sharing their faith publicly, our European counterparts are all too happy to publicly display their hostility toward it. Our expressions of spiritualism and personal displays of religious behavior make most Europeans uncomfortable. Yet considering that their continent has been repeatedly ripped apart by naked, brutal, *humanist* ambition, it is remarkable that modern Europe continues to bank on open secular humanism as the ultimate solution to global problems.

I witnessed this attitude at a dinner in London in September 2008. It was at a posh three-story town house across from Regent's Park in a very wealthy, leafy part of the city. The guests were all part of Prime Minister Tony Blair's old brain trust. I was seated at the foot of the table between two of their wives. Both were classy and proper, and I felt like the quintessential Ugly American. The conversation dipped in and out of politics—why current PM Gordon Brown was such a loser, why George Bush was such a loser, how many forks are used at Buckingham Palace in a typical state dinner (my question), etc.

One of the women segued from Brown's dour demeanor ("His religious upbringing caused that") to Bush's "unhealthy dependence" on religion to a biting but sophisticated critique as only the British can make of Sarah Palin, who had just recently been selected as the Republican vice presidential nominee, and her membership in a conservative evangelical church where people occasionally speak in tongues. Did I find that amusing or scary? I was asked. Why was Bush so religious? What is it about Americans that makes them so religious? Why do they wear their religion on their collar? The questions were genuine, but I could hear a tone of hostility and contempt just beneath the surface. So I asked both women a rather blunt question for a British dinner party.

"When was the last time you went to church?"

For several minutes, the woman on my left gave me a running history of her religious practice, beginning with an event when she was eight years old, and then as a teenager, and ending about six minutes later with something that had happened to her in her twenties. I had asked her a simple question, and she was rambling. So I took a calculated risk and asked again: "I don't mean to be rude, but you don't go to church, do you? You don't believe in God either, do you?"

The answer was no, and no. I could tell by her lengthy nonanswer answer that she was part of the British elite who resent and reject religion. They think faith is for the poor and weak. Something of the past. Silly for clear-thinking citizens of the modern world to believe in fairy tales.

For irreligious societies like those of our friends in much of Europe, *any* religion looks like *über*-religion. They don't recognize the spectrum of belief that exists within the true statement that "Americans believe in God." To them, anyone who talks about their religion in public is an extremist, and everyone who prays is a televangelist. (You'll find this view in much of Manhattan and Hollywood as well.) These would be the people sitting on the slower side of that highway George Carlin talked about, aghast at how every single car on the road was speeding by at a lunatic pace.

Considering that most Americans are timid about discussing our faith and our politics in public, we sure mix them together in the voting booth. The single best indicator of how a person will vote is how he or she worships God. This is why we are so curious about the faith of other people. It's a great way to know a person's life story without sitting through the boring parts. Where you worship explains your values. Your values inform your vote. When you discover what church someone attends, you identify them through the prism of your own religion, or lack thereof.

If someone is identified as a "God-fearing Christian"—(or, more accurately, God-fearin')—it is shorthand for "They're one of us." You know how they vote (Republican), how they live their lives (married with children), their relationship to their job (satisfied) and their community (involved). If I identify myself as a Republican or a Democrat, it tells the listener much less about me than if they know my religion. Conversely, knowing their religion and how often they attend church virtually guarantees you know their electoral preference.

As a nation full of religious people—who don't really like to talk about it—we have come to rely on code words and short phrases to identify when someone shares our beliefs. Consider, for instance, the great difference in our American vernacular between a "person of faith" and a "spiritual person."

Identifying someone as being a "person of faith," "born again," or "evangelical" has come to signify a more devout approach to Christianity founded in a literal application of Scripture. Those who consider themselves to be evangelicals will be offended by the very title of this chapter. To them, it should never be about what Americans want from God. It should always be about what we do to serve Him. Similarly, some Orthodox Jews might even refuse to read this chapter because "God" is spelled out rather than presented acceptably as G-d. Those who self-identify with any of the terms above vote overwhelmingly Republican. They are a minority in the American political process, but an active and powerful minority because of how they vote.

On the other hand, a majority of Americans would be much more comfortable being called "spiritual people." *Spirituality* is the least explicit, least offensive, most easily articulated aspect of religion. It is less definitive and therefore less aggressive than "faith." Faith indicates a specific belief and suggests a religious behavior or judgment, whereas spirituality is more of an attitude. Four in ten Americans attend a place of worship on a weekly basis. More than 80 percent say they are people of faith. But more than 90 percent claim some form of spirituality. Even an atheist who doesn't believe in God can still define himself or herself as spiritual.

But consider how these camps view *each other*. Persons of faith hear "spiritual" and think Shirley MacLaine. Spiritual people hear "evangelical" and think Jerry Falwell. And neither means it as a compliment. Buzzwords cut both ways in our American religious dialogue. Handle with care.

CHURCH AND STATE

We know there is a partisan difference in religion. Sixty percent of Republicans attend church on a weekly basis; only 25 percent of Democrats do. Evangelicals are heavily Republican; atheists and agnostics are almost exclusively Democrats. These are consistent conventions of our modern American political system. Republicans allow and even expect candidates to tell them about their experience with God. Democrats are much more uncomfortable with the conversation, though Barack Obama made a genuine effort to explain his faith during the 2008 election. However, there is a world of difference between discussing your beliefs candidly and disparaging your opponents' beliefs. Make that mistake and kiss your election good-bye—even in the Bible Belt and even if you're an incumbent Republican.

Former senator Elizabeth Dole (R-NC) committed the cardinal sin of electoral politics, connecting religious beliefs to a political attack. Dole ran a thirty-second ad against Democrat Kay Hagan, harping on a fundraiser hosted by two people the campaign described as antireligious activists. The ad said, "Godless Americans and Kay Hagan. She hid from cameras. Took 'godless' money. What did Kay Hagan promise in return?" Hagan fought back, reminding voters that she was a Sunday-school teacher and an elder at her Presbyterian church in Greensboro. The hapless Dole campaign actually released a second ad asking, "If godless Americans threw a party in your honor, would you go?"

Dole was thrown out of office . . . in North Carolina, where they don't just *say* God Bless You when you sneeze—they really *mean* it. Can't blame the Obama Effect; he won by only about 14,000 votes (.32 percent) while she lost by more than 360,000 votes (8.47 percent). Americans are intolerant of religious intolerance. Period.

As for Barack Obama, he may be the best communicator in politics today, but he is dangerously flippant when it comes to religion. He was born poor and raised in working-class communities where a belief in God was expressed in a daily ritual. But Obama's religious upbringing was nonconventional and somewhat chaotic. His father was a Muslim who later became an atheist. His mother was a Christian who became secular as she explored many faiths. She took her children to Catholic services as well as a Buddhist temple. The ambiguities that inevitably result from such an upbringing periodically surface in his language about religion. Obama, due primarily to guidance from his wife, settled on Trinity United Church of Christ, a black church in Chicago, where he was baptized in the early 1990s. He was married in the church and his children were baptized there.

Enter the Rev. Jeremiah Wright and the infamous sermons—offered for sale by the church—that threatened Obama's nomination and election. Reverend Wright regularly took issue with the treatment of the black community in America. Here are his words in full context:

> *The government gives them the drugs, builds bigger prisons, passes a three-strike law, and then wants us to sing "God Bless America." No, no, no, God damn America, that's in the Bible for killing innocent people. God damn America for treating our citizens as less than human. God damn America for as long as she acts like she is God and she is supreme.*

Obama had sought to downplay Wright's comments as being similar to those of a cranky uncle. But the minister's repeated denunciations of the United States from the pulpit ultimately forced Obama's hand. A religious figure condemning the United States from the pulpit was more than extreme or radical—it was unacceptable. Obama may have attended Wright's church for two decades and listened to these sermons as the voice of religious authority in his life, but he was not going to allow his pastor to derail his political campaign.

Less than two months later, Obama once again found himself in religious hot water. In what came to be regarded as the single greatest "slip" of the campaign, he suggested that the religiosity found in rural communities like central Pennsylvania was born of frustration rather than faith. Here's the entire quote:

> *Our challenge is to get people persuaded that we can make progress when there's not evidence of that in their daily lives. You go into these small towns in Pennsylvania and, like a lot of small towns in the Midwest, the jobs have been gone now for twenty-five years and nothing's replaced them. And they fell through the Clinton administration, and the Bush administration, and each successive administration has said that somehow these communities are going to regenerate and they have not. And it's not surprising then they get bitter, they cling to their guns or religion or antipathy to people who aren't like them or anti-immigrant sentiment or anti-trade sentiment as a way to explain their frustrations.*

Obama made this astonishing statement at an April 2008 fundraiser in San Francisco, ostensibly closed to the press and public. His comments clearly weren't meant for public consumption, and I have provided the entire quote to demonstrate that his words were taken out of context to some degree. But he knew his audience—a group of well-heeled Democrats in one of the least religious cities in America—and he understood the ramifications of what he was saying. A tape recording of the speech made its way to a blogger, and then to cable news, and we all know what happened next. He found himself playing defense— and losing—on the eve of the Pennsylvania primary, where guns and religion are indeed cornerstones of life—as is an economy that for much of the state has been resistant to recovery for years.

On reflection, it is too bad that Barack Obama said that people of deep conviction cling to religion out of *despair,* because the truth is that living a religious life is simpatico with his signature refrain of *hope.* He missed a golden opportunity to connect spiritual satisfaction with economic fulfillment.

All of our recent presidents have been people of faith, and most presidential campaigns have featured at least one major faith-based event or moments that have crystallized our understanding of those who lead us. The most historically significant was Jimmy Carter's expression of

WHERE AMERICANS WORSHIP

These are the top five churches in the United States, based on membership reported to the National Council of Churches USA in 2008:[45]

1. Catholic Church, 67,515,016
2. Southern Baptist Convention, 16,306,246
3. United Methodist Church, 7,995,456
4. Church of Jesus Christ of Latter-day Saints, 5,779,316
5. Church of God in Christ 5,499,875

faith during the 1976 campaign and his acknowledgment that, "I've looked on many women with lust. I've committed adultery in my heart many times. God knows I will do this and forgives me." The words were shocking for a presidential candidate, even more so because they came from an interview he did with *Playboy* magazine.

In the 2008 campaign, one of the seminal moments occurred at the Saddleback Church in Orange County, California, one of the largest churches in America, in a forum moderated by the Rev. Rick Warren, author of the bestselling book *The Purpose Driven Life.* The Saddleback Church has 22,000 members and is one of the so-called megachurches that seek to provide far more than just a weekly sermon. They are more like a Vegas buffet, offering a wide menu of services for their members, including actual menus at food courts and restaurants.

Warren proved to be a brilliant moderator, asking questions that probed the thinking process and moral compass of both candidates and without the "gotcha" style that had infected most of the presidential debates. What does Christianity mean to you? What does it mean to trust in Christ? What does that mean to you on a daily basis? Obama answered in language clearly indicating he was familiar with Scripture:

As a starting point, it means I believe in—that Jesus Christ died for my sins, and that I am redeemed through him. That is a source of strength and sustenance on a daily basis. Yes, I know that I don't walk alone. And I know that if I can get myself out of the way, that I can maybe carry out in some small way what he intends. And it means that those sins that I have on a fairly regular basis, hopefully will be washed away.

Obama also talked of acting justly and walking humbly.

"Does evil exist?" Warren asked.

"Evil does exist," Obama said. He then pointed to evil against innocent civilians in Darfur, but surprising his audience, he also referenced the evil in America's inner cities and by parents who abuse their children.

Segue to McCain. He talked about what his faith means to him. "It means I'm saved and forgiven." He acknowledged his greatest moral failing was the failure of his first marriage. Then he told a story about his years as a prisoner of war, how he was kept in solitary confinement and physically tortured. But one guard would surreptitiously loosen the ropes when no one was looking. Said McCain:

> *The following Christmas, because it was Christmas Day, we were allowed to stand outside of our cell for a few minutes. In those days, we were not allowed to see or communicate with each other, although we certainly did. He [the guard] stood there for a minute, and with his sandal on the dirt in the courtyard, he drew a cross and he stood there. After a minute he rubbed it out, and walked away. For a minute there, there was just two Christians worshiping together. I'll never forget that moment.*

Our nation would benefit from more discussions like this, not fewer. We look to elected officials to set examples and seek common ground; if they can enter a public forum to talk with civility about what faith means to them, maybe we can muster the courage as mere mortals to listen without immediate moral judgment. Nobody wants religion to control the public sphere, and nobody wants government to govern faith. But we cannot and should not ignore the real role that religion plays in the creation and fostering of societal morals and values—and how those beliefs affect our views of government, of business, and of American culture.

This discussion of faith between Obama and McCain, in the heat of a campaign for the highest office in our land, simply would not occur in any other nation in the world. We should be grateful that America maintains this commitment to what makes us unique and cautious in our drive to be like the rest of the world.

YOUTH AND GOD

Parents really want their children to share their religious commitment. But younger Americans simply don't have the same level of faith or the same level of religious activity.

Allow me a personal story that I could not tell when I was younger, but it illustrates the disconnect between religion and youth. Young people are notoriously skeptical of organized religion, and I was no exception. Against my wishes, my parents would drag me to my local synagogue throughout high school and whenever I came home from college. It wasn't that I disliked religion. It's that I disliked the rabbi, who was a hard-core liberal at a time when I was discovering my own conservative beliefs. This was September 1981, in West Hartford, Connecticut, at the Beth Israel congregation, a Reform temple where everyone was a registered Democrat. My mother would insist that I attend services with her (because she wanted to show off her Ivy League son), and my father joined in because he wanted to make her happy. At one particularly contentious moment, my mother demanded to know why I was so obstinate. I told them the truth: I didn't want to sit for an hour and listen to the rabbi criticize my political beliefs. After more than an hour of arguing, I finally relented, but with a small caveat. I told my father, "I'll make you a bet. If Rabbi Silver doesn't mention anything about Republicans or conservatives or Reagan, I'll pay you fifty bucks. But if he starts complaining about the NRA, the religious right, or Republicans, every time he complains you pay me twenty bucks." My mother was really annoyed at this conversation, but it was the only way to get me to go, so she relented.

This is a true story, no embellishment whatsoever. I remember it as though it happened this morning, and it brings both pleasure and pain to retell it. We got there early as usual ("We have to beat the traffic," my mom would say) and sat where we always sit—on the aisle, somewhere between rows 5 and 8 so that we could be close enough to see the rabbi's eyes but not so close that our necks would hurt. About forty-five minutes into the service, the rabbi got down to his sermon. After a few opening remarks, he launched into what I knew was coming: "In this time of great challenge and change, in this era of intolerance and misunderstanding, we have to look objectively at where our country stands and whether the president of the United States and organizations like the Christian Coalition and the NRA are doing what's good for all of America."

I whispered loudly, "Bingo! Pay up, Dad!"

My mother was mortified.

The sermon lasted eight minutes. The rabbi wouldn't let up. "Reagan said this . . . the NRA did that . . . the Christian Coalition is a threat to . . ." On and on. It was like a Jackie Mason routine. And every time the rabbi hit one of my bugaboos, I yelled, "Pay up," just loudly enough that people within about five seats (and my mom) could hear me. At one point I looked at my father and said, "Just give me your wallet." We were both laughing, the only time he and I ever laughed in a synagogue.

He wasn't mad at me. He wasn't mad that he lost the money. He was mad that the rabbi went after the NRA. My father was surely the only gun-toting Jewish dentist in all of Connecticut. He'd spent twenty-six years in the National Guard and was the state pistol-shooting champion. Guns were a God-given right as far as my father was concerned.

But the story, and the lesson, doesn't end there. After services, we went to a nearby Howard Johnson's, as we always did, for a bite to eat. I was still high from winning the bet ($180!) in such a spectacular fashion and was bragging loudly about it. My father shushed me. I mentioned it again, and this time he sternly told me to keep quiet. Turns out it was OK to talk about religion, even make fun of it in the temple, but not in a family restaurant one mile away. The scene was too *public*; the subject too *private*. It was a generational thing. You just don't talk about religion in public—particularly if you're Jewish. That about killed religion for me.

The National Council of Churches says people in their twenties and thirties attend churches but resist becoming members. Young people are least likely to describe themselves as very religious or to pray at home. Some of this can be traced to moral conflicts over gay marriage. Two big denominations—the Episcopal Church and the Presbyterian Church USA—both reported declines in membership at a time of roiling debate within those faiths about the role of gays in the church and interpretation of biblical teachings. Into this atmosphere, the United Methodist Church launched a new slogan: "Open hearts. Open minds. Open doors."

Scandals in religion are deeply damaging, especially to young people already skeptical of organized religion. The Catholic Church disillusioned followers with its cover-up and subsequent silence about priests who were sexual predators. This shattering of faith in the Catholic Church was a defining moment and not just for Catholics. It caused real damage to our collective psyche regardless of our religious affiliation. We assume the clergy is the most trusted profession in America. For the Catholic Church to go through such a meltdown affected everybody's faith and trust in religious institutions.

Americans believe there are clear and absolute standards for right and wrong, a moral compass drilled into us almost from birth. Yet most

HOW AMERICANS *REALLY* BEHAVE: THE SEVEN DEADLY SINS

We are envious. More than 40 percent admit buying something they really didn't need and couldn't afford simply because someone else had it. Television ads are especially effective in provoking the "I want it" hormone. Who wasn't envious when you first spotted someone with an iPod or iPhone?

We are greedy. Asked what you would do if the IRS made a $5,000 error in your favor and you knew it wouldn't be discovered, 44 percent said you'd keep the money and spend it. Republicans and Democrats equally.

We are gluttons. Americans are the fattest people on the globe. We are a nation of supersized appetites, and it shows in rates of obesity and alcohol abuse. Eleven percent say they drank so much it made them sick in the last year alone. Thirteen percent ate until they got sick. Six percent admitted to both.

We are vain. Most of us think we are more attractive than the average American, and we definitely think we're smarter than the average Joe.

We are wrathful. A third of us admit to losing our temper in public in the last year. Road rage is Exhibit A. Queue up in any line—post office, fast-food restaurant, the grocery store, the Motor Vehicle Department—and you'll witness bad behavior.

We have lust. Twenty percent would definitely or probably have an affair if we thought we could get away with it. Another 16 percent would "possibly" do it. Still, 46 percent said definitely *not*.

We are slothful. Some of us, anyway—three in ten admit to taking a day off work and claiming to be sick when we weren't.

people cannot recite even half the Ten Commandments, let alone live by them. Same with the slightly condensed Seven Deadly Sins, polished and refined by clergy through the centuries to keep Christians in line.

For the most part, sin is gender-neutral. There are just as many men with one foot in the pit of hellfire as there are women. Surprisingly, household income, education, region, and race also didn't matter. There was a generational gap, however. Nearly *half* (44 percent) of Americans between the ages of eighteen and twenty-nine admit to committing four or *more* of the Seven Deadly Sins—almost three times more likely than their parents.

The upshot is that although 92 percent of Americans believe in God, there are increasing signs of religious erosion. For those who believe in the importance of religion in family and community life, we must recognize that we can't get there just by worrying about it. We have to overcome our reluctance to talk about God and learn how to do it in a constructive, respectful fashion.

TALKING ABOUT RELIGION EFFECTIVELY

It starts with building credibility. While we are so deeply and universally religious, the mere effort to discuss religion in a public forum often draws howls of protest. I have argued that if there was an Eleventh Commandment, it should read "Thou shalt not judge the other ten." In truth, you can talk about religion, as long as you talk about *your own* religion. It's acceptable to talk about *your* faith. It's when you talk about or evaluate someone else's religion that you get into trouble.

The religious community has had its share of good communicators, but some fell from grace because their private behavior did not match their public image (Jim Bakker, Jimmy Swaggart, Ted Haggard), while others came to be seen as a fund-raising machine rather than a fountain of inspiration (Oral Roberts). They rose to great fame because of their perceived authenticity, but then crashed and burned because of a very real hypocrisy. We remember their public displays not just for the salacious details or outlandish demonstrations but for how they fell from grace.

Billy Graham was different. Graham was a public figure for more than half a century. You didn't just believe that he actually *lived* what he believed—you knew it. You allowed him into your life and paid attention to his teachings because *he* was *sure* he had a friend in Jesus, and he wanted to introduce you to his friend. Maybe his beliefs were right, maybe not. It really didn't matter. You might not have agreed with him, but you knew he meant what he said because of how he lived.

It was entirely natural to see Billy Graham in meetings with presidents from Harry Truman to George W. Bush. Even though the White House belongs to the American people and is therefore a "public" institution, Americans didn't mind seeing Billy Graham there. He met with Democrats and Republicans alike, and it didn't seem strange. We knew he wasn't there to lobby or insert God into politics. In fact, we admired him because his message was the same to Republicans and Democrats—and that's because it actually had nothing to do with Republicans and Democrats. And we endorsed him when he said the following in explaining why he would not affiliate with Jerry Falwell's Moral Majority:

> *I'm for morality, but morality goes beyond sex to human freedom and social justice. We as clergy know so very little to speak with authority on the Panama Canal or superiority of armaments. Evangelists cannot be closely identified with any particular party or person. We have to stand in the middle in order to preach to all people, right and left. I haven't been faithful to my own advice in the past. I will be in the future.*[46]

A little humility goes a long way. When it comes time to share your beliefs, be honest *about* them—but also be honest *to* them. Americans revile hypocrisy. We revere authenticity.

Sarah Palin is the perfect case study for those seeking to uncover the secret to religious messaging and communication. She clearly recognized the connection between religious values and small-town values—and sought to make that connection the centerpiece of her campaign message. It was a genuine appeal from a devout Christian. She was baptized Catholic and was drawn to a Pentecostal church as a teenager. As an adult, she eventually joined the Wasilla Bible Church, a conservative evangelical congregation.

Throughout the campaign, it was impossible to tell where her political beliefs ended and her religious beliefs began—they were so intertwined. When McCain anointed her as his running mate, Palin was immediately embraced by the evangelical wing of the Republican Party, which had been lukewarm toward McCain. They celebrated her religious convictions, and she didn't let them down.

At the GOP convention, she delivered her own version of the well-known Ecclesiastes passage about a season for everything: "There is a time for politics and a time for leadership . . . a time to campaign and a time to put our country first." More subtle but just as important was a line later in the speech, when she said, "We are expected to govern with integrity, good will, clear convictions, and a servant's heart." Non-evangelicals probably missed it, a reference to the Bible's model of servant leadership, to put others first. She didn't mean it in the political sense; she meant it in the religious sense. She used a code phrase that communicated to every Christian that she was one of them, and so was McCain. It was a great speech, one of the best of the campaign, and it (briefly) rocketed McCain ahead of Obama. Her subtlety allowed her to touch both religious and secular Americans without insulting either.

She was much more overt, and much less effective, in an interview with evangelical leader James Dobson a few weeks before the election and the reaction was much more polarized. She sought God's help and that of his followers in the election. "It is that intercession that is so needed and so greatly appreciated. And I can feel it too, Dr. Dobson, I can feel the power of prayer, and that strength that is provided through our prayer warriors across this nation."

She continued: "When we hear along the rope lines that people are interceding for us and praying for us, it's our reminder to do the same, to put this all in God's hands, to seek his perfect will for this nation, and to of course seek his wisdom and guidance in putting this nation back on the right track." These words are not polished, political buzzwords designed to signal to the faithful without irking the faithless. These are the same words you'd hear in her church, not in the public sphere. And these words, while balm to the religious community, were like fingernails on the chalkboard to everyone else.

Just as 2008 was viewed as an opportunity to talk about race in America, it is my hope that over the course of the next few years we engage in a renewed national dialogue about the role of religion in America. And because dialogues are always *at least* a two-way street, we need to make a concerted effort to improve the *way* we communicate our beliefs to one another.

CONCLUSION

The following "Rules for Religious Discussion" have been prepared for people who have devoted their lives to spiritual outreach, and are based on years of research into how we articulate our faith and how religious leaders can best lead the conversation.

We are painfully—and dangerously—shy about discussing something as clearly important as religion. So ask more questions than you offer imperatives. Stop hiding behind code words and hurling them like hand grenades. Listen. Understand. "Do Unto Others as You Would Have Them Do Unto You" applies to communication, not just behavior. You'd like others to understand where you're coming from, right? They are much more likely to listen to you if you listen first. And after all that listening, you'll have earned the credibility you need to share your own beliefs. Just remember, when the time comes for you to preach . . . practice, too.

LUNTZ LESSONS

THE RULES FOR RELIGIOUS DISCUSSION

1. **First, admit there is no perfection.** One of the core tenets of all religions is the fallibility of its practitioners. The same is true for those who seek to engage in a religious dialogue. By acknowledging at the outset that "we all make mistakes, but that our mission in life is to learn from them," you will have found common ground on which to begin.

2. **Second, acknowledge that "all points of view are welcome."** This is going to rankle the leadership of certain faiths, but let me explain. Welcoming differing views or interpretations isn't the same as agreeing with them or affirming them. What it does do is affirm a person's right to disagree—an essential component in any open and fruitful dialogue.

3. **Talk about the decay of morality and the disintegration of the family.** More than 70 percent of Americans have serious concerns of the moral kind: the increasing coarseness of the culture, the lack of respect we have for one another, the millions of children who are growing up not just in one-parent families but in no-parent families. You will be far more successful entering the conversation by addressing issues of morality and values than applications of religion. Bill Clinton understood better than any modern politician that if you connected with people based on your articulation of the problem, they would be much more likely to accept your solution.

4. **Acknowledge a "separation of church and state."** Contrary to popular myth, the principle is enshrined in the Constitution but the phrase is not. Thomas Jefferson talked about a "wall of separation" in a letter written fifteen years *after* the Constitution, and it wasn't until 1878 that the Supreme Court specifically referenced it. Nevertheless, it is an accepted doctrine among all but the most devout in America, even as we disagree about its application. We cringe at the idea of Sharia—the body of Islamic religious law that has binding judicial power over citizens of multiple countries. Could you imagine if the Supreme Court cited Deuteronomy as the basis of a holding, rather than the Constitution? Americans of *all* religious intensities would oppose that. But just because we don't want our government to establish a religion doesn't mean we should pretend religion doesn't influence our government at all. The fact is, we pick our politicians *after* we pick our God. Just don't say it this way.

5. **Dispense with the "code."** Americans want to get past labels that have been buried under the weight of use and abuse and understand the under-

lying beliefs. If simple utility requires using the words themselves, first establish a mutually satisfactory definition. For example, ask a person what "evangelical" means *to* them, before you use the label *on* them. Ask your counterpart to explain how their "spirituality" guides their daily decisions. A belief system is simply too complicated a thing to be summed up in one word. Spend your discussion time understanding the meaning behind the words rather than batting the same words back and forth like a tennis ball.

6. **Stop lecturing; start listening.** Americans have spent almost all of our time in public discussions about religion on *telling . . . lecturing . . .* even—gasp—*preaching.* Make a deposit on the listening side of the account. See how long you can go in a conversation without saying, "What I think is . . ." Americans feel their beliefs are not understood in the public realm; listening is the cure. Conveying *understanding* is a precondition to credibility, and you can't understand if you don't listen. We might not reach a final accord about the true nature of Truth, but listening to what it *might* be is the start that fosters mutual credibility.

7. **Answer questions with questions.** Too often we take a question as an invitation to launch into a lecture, when really we should use questions as vehicles for *more* back-and-forth conversation. The Jewish faith has had more than its share of great communicators through the ages because of its exploration for answers through a series of questions.

6

LIVING AT THE SPEED OF LIFE:

The 2020 Generation

Before these kids know about excellence, they know about money, and that's a shame.

—MIKE KRZYZEWSKI,
2008 OLYMPIC GOLD MEDAL BASKETBALL COACH
COACH, DUKE UNIVERSITY BASKETBALL (1980–PRESENT)

Never in American history has one generation lived a life so fundamentally different from what their parents experienced. Sure, this was said about Baby Boomers, and then the Gen-Xers. Fundamental change is a natural trend in our modern era of technological development and the increasing speed and breadth of communication. But the generational change we see today is exponential. Put differently, Generation 2020, individuals born between 1980 and 1991 and occasionally referred to as Millennials, are *drastically* less like their parents than Gen-Xers are like theirs. Politically, technologically, economically, and socially, kids today are growing up with expectations, assumptions, and experiences that simply did not exist thirty years ago.

To provide a framework for this entire chapter, let's take a moment to survey the world landscape as members of the 2020 Generation have come to know it. Born between 1980 and 1991, they are too young to remember Vietnam, Watergate, Arab oil embargos, Iranian hostage-taking, and Ronald Reagan. What they will never forget is the collapse in personal security that took place on 9/11, as well as the collapse in their economic security in 2008—leading to a collapse in confidence. As stated in the Introduction, it would be equally appropriate to call them Generation Zero, for they are the first and only generation of Americans who don't necessarily believe that the future will be better than the past. Their world has changed in ways their parents and grandparents couldn't even imagine.

Globalization isn't just an economic term to young people. It's woven into their daily lives. They don't have to wait until spring to buy strawberries or summer to eat plums because they have access to global imports. Their breadth of travel options has grown dramatically. Social networking sites have made borders less relevant. Thanks to the Internet, they can follow and "friend" someone anywhere in the world they've never met, and likely never will, via Facebook (or Twitter). They aren't as interested in the Olympics as their parents were because they don't really like international competition—the whole country-versus-country thing—U.S. versus Russia, U.S. vs. China. They admire individual excellence (one reason why the television ratings for the 2008 Beijing Olympics on NBC remained so high during Michael Phelps's quest for eight gold medals and then collapsed after his final race). They can't relate to superpower competition on any field—of battle, or otherwise. This generation is the first to reject "American exceptionalism," preferring a "We're all in this together" philosophy.

Video is more real for young people than the actual experience. That's because they've learned more about the world through video than they have through actual experience. At a game or event, their parents will watch a sporting event itself, even if there is a huge TV monitor nearby and they're in the very back row. The 2020 Generation will watch the television monitor even if they're up close to the action itself. I saw the final Yankees game at Yankee Stadium from the comfort of the Fox box overlooking home plate. I was a guest of Bill Shine, senior vice president of programming for Fox News, who had taken his son to see the historic event. Bill was watching the *actual* game as it played out in front of him. His son and several older teenagers were watching a nearby television monitor. I looked around. All the adults in the box were watching the *real* game. All the younger people were watching the *digital* version. Remember, this was the *last* game ever to be played in the House that Ruth Built,

Gehrig blessed, and Mickey Mantle wowed. From that day forward, the only way you could *ever* see a game in this building was on film. Last chance to experience it as it really was. Only sixty thousand people could ever claim to have seen the final spectacle at the Mecca of baseball. And these representative members of Generation 2020 were content with the digital version—the version that would be available online the next day and forever.

Even if this trend is regrettable, it's certainly understandable. To a generation that grew up with the soft, electric glow of TV and computer screens, what's broadcast over the air and through fiber-optic cables is more real—more familiar—than reality. Perhaps it's because they are the first generation whose parents had video cameras to chronicle every event in their lives, so it's no surprise that they are living out their young adulthood on YouTube and other online outlets. Perhaps it's because it's easier to find excitement when it's piped into your home, rather than choosing the harder, if more fulfilling, route of finding excitement in the real world. Whatever the reason, the habit is now as hardwired as their broadband connections.

The best things really do come in small packages for this generation. Their parents boast of their big-screen TV, but the 2020 Generation would rather watch video portably on their small handheld devices. My generation created the market for SUVs, which grew bigger and bigger over time. Young people today wouldn't be caught dead behind the wheel of a Chevy Suburban. That's Mom's car. Gen-Xers only had the privilege of rebelling against minivans (*their* moms' cars).

Generation 2020 can get what they want, when they want it, and how they want it. Right now. Immediately. Forget about them going to the music store to buy CDs to make a mix tape, or sitting patiently through a block of commercials so that they can watch their favorite TV program. That's their parents' behavior. That's the way things *used* to be.

To understand Generation 2020 is to understand the seamless integration of modern technology into daily life. Multitasking is an insufficient way to explain how Gen 2020 lives because it suggests handling two or three tasks at a time. For Gen 2020, it's more like everything, all at once, always. Call it omni-tasking.

They are always connected and therefore never alone.

Their lives are fully interactive, yet they have trouble communicating face-to-face. They've even started breaking up with each other via text message.

They can manipulate a cell phone keyboard far faster than their parents, yet they never learned how to type properly.

They are the "participation trophy" generation who won awards just for showing up, yet they spend less time outdoors than any generation before them.

They have created a new language for their online relationships, yet they haven't mastered English.

They are experts at locating individual bits of information, yet they have little knowledge about how governments or economies work.

Every thought is expressed via MySpace, Facebook, or Twitter, and therefore no thought is ever left unspoken.

And thanks to an abundance of bandwidth, YouTube produced more video programming in the last six months than all of the big three television networks combined in the last sixty years.[47]

No need to troll the dive bars applying hackneyed pickup lines anymore. Generation 2020 doesn't want or need to meet people the old-fashioned way. They don't even need to fill out online questionnaires like those used by Eharmony.com. Thanks to the ability to track user habits on the Web, they'll be able to match people based on the sites they like to visit. Similarly, with Social Plan, subscribers will be able to track what friends are doing online and at real-world events. It's part Twitter and part GPS—and it's all instantaneous.

But don't let their demand for immediacy fool you. They're still living for the journey, not just the arrival. Gen 2020 has embraced an independent culture that isn't as much a rejection of the present as an embrace of the future, with a sprinkling of the past. From Yahoo! to YouTube, they see life as one big buffet—ready-made for sampling. They watch cartoons on Adult Swim, only these are of the mature variety. *Flight of the Conchords* is their *Monty Python*. They listen to mash-up remixes of music that often originated decades ago. Since history is online and at their fingertips, they have the luxury of being able to pick and choose what they like about the past and import it into their future—thus making it "retro" and acceptable. They buy clothing styles popularized in the 1980s not because it is in style now but because it is not—which makes it in style. They're into irony, even if most couldn't define it.

They have no Cold War memories to shape their world vision. Life is not black and white. They know nothing of generation gaps, battles for integration, or the sexual revolution. They reject absolutes regarding morals, values, and ethics. There is no absolute right and wrong. Everything is shades of gray. Or perhaps green—green as in the environmental condition they seek for the planet. This generation doesn't just talk conservation. They live it in their day-to-day lives. Most of them recycle, and few of them litter.

So get ready to slide open the door and peer inside America's future. You might not like what you see. But in order to shape their worldview as a parent or market your product to them as a business or earn their increasingly important electoral loyalty, it is crucial to understand how they think—scary though it may be.

SCHOOL'S OUT FOREVER

For Generation 2020, it all starts—and ends—at the classroom door. The youngest of them are just entering college, while the oldest are beginning to have children of their own. While the difference in age

THE GEN 2020 DIFFERENCE

It's not just political allegiances that differentiate Gen 2020 from the rest of America. On a host of issues, attitudes, behaviors, and expectations, this generation is nothing like their parents. Here are the five areas where Gen 2020 and the American population overall are most at odds (see Appendix for questionnaire, response wording, and numerical results):

1. **Immediate gratification.** More than half (53 percent) of Gen 2020 agree with the statement *"I want it all and I want it now."* To them, gradual intergenerational improvement isn't a cozy definition of the American Dream. It's a command. By comparison, only a third (35 percent) of the American population has similar demands. Gen 2020 is in a big hurry, and nothing—and no one— better step in their way.

2. **Ongoing happiness.** When given the choice of 15 priorities for life, both Gen 2020 and adults overall picked a loving family as their first choice. But that's where the similarities ended. For Gen 2020, happiness was a very close second.

For adults overall, health and financial security were second and third, with happiness a very distant fourth. Once again this is evidence of the desire among Gen 2020 for products and people that offer a pleasant, positive impact rather than the comparative/negative messaging that worked well with older generations of Americans.

3. **The decreasing importance of religion.** One-fourth (26 percent) of all adults consider *"the church"* to be one of America's two most important institutions for the future—second only to schools. But among Gen 2020, only half that level (13 percent) pick the church in their top two. To them, schools, the federal government, business, hospitals, local government, and financial institutions are all more important. Now is not the time to invest in new church construction.

4. **The value of equality.** One-third (35 percent) of Gen 2020 chooses "equality" as one of the two most important American values, second only to "opportunity" at 41 percent. Yet among all Americans, equality (at 24 percent) comes in a distant fifth, behind liberty (45 percent), opportunity (33 percent), justice (30 percent), and democracy (28 percent). Politicians talk about a color-blind society, but Gen 2020 lives it.

5. **No news is . . . no news.** Gen 2020 is certainly on the Web and still watching television—but they're actively avoiding news. In fact, the behavioral difference between them and Americans overall when it comes to news consumption is staggering. Only one-quarter (24 percent) of Gen 2020 spends more than an hour each day collecting national or international news. For all adults, news consumption doubles; 46 percent spend more than an hour.

means a difference in day-to-day priorities, one area that unites them—and their parents—is the nagging feeling that their educational experience could have and should have been more challenging and informative. Almost everyone can name a teacher or two who inspired him or her with passion and commitment to education, but there is universal agreement that America's public education system falls short of the desirable (and in some cases short of the acceptable). In many cities, the schools are considered an embarrassment by some and a joke by others.

While it's too late for Generation 2020, the next crop of kids are working their way through the system—and for them, it is worth examining what Americans really want, not just for their own children but for the next generation. The Bill & Melinda Gates Foundation and The

Broad Foundation have been particularly active in pursuing education excellence and fundamental reform at the local school level. Standing in their way are the federal and state teachers' unions, which, while fighting for higher teacher salaries, have a vested interest in maintaining the status quo. Having interviewed hundreds of recent graduates and thousands of their parents, here are the ten aspects of the public education system that Americans want most:

WHAT THE 2020 GENERATION (AND THEIR PARENTS) REALLY WANT FROM AMERICA'S PUBLIC SCHOOLS

1. **The Principle of Parental Choice and Control:** Americans want to increase the role of parents in the day-to-day decisions about the education of their children. Every piece of research data ever conducted has shown a direct link between parental involvement in their children's education and the intellectual success of the child. Education starts in the home, not in a government building. Parents have the right to know how their children are doing and how their schools are faring, and the right to have the ability to influence both.

2. **The Principle of Positive Thinking:** Americans will turn against anyone who universally condemns public education. A majority believe a quality public school education is now a right, not just a privilege, and they will rebel if they don't hear your *solutions* to address the *challenges* you raise, and giving up on public schools is not an option.

3. **The Principle of Safety:** Above all else, children have the RIGHT to a violence-free and drug-free environment. Children simply cannot learn if they are afraid. In fact, the only fear a child should have is of the next exam, not the child sitting next to him or her.

4. **The Principle of Child-Centered Education:** Education is first, last, and always about the children and teaching them what they need to know to succeed in a twenty-first-century economy. The objective of education is not to measure attendance or teaching. Rather, it should measure *learning*—and that depends on putting the child front and center in the education equation. Teachers deserve our respect, but children deserve our primary focus.

5. **The Principle of Equality:** Every child, regardless of race, income, or family status, should have the right to a quality education, and no child should be

denied the opportunity of a quality education just because of residence or the family's financial situation. We may not end up at the same place, but we firmly believe in the principle that every child deserves an equal start in life.

6. **The Principle of Effective Education Investment:** When measuring success, it's not how much you spend, it's how you spend it. Similarly, it's not what's taught that matters; it's what the child learns. Attendance is important, but learning is vital.

7. **The Principle of Back to the Basics:** Children need to study and master reading, writing, math, science, and history regardless of where they are, from Massachusetts to Mississippi. The arts are important, but these basics are essential. Experimentation is out. Common sense life skills are in.

8. **The Principle of American Exceptionalism:** While it is true that Generation 2020 does not respond well to global competition—choosing cooperation instead—when presented with the fact that American schools do not rank in the top ten globally in either reading, math, or science, the information is received with a strong sense of embarrassment and shame. They agree that you can't have a great country without having great schools.

9. **The Principle of RESULTS and CONSEQUENCES:** Americans want education results measured and success rewarded. Parents want the right to demand *accountability* from the schools and *discipline* inside the classroom. And everyone except the teachers' unions wants outstanding teacher performance rewarded.

10. **The Principle of a Common-Sense National Education Policy:** Keep politics out of school policy. Only fund education programs that work. Fix or end those that fail.

WHAT PARENTS DON'T WANT TO KNOW

Warning: If you're a squeamish parent with 1950s values and twenty-first-century kids in high school or college, you might want to skip the next three pages.

First, let's start with what they think of you.

For so many, you aren't their parent. You're their best friend and confidant. You're less an authority figure and more a life advisor. Somehow you successfully bridged the generation gap that you faced with your own parents growing up in the 1960s.

Yet one theme that comes through loud and clear in listening to

Generation 2020 is the sense of pressure for status and success from their very first recollections. Beauty pageants for three-year-olds who can barely walk, spelling bees at six for kids who can barely read, pee-wee hockey for kids who can barely skate—they were put into competitive situations at younger and younger ages. But what is even more disturbing is their perception that their own *accomplishments* were used by you parents as symbols of *your* parenting success. The sports trophies, honors classes, countless extracurricular activities, and SAT scores were achieved not just for *their* personal betterment but for *your* bragging rights. And you wonder why some of these kids come out of college already worn out from life.

And if you're still reading, here's the scoop. Your teenage children are likely having sex with their friends as a way to exercise their overactive libidos. There, I said it. And no, this is not the sexual revolution of the 1960s and '70s between two (or more) consenting adults. It's not about "making love, not war," because they don't need love. It's not even about relationships. It's called "friends with benefits." Or FWB for the textually inclined, as many of them are. No strings attached (NSA), no expectations, no commitment. Just sex. And everyone's doing it. You may have heard this term before. What's new is that kids as young as middle school have taken it and run with it. It's not that they resigned themselves to loveless relationships after a series of heartbreaks. They just dove right into it as soon as they started dating. Now they're in their twenties and utterly inclined to the most casual of physical relationships.

If you want to understand the mentality of today's youth before they become tomorrow's leaders, just think of the Nike slogan that captured the imagination of the last generation of young people: "Just Do It." For them, it was a direction. For kids today, it's a mission.

I had the distinct opportunity to enlighten a number of parents about the term and the practice of "friends with benefits" during a focus group for Rupert Murdoch's leadership team in 2006. We had gathered a group of kids in their late teens and early twenties. They were a window into the future for the most powerful, successful media conglomerate in the world. My job was to enlighten the audience of three hundred business elite to the world of tomorrow, to let them hear what young people really think, say, and do.

The phrase came up in response to a question inquiring what these kids do that would make their parents blush. I asked the group of twenty-two participants how many of them knew what the term "friends with benefits" meant. All twenty-two hands went up. Then I asked, how many of *you* have friends with benefits? Nineteen hands went up. I turned to the audience and asked if they'd heard of friends with benefits. Half the hands went up, mostly men. I turned back to the kids and asked, "Who wants to explain it?" *No* hands went up.

I could hear a buzz out in the audience as the clueless sought information from the clued-in. One mother told me later, "I am grateful you told me about this . . . and I will never forgive you for telling me about it." I wonder how many parents asked their own children about it later. I have polled parents ever since, asking them whether they'd want to know the truth about what their children do when the lights are off. Most have told me no, but the price of not knowing might be more than you can afford. As a parent, not knowing might cost you your relationship with your child—or worse. As a company, not knowing what the youth of today are thinking and doing *will* cost you your bottom line.

The purpose of this chapter isn't to sling attacks at the behavior of today's youth. After all, in so many ways they're just like their parents: drinking, drug experimentation, and late-night partying are a regular occurrence—nothing out of the ordinary there.

But there are other aspects of their behavior that would frighten any mom and dad. Booty-texting for a late-night hookup; posting photos of themselves in a drunken stupor or in various stages of undress on Facebook or MySpace; robo-tripping on the cough medicine Robitussin.

Even the geeks are getting laid—at just about the time they get their driver's license. This generation celebrates the coming of age of the "beta male," the somewhat awkward, very intense, entirely unconventional and totally lovable teen who would have spent his weekends in the library in the 1980s but is now the center of sexual attention on today's college campuses. Sure, the college jock still gets his share of women, but he now has competition, and you can credit Hollywood's influence for the turnaround. The acclaimed writer, director, and producer Judd Apatow (*The 40 Year Old Virgin, Superbad*) and actors such as Michael Cera (*Arrested Development, Juno,* and *Nick and Norah's Infinite Playlist*) and Seth Rogen (*Knocked Up* and *Zack and Miri Make a Porno* . . . yes, you read that movie title right) have made a career of creating and playing the outcast who gets the girl. By the way, the lead actress in those movies is every bit as attractive as you're accustomed to seeing in films, if not more so. It's good to be the beta male. Especially since now life has come to imitate art. The computer nerd, beaten up in junior high for wearing glasses and reading comic books, is no longer lonely—or alone. In fact, until 2008, more people under age thirty had sex at least once a week than voted for President once every four years.[48]

For this generation, their personal habits veer toward *excess*—at least in comparison to traditional behavior. This group claims to be far more sexually active than any generation before them, and we know that they are experimenting with sex at an earlier age, though they are less likely to be adventuresome. And while they may be having a lot more sex than their parents did at that age, they define sex much more narrowly. Most adults believe oral sex does indeed constitute sex, but more than a third of young people disagree. And who can blame them? Having a former president set that bar for you makes arguing with your parents about it much easier. It's all part of their "hookup culture."

Their behavior is an overall reflection of a paucity of ethics. As the Josephson Institute, which publishes a report on high-school student ethics,[49] puts it, "There's a hole in our moral ozone and it's getting bigger." A sampling of dismaying results from the youngest of the 2020 Generation:

- **Stealing:** 35 percent of boys and 26 percent of girls admitted stealing from a store in the last year. Even honors students (21 percent) and student leaders (24 percent) admitted stealing. More than one in five stole something from a parent or relative or a friend.
- **Lying:** More than 80 percent acknowledged they lied to a parent about something significant.
- **Cheating:** Two-thirds admitted cheating on a test; 38 percent cheated more than twice. More than a third said they used the Internet to plagiarize an assignment.

And now, the kicker. Compare the stats above to this one:

- **Phony self-evaluation:** Astoundingly, 93 percent said they were satisfied with their personal ethics and character, and 77 percent said they're better at doing what is right than most people they know.

Ouch.

The teenagers claim that their parents always want them to do the ethically right thing, no matter what the cost. They overwhelmingly say trust and honesty are essential in personal relationships as well as in business and in the workplace. Yet here is the disconnect: *Six in ten teens say successful people in the real world do what they have to do to win, even if others consider it cheating.* And these are the people who will be assuming positions of leadership in politics, business, and culture in the year 2020.

Sure, leaders across society today show a glaring lack of ethical standards. At a time when cheaters are being exposed throughout sports (Bonds, A-Rod, Ramirez), finance (Madoff, much of Wall Street), and politics (Edwards, Spitzer), it would be wrong to cast dishonesty as a generational phenomenon. From football star Michael Vick to television diva Martha Stewart, people in the limelight are behaving badly, and it's bound to have repercussions on America's youth. Today's young people have a much shorter climb to moral turpitude than their parents.

Young people own their e-universe and are fiercely protective of it. They surf the Web *alone* in their rooms. They have their earbuds in, listening to music and ignoring the world outside. Their cell phones are standing by for incoming text messages and, less frequently, calls. The TV may be on in the background, and they'll rewind it (thanks to DVRs and TiVo) and turn up the volume if something catches their eye, but their computer is more important because it offers an ever-changing flow of information and communication. Here's a little experiment you can try. Go ask your teenager or the college intern working at your office which technological luxury they'd give up if they could only have one: cable television or wireless, high-speed Internet. I'll bet you a dollar to a doughnut they'd pick wireless Internet over their own dog if it came to that. It matters that much.

I call this phenomenon "Living at the Speed of Life." Contrast their

AM I REALLY THAT OLD?

If you are a typical college freshman this year, you were probably born in 1991. And if you bought this book in a bookstore, on average, you were born in 1967. That's not a twenty-four-year awareness gap. That's a consciousness chasm. But thanks to the annual Mindset List produced by the folks at Beloit College, there is a highly respected source to help you remember what these college freshmen never learned. Before you even think of fashioning a marketing campaign, advertising effort, or public-relations project, consider the events that seemed like yesterday to **you** but seem like ancient history to the 2020 Generation:

From the world of politics and current events:

- Ronald Reagan and George W. Bush's father
- The fall of the Berlin Wall
- Leningrad and, for that matter, Stalingrad
- The O.J. Simpson trial
- The Tiananmen Square Massacre
- The Space Shuttle *Challenger* explosion

From the world of science and technology:

- Free directory assistance
- Typewriters
- Car window cranks
- Getting tangled up in a long kitchen phone chord
- Setting the clock on your VCR
- Floppy disks
- The need to use various unpleasant parts of the body to take your temperature
- A gas-station attendant offering to "check under the hood"

From leisure activities and pop culture:

- Johnny Carson
- When Michael Jackson and the Moonwalk were cool
- X-rated films (they're now NC-17)
- Pete Rose (when he was Charlie Hustle)
- Howard Cosell
- Dress codes in restaurants
- Sex before AIDS
- Walkman, cassette tapes
- *Playboy* magazine as porn

choice with the fact that a strong majority of their parents would choose cable TV. And their grandparents? Please. Nearly unanimous to keep the TV going.

Some college freshmen have never written a check, and most college seniors have never balanced a checkbook. Young people pay their bills online, and their PIN numbers are as important to them as their phone numbers. Their debit cards wear out from use years before the expiration date. They wonder why their parents still fiddle with cash and change when it just keeps you at the restaurant five minutes longer. You could download five albums on iTunes in that time. They'll only mail a note or card via the post office if they're trying to impress someone. They probably don't have a stamp, so they'll borrow one from an "old" person. They're not surprised when a wedding invitation arrives by Evite or Facebook—though, in their defense, such an electronic communiqué does break through clutter, even though it is still perceived by their computerized minds as a breach of etiquette.

Music is the narrative of their lives. It is how they express themselves and how they relate to others. It's also the gateway for others to reach them. Music has always played a role in connecting Americans to other aspects of the culture, but never has it been so important and omnipresent. They'll watch a TV show or go see a movie if the music used to sell the content touches or provokes them. They'll buy an item of clothing if it has a direct association with a song they like. The iPod is to the 2020 Generation what television was to Baby Boomers and cable was to Gen-Xers—the right invention at the right time for the right audience.

Consider what weekly broadcasts of *All in the Family* meant to Boomers. Remember what the daily availability of MTV provided for Gen-Xers. And then you'll realize exactly what the constant availability of downloadable music is to 2020ers. It's transformational. It's definitive.

That's why I tell my corporate clients that no decision is more important in their advertising and marketing efforts than the choice of music. It should no longer be added as an afterthought. On the contrary, it should come first—with the words and visuals built around it.

How strange, then, that so few of the 2020 Generation pays for music. They grew up able to download it from Napster and other websites offering illegal content, but it's not an issue of "stealing" to them. Why pay $18 for a CD from Virgin or $25 for a book at Borders when you can download a copy off the Web or "rip" a digitized copy from a friend? If the Web offers music for free, no matter how the site obtained the content, it *must* be OK. The risk of getting caught is also no deterrent since "everyone does it and you can't put everyone in jail." The Recording Industry Association of America (RIAA) learned this the hard way when they started suing their own consumers for illegal downloading. The more they sued, the more the kids downloaded. By the time Apple came up with iTunes, a hassle-free, comprehensive online music service, the damage had already been done. Kids who would have gladly paid $2 for a song two years earlier now wouldn't even pay 99 cents. No industry in modern times has so misjudged the market and so alienated the people they most needed—a classic, textbook case of not knowing what Americans really wanted, or worse, simply not caring.

It didn't have to end up that way. Years ago, almost at the exact moment illegal downloading of movies and television shows had begun, I brought a dozen kids, seventeen-to-twenty-year-olds, to the Television Hall of Fame in Beverly Hills to explain to the Hollywood elite *how* and *why* all the creative arts were in jeopardy. The CEOs of the major studios and some of the most influential producers and directors were there: Les Moonves, head of CBS; Peter Chernin of NewsCorp; Jim Gianopoulos, head of 20th Century Fox; Jonathan Dolgen, then-CEO of Paramount; producers Brian Grazer and Brad Gray, the latter of whom is now CEO of Paramount Pictures. It was a star-studded panel, and they eagerly awaited their conversation with the kids who threatened not just their profit margins, but their very livelihood.

It didn't go well. The "suits" (yes, someone actually used that expression) listened incredulously as the kids boasted about ripping off movies and music because the studios and their "overpaid" (yes, they used that word as well) executives deserved it. On top of inflicting some social justice on overpaid authority figures, these kids also felt that ripping off content was justified because the industry was charging too much for an inferior product. After the bigwigs had a bellyful of criticism, I was tasked by the executives to deliver a challenge to the kids: Prove how easy it is to steal movies by obtaining five that had not yet been released.

Now, this was a challenge a young person could rise to—and they did.

We sat the kids down in a separate room on the top floor of the building with high-speed Internet connections and gave them a list of three movies that had come out the night before and two movies that were to be released in the next thirty days. You probably already know the ending to this story. The kids were able to find and successfully download all five of those films, to the horror of the executives. It was a piece of cake. The executives came in about an hour into the process to check on their progress, and what ensued could only happen in Hollywood. The kids, now empowered because of their downloading prowess, addressed the executives directly and told them point-blank what they were all thinking but were initially afraid to say:

"Why should we pay anything when all you sell us is crap?"

Jim Gianopoulos from Fox rose from his chair and approached the students: "How do you know that it's crap? What's crap to you might be great to someone else."

The kids had a ready response: "You entice us to come to the theater with misleading and phony trailers and ads, you give away the best bits, and you waste our money. As long as you keep doing that, it's our responsibility to rip you off." The studio execs viewed the kids as Internet *hoodlums*. The kids viewed themselves as *Robin Hoods* of the Online Forest.

It's not news that people want reliability and dependability if they're going to fork over ten bucks for a movie. They think they have a right to be entertained, to laugh or cry, and if the movie is not what they expect, they feel cheated. And suddenly, for the first time, they had the means and the technology to take control of the consumer experience.

Baby Boomers signaled their displeasure with Hollywood by simply not going to the theater and by buying less music. It was a consumer twist on the boycotts that had worked for societal change while they were growing up. The 2020 Generation takes a different tack: revenge. Whereas you might have boycotted a business for unfair hiring practices, these kids would rather firebomb it (digitally, of course). Yes, it was and is about saving money. But it is also about *punishment*—teaching the industry a lesson. They rationalize their thievery: "It's sharing, not stealing, and it's the industry's fault for selling me music I don't want and movies that don't entertain." I know it sounds harsh. But I have extensively researched this issue and consistently found a darker motive behind the obvious financial incentive. Whatever their argument, the result is the same. They get products for free and threaten the viability of whole industries as a result.

So, what to do with this blinding, even dogmatic allegiance to illegal downloading? How do you as a business deal with someone half your age who is convinced that they can rightfully steal your product? First, don't firebomb them back. Lawsuits didn't, and will not, work. And second, give them a genuine alternative that is affordable, available, portable, and specifically targeted to their generation.

The Hollywood moguls and the music mavens may have missed the opportunities offered by the Web, but Bill Gates, Steve Jobs, Michael Dell, and the techno gurus have been much more effective in connecting to the 2020 Generation. Whereas their parents wanted everything big— remember their big-screen TVs, their big stereo speakers, and their big cars—young people are immersed in their own increasingly small world of palm-sized cell phones, tiny digital devices, and gigabytes of data stored on drives smaller than a tube of lipstick. Young people will text-message or IM the person sitting next to them—literally. They ring up as many text messages on their cellular bills as actual cell phone calls, and often many, many more. Everything is automated and everything is electronic. They are living the eLife and loving it.

Their parents bought into the "new-and-improved" shtick. But for these kids, it's all about smaller and lighter. Apple's phenomenal iPod has already given way to the iPod nano, iPod shuffle, iPod touch, and several generations of each. It is almost socially unacceptable to have anything but the tiniest of every electronic gadget. You'll never see any-one walking around with a portable CD player anymore. It's too taboo.

This switch to miniaturization is so significant because the switch to smaller masks something much larger. Unlike their parents, you connect with Generation 2020 through technology, not television. Only in instances TV has *used* technology, such as DVR and TiVo, or on shows like *Gossip Girl* that acknowledge and reflect their always-connected lives, has it maintained a hold on the youth attention span. Technology has taken an already limited attention span and dispersed it—particularly television viewing. This point can't be stressed enough: People younger than age thirty spend more time in front of a computer screen than a television screen—and the gap is widening. They time-shift the television they do watch, making network scheduling decision making both easier and harder at the same time. They speed through the commercials on their DVRs and still don't have the patience to watch the entire hour-long drama or half-hour sitcom. They will watch TV in "chunks"—two or three edited episodes in less time than a full

DECODING THE OMG GENERATION

A few words and phrases that matter to the younger set, as translated for an AARP audience:

Cupcaking: engaging in a public display of affection

Brodown: boys night out

NGA: no girls allowed

GTG: got to go

BRB: be right back

Frenemy: a friend-enemy, someone close to you who often hurts your feelings

Check vitals: to check your e-mail, cell phone, or other tech devices

Sick: extremely cool

Totes: totally[50]

episode would take on broadcast television. Ask them why and they'll tell you, "Why watch the whole show when I can get the best bits on YouTube in half the time?"

The Internet is not just a source of information or entertainment; it is the canvas for their lives. They write blogs. They post videos and photos. They create their own websites, post profiles on social networks, and message one another within the walls of those sites. They have their own language, some of it born of the shorthand they use to text-message and some of it simply the cool words created by every wave of teenagers.

And all of this is done behind closed doors and in front of computer monitors. Nothing matters more to the 2020 Generation than the sanctity of their thoughts and the privacy of their online experiences; odd, because many of their online experiences make their private information very public. They *feel* in control of their online universe, even if they really aren't. Online researchers have been able to measure clicks and visits, but it has been impossible to flesh out the whys of the online experience because the kids wouldn't talk about it—until now.

TWENTY DAYS AND NIGHTS IN STUDIO U

In the summer of 2007, my company did an unprecedented anthropological study of young people aged seventeen to twenty-three that we dubbed Studio U. We handpicked fifty people from the 2020 Generation to represent a cross section of Young America from across the country and studied them for twenty days and twenty nights 24/7. Every "student" had a laptop and free wireless access to the Web. The "campus" was the studio lots for NBC Universal and 20th Century Fox, and the classrooms were specifically designed to encourage personal and technological conversation. And every night there was "homework" in the shape of Internet assignments to create the ideal website for viewing entertainment content—the holy grail of program delivery—the elusive intersection of technology and television. For three weeks, we monitored every click of their computers, observed their online interaction, and listened closely to what they had to say (Mom and Dad, eat your hearts out).

There was a method behind this research madness: the creation of Hulu.com, an online alternative to YouTube that allows users to watch content from the NBC-Universal and Fox television and movie vaults in unedited, pristine condition. Hulu.com was a generation ahead of existing entertainment websites, prompting *Time* magazine to name it it's "4th Best Invention of 2008" and one of the "50 Hottest Websites" because it offered fewer commercials and a better viewing experience. As *Time* summarized:

> *Hulu was at first roundly mocked as "a ham-fisted corporate knockoff of the grassroots glory that is YouTube." (It was also mocked for its weird name.) Instead it proved that "suits can play in the Internet video space too" and that studio content can coexist online with the user-generated kind.*

What the author did not know was that the insights applied to Hulu were fashioned not by the *suits* at the studios but by the *kids* at Studio U. But that's only the tip of the iceberg. We discovered what their parents already knew: These kids were brutally honest—and brutally amoral when it came to entertainment and the Web.

As with every group of teenagers I have polled, focus-grouped, and otherwise analyzed, almost half of the Studio U participants admitted to not paying for any music in the last twelve months, and all but three had illegally downloaded music in that time frame. In fact, most of these kids had full music libraries they had compiled illegally—and almost none felt guilty about it. Lesson to the music industry: Don't sue your best customers, or they'll turn into your most passionate thieves. The heady days of the content-controlled past are over. Stop fighting to bring them back. It's sad but true that these Internet bandits have seized the upper hand. They won. You have to concede to at least some of their terms in order to achieve a cease-fire.

Think of it as if you are meeting them in the middle, even if the middle of today seems far skewed in the young consumers' favor than it used to be. You will agree to:

- Lower your costs—99 cents is a dollar, and a dollar is too much for today's consumer.
- Give them more for less. They'll buy entire discographies if you make it economical.
- Offer some unique and free content that they can only get from you; and . . .
- Oh yeah, stop suing them.

In exchange, they will agree to:

- Spend more time on *your* sites and take in *your* ads,
- Buy at least *something*, and . . .
- Oh yeah, stop stealing from you (at least, as much as they used to).

Just accept the new reality and move on. Give them the most comprehensive music library in three clicks or less and they may buy some of its content, but they're never going to return to CDs no matter how hard you try. Better own the concert-promotion business if you want to protect your music revenue.

Two-thirds of Gen 2020 acknowledged illegally downloading TV or media content in the last year. Lesson to the television and movie companies: Make your content immediately available over multiple technology platforms and in a high-quality format, and make users pay for the privilege by requiring them to watch up to 30 seconds of ads. They won't pay for your product, but they'll give you half a minute of their time.

Many of them are sellers on eBay. One kid admitted he'd been kicked off eBay forever because he and his brother had sold hundreds of bootleg CDs and DVDs. Message to the millions of Baby Boomer eBay users: If you're buying entertainment content of any kind, more likely than not you're buying illegal, bootleg, and knockoff copies made by people young enough to be your children. If it's not sold by the studios directly, or on a site like iTunes, you can be pretty sure it ain't original—or legit.

Virtually all were big fans of YouTube, especially user-generated videos and mash-ups (the altering of professional music and/or video content by viewers to create a new and different entertainment experience). Lesson to all entertainment companies: The more you democratize your product, both in terms of access and involvement, the more popular that product will become and the more dollars you will earn.

And before we leave the Internet, half the guys and a quarter of the girls admitted they were at least occasional visitors to porn websites. I'll let you draw your own conclusions on this one.

Generation 2020 is more accepting of ad-based Web content than previously assumed. They do not rebel against advertisements online or on their wireless gadgets. They grew up with ads; they expect them. In fact, they think it's a fair deal to see a promotion in order to get the free content and quality they want. However, they do want to be entertained while waiting. In fact, they have a message for Madison Avenue: Make the ads as interesting as the content and you can sell me. But if you make ads lame like what I see on television, I'll be checking my messages during the thirty seconds it takes before the program begins.

This is a key distinction. Do not mistake an *impatient* attention span with the *lack thereof.* These viewers are happy to spend hours online if you give them a compelling reason. They've been conditioned to scour their online universe for things that interest them. Exploring the Internet is a perpetual journey down a multitude of rabbit holes. So give them an individualized, personalized reason to explore your product. Present them an opportunity to touch it and feel it (virtually speaking, of course, but in an online universe, it feels every bit as real as reality to them anyway). And if you really want them to watch your ads, tell them something they've never heard before and show them something they've never seen before.

The Studio U students offered this advice to the ad makers:

ADVERTISING TO THE 2020 GENERATION

Make the ad a thirty-second show unto itself. If you insist on the same length as a television spot, give me a theme, a plot, and characters I care about, and I'll pay attention.

Make it interactive. Give the users a chance to play with the ad content: a website with additional information or *"clues,"* or the chance to "vote" on a desired outcome (words in quotes are their words).

Connect it with the content they're waiting for. Make it a seamless experience. Example: a show situated in New York (*CSI: New York* or *30 Rock*) could feature advertising from the New York City Convention and Visitors Bureau. Tina Fey's acclaimed show *30 Rock* periodically and pointedly pokes fun at her parent company's (General Electric) penchant for product placement and cross-promotion. But GE does it because it works, and others are following. You know you've reached critical mass when Tina Fey takes aim at you (e.g., Sarah Palin, circa 2008).

Make it special with bonus clips, secret footage, etc. This is a message to the studios: No longer is their entertainment limited to the broadcast version of half-hour sitcoms or one-hour dramas. People want creativity and flexibility in what they watch, including the scenes that weren't meant to be shown.

The Rookie, a spinoff of the show *24,* is a great example of how this can work. With high production quality, it mirrored the elements we've come to love about *24* while advertising a product. Here's how they promoted it:

Catch the Action When and Where You Want It. Degree Men protects men like the Rookie . . . men who take risks and meet any challenge head-on. Because those men are always on the move, Degree Men is giving fans access to The Rookie: Day 3 Extraction *when they want it, where they want it. The shorts, which will debut on Monday, March 17, will be available in the Searchlight section of Comcast's On Demand service, www.DegreeRookie.com, while DirecTV will debut the content on Monday, April 7, on channel 115.*

Home run. "When you want it, where you want it" is perfect for this generation. The content was high quality. And the product placement was just obvious enough to catch buyers' attention while subtle enough to avoid scaring off younger viewers.

To deliver an effective message to young people, today's ads must be louder, faster, funnier and, at times, darker. It's no longer enough to just put an advertising message into a young person's head. It has to be *extraordinary*. And I mean that. It has to stop them cold. Otherwise, it will have no resonance and no staying power. They simply have too many other messages and media competing for their very limited attention spans and precious time. Brand loyalty is also more difficult to achieve. It's harder to change the behavior of the 2020 Generation because they are so random and inconsistent. Their experiences are less deep and more fickle, which leads them to float from message to message and product to product. This generation has scores of blogs and online communities to go to, all of them offering competing information (in some cases misinformation) about your product. They can instantly share their own preferences and experiences with one another, meaning they can find out if your widget is any good or does what it says it will before buying it. What you say is infinitely less important than what they hear.

In this new seamless, digital world, how you grab their attention becomes paramount. A decade ago, Mountain Dew created ads that showcased kids engaged in death-defying activities on bikes, snowboards, skateboards, and Rollerblades, climbing dangerous mountains and high-diving into lakes. The ads played off their admiration for extreme sports. Drink a Mountain Dew, go do something extreme. Mountain Dew gives you the energy, the intensity, the boost to do what you want to do. Mothers hated those kinds of ads, of course, but the 2020 Generation loves them because they represent life and all its intensities.

In 2007, a YouTube music video called Chocolate Rain, created by a then-unknown musician named Tay Zonday, debuted to almost immediate Web acclaim and has 38 million hits and counting. Dr Pepper seized on the Web hit, creating a parody of the video to unveil its new "Cherry Chocolate Dr Pepper." That parody itself generated almost 10 million hits—and the perfect connection to its target generation.

THE INTERNET HABITS OF THE 2020 GENERATION

The real value of the Studio U project was the ability to track every click of every keyboard for three weeks. We were able to observe what websites they went to, how long they stayed, what they posted, and then engage them in conversation to explain their Web behavior. From that research, we developed five distinct Generation 2020 Web profiles:

1. **The Posting Junkie.** These are incurable Internet surfers who participate in all the latest trends. Posting junkies are the Johnny Appleseeds of the Web. They're the engine behind the latest fads. They don't actually create trends, but they give fresh trends oomph by turning on their friends—"Hey check this out"—the way teenagers in the 1960s turned one another on to music and hallucinogens. They have an opinion on everything, and unlike Gen-X, who are relatively positive in their outlook, Generation 2020 is quite willing to deliver a thumbs-down review publicly. They're the ones who diss a new CD or bust a fake blog or otherwise wreak havoc on the Establishment. They're compulsive about keeping threads alive, and they provoke interest and emotion from other posters. Their behavior is critical to popularizing a new website or blog—and they will make or break you and your competitors. Find fifty of these people and you'll not only have your finger on the pulse of America 2020, but you'll *be* the pulse of Generation 2020.

2. **The Utilitarian.** Their online activities are primarily used to enhance (socially and financially) their offline activities. They conduct "business" within their online network. Example: One Studio U student took the NBC Universal "front of the line" pass that we gave the students, and *sold the freebie on eBay.* Others enter blogs looking to score tickets for hot events. They are frequent posters, but it's all about practicality. They announce their weekend plans online because it's more efficient than e-mailing or calling their pals. Facebook was designed for them, but Twitter has just as much potential, perhaps more, because it requires minimal thought and minimal effort. On a broader scale, a more social, all-encompassing eBay will eventually be created for this well-connected, economically powerful segment of the online community.

3. **The Gamer.** These young people are more narrowly focused but enjoy exploring the full breadth of their special interest. They might focus on trance and techno music, Asian culture, or fantasy sports. The focus matters less than their behavior: Their interests are an inch wide but a mile deep, and they're the ones who are pressing the establishment hardest to innovate to match their interests, curiosity, and creativity. They identify not through their real names,

but instead, through their gamer tags and screen names, and their universe is literally the globe. They play World of Warcraft or Grand Theft Auto or the latest cool game with other gamers from everywhere. Note to business: Find a way to affiliate with the games or the gaming websites, and you'll extend your reach. Movie studios have already found ways to turn popular comic books into popular movies, but someone will tap into this segment to turn popular games into movies and vice versa.

4. **The TV Junkie.** They're driven by humor. These young people grew up watching entire seasons of their television comedy favorites in a single sitting. *Family Guy* and *The Simpsons* are typical favorites—and thanks to a new interest in politics, they are fans of *The Daily Show* and *The Colbert Report* as well. But they're not wedded to professional content. They're open to any kind of comedic postings, including funny videos and mash-ups that are user-generated. They scour the Internet daily for random TV clips, which they then post on their social networks, and their friends are in turn challenged to find something even funnier. Reach these people and they'll spread your content far and wide.

5. **The Internet Rookie.** This cohort uses the Internet because they have to, not because they want to. It is a means rather than an end to a specific result. They go online to find what they're looking for, and then they sign off. They are observers rather than doers. But they *will* follow the crowd because they feel pressure to keep up with the latest and greatest. They don't want to get caught saying "no" when someone asks if they saw the video of Miss South Carolina making a fool of herself on YouTube. They're just not interested in anything too technologically difficult. For business, their message is simple: KISS (keep it simple, stupid). Use them as a guidepost to balance sophistication of a new product with ease of use.

Here is some additional information about the 2020 Generation for those interested in reaching them, marketing to them, and connecting them to their products and services.

The Internet for this generation often starts with Firefox (not Microsoft's ubiquitous Internet Explorer) and IM. They tab up their browser—tops are Facebook or MySpace, YouTube, Google, and Gmail. Then they jump tabs seamlessly throughout the day. Updates and messages will bring them back to their tabs over and over. IM is a primary communication tool. They use it not just to chat, but to send links, files, and music. They even create their own chat rooms for school projects or just for the hell of it.

The social networking phenomenon was created for and is being fed by the 2020 Generation. In 2009, they spent more time on the Web than in front of the television—and a majority of that time was on social networking sites. Here's where they went:

THE FIVE MOST POPULAR SOCIAL NETWORKING WEBSITES[51]

(May 2009)

1. Facebook	83 million visits monthly
2. MySpace	66 million
3. Twitter	15 million
4. LinkedIn	12 million
5. Classmates.com	11 million

If they're looking for information, the Studio U kids immediately turned to Google. It dominates all other search portals. In fact, it's less of a search portal than an active verb. Want to go out for dinner? Type in "spicy food Century City CA" and take it from there. Then click onto a blog to get more detailed information or reviews. Forget traditional sources of information like magazines and newspapers. Here are examples of websites they frequent when they search for specific information. Look at these sites and learn from them.

- Reference: Wikipedia, even with its accuracy issues and teachers' antipathy for it
- Entertainment: IMDB.com, movies.com, Rotten Tomatoes
- Music: MySpace, Pitchfork, Stereogum, Pandora
- Fun place to go out: Facebook, CitySearch, Yelp.com

Traditional "video" still has a place, but it, too, is changing. For the social experience of hanging out with friends, the younger half of the 2020 Generation will occasionally and begrudgingly spring for the $10+ ticket at the movie theater and the $10 popcorn and large cola "special"—especially for blockbuster movies on opening weekend. In fact, most of the Studio U students have at least one movie poster hung somewhere in their room or home. However, they think movie quality has suffered since they were "kids," the theater experience has become

DESIGNING THE PERFECT WEBSITE
FOR THE 2020 GENERATION

While music is their lifeblood, video is their intellectual stimulation. If the Studio U kids were hired to create the perfect standard websites for their music, video, gadgets, clothing, food, and everything else they do online, it would be built on four pillars:

1. **Innovation.** They want the look and feel of their Web experiences to be a generation ahead of what they already do online. The worst mistake a Web company can make is to copy what already exists. If it looks just like a popular, well-known site, they'll stay with what they already know and use. The only way to get them to change their habits is to give them something that is immediately more appealing both visually and content-wise. The "build your own" sites for automobiles like Lexus and MINI Cooper are really popular because they allow users to create something that comes to life on their computer. If it doesn't grab their attention in ten seconds, they're off looking at something else.

2. **Fluid in form and function.** They are attracted to sites that are smooth in transitions and logical in their links. This generation doesn't want to think, and they don't want their experience interrupted. Stop with the boxy design; it's so 2000. Rounder edges, more pictures, and links that take you right to where you want to go will capture their attention. Nike's website is attractive because it feels alive, as in when you click a link, the new information seamlessly comes into view as if it were coming to life. Equally important, having to use the Back or Previous button is tantamount to Web-design failure. This is particularly important in sites that are selling merchandise—they'll punish *you* for their mistakes. In some cases, a third of all commerce is lost because someone makes a mistake, is sent back to the start of the buying process, and decides to disconnect rather than try again. They will punish you for technological failures, whether they are your fault or their ISP's, or even their own computers'. Some of this you can control, some of it you can't. But if your site's design itself makes the buying process anything but perfectly seamless, you've just attacked your own bottom line. Gen 2020 is unforgiving. Not only will they quit trying to buy the product that day; they won't come back to your site again.

3. **Deep vaults of content.** When I'm asked which attribute or characteristic is most important in a Web design, I answer in one word: "**content.**" The 2020 Generation wants it all in one place at one time. That's why Google and Wikipedia are "must-bookmark" sites for this generation. The closer you are to the concepts of "comprehensive" and "all-inclusive," the more appealing your site.

But don't say it unless you can deliver. Nothing destroys traffic potential faster than bad word of mouth.

4. **A breakthrough viewing experience.** There is a false assumption that younger Web users are willing to sacrifice visual quality in favor of other benefits. Not true. The more breathtaking the visual experience, the more likely they are to return again and again—as long as it doesn't take forever for the visuals to load. The fact is, from retail buying to apartment hunting, it is the website visuals that sell the product more than any other attribute. As for entertainment sites, young Web users accept advertisements as a fair price for so much free content; but if you cross the clutter line, you're just telling them to get the same content elsewhere.

too expensive, and the studios are producing crap. The eighteen-year-olds who would have stood in line ten years ago have given way to the eighteen-year-olds who are equally willing to watch a *free* movie on their home computer screen (the more technologically proficient will hook up their laptop to a larger TV). They watch as many movies as ever, just not in the movie theater.*

40 HOURS FOR YOU . . . AND THE REST IS FOR ME

My polling firm has often been tasked with the responsibility to craft employee-retention plans for young workers. Why? Generation 2020 has abandoned the concept of company loyalty.

Young people have an unusually strong sense of entitlement about their careers. Previous generations assumed they would have to work long and hard—and hope that the rewards would come in the end. The Generation 2020 crew isn't willing to wait. They're ready to demand. Some of this has been tempered by tougher economic times and the prospect of fewer jobs at lower wages as they graduate from college. But they grew into adulthood in an education environment that celebrated attendance rather than achievement and turned everyone into winners

---

* Still 2009 is one of the best years for movie attendance. People who can't afford a new flat-screen TV or a weekend getaway are choosing a night out at the movies. People in their thirties who gave up on theaters a few years ago are back in droves.

even when they weren't. The 2020 Generation grew up with more gadgets and less restraint than any previous generation—abundance without limitation—and now they expect to be treated accordingly.

This has led to expectations of compensation and quality of life among young people that are unlikely to be fulfilled at work. They want higher pay (74 percent), flexible work schedules (61 percent), a promotion within a year (56 percent), and more vacation time (50 percent)—all at a time of greater international competition and reduced profit margins.[52] There is nothing so out of the ordinary about their desires—only the likelihood that their wish lists will go increasingly unfulfilled.

There is also apprehension in the corporate suites because younger workers show little propensity toward the loyalty that drove their parents to stay with the same company for decades until retirement. "Why have one career when I can have several?" This disloyalty—and it's mutual—can damage both American employers and workers. A workforce that "surfs" from job to job translates into higher training and retention costs for companies. A company that sends jobs overseas undermines not only employee loyalty, but the enduring belief in the American Dream. Such corporate behavior may be good for the people of China and India but it does nothing to endear Americans to capitalism—and explains why Generation 2020 is more hostile to Wall Street than any generation in modern times.

At the same time, the American economy can benefit from the new spirit of adventure, innovation, and movement that permeates its youngest working class. Employers must harness this energy and reward it—even if it means accepting the consequences of declining loyalty. Let young employees know that you don't require a lifetime of service, but that your company makes it a priority to reward loyalty with life-changing experiences. This language approach should do the trick:

WORDS THAT WORK

"We want this to be the place where those who have a sense of drive, discipline, innovation, and adventure want to come to and want to stay. We don't want to be a stopping-off point. We want to be an end point in your search for an enriching experience and a stable career."

At the other end of the spectrum are the alarming numbers of young people who do not even finish high school. This has long been an inner-city shame in cities like Detroit, where only 25 percent of teens get a high school diploma, and Cleveland at 34 percent. In the nation's largest fifty cities, the graduation rate barely tops 50 percent.[53] For them, America really is, to quote from a Green Day song, a "boulevard of broken dreams." For us, we will have created a permanent underclass that will have not only fallen behind, but probably dropped out by the time 2020 rolls around.

Some of the decisions being made by the 2020 Generation are based on an effort to set quality-of-life priorities. If the 1980s represented the "greed is good" decade, and the 1990s the rise of Silicon Valley and the limitless tech boom, the decade we are now closing has been about a recognition of boundaries and limitations in our national economic condition at the very same time we are given unprecedented choices and opportunities in our personal lives. No longer is money the primary motivator in job decisions (health care is a higher priority).

Similarly, an overwhelming majority of the 2020 Generation would pick a job they love that pays a lot less over a job they hate that pays a lot more. And there's one more factor that did not exist even ten years ago: The 2020 Generation wants to do good as they do well. They have a belief in the need for corporate social responsibility that sets them apart from previous generations and occasionally puts them at odds with their own employers.

Not surprisingly, the *"Made in America"* slogan and *"Buy American"* appeal doesn't work on a generation far more concerned about human rights in Darfur than economic rights in Appalachia. Young people grew up living in an interconnected world. They do not recognize competition between the United States and other nations—they see one huge, global economy. Don't bother making an "America is exceptional" pitch to them. It's not that they are unpatriotic; they simply grew up with a more holistic worldview. In their lifetime, Japanese cars have always had a better reputation for reliability and fuel efficiency than American cars, and that's what matters to this generation. So the American-heritage-heavy pleas from Ford and Chevy are met with a collective "ho-hum." This generation sees poverty in Africa as just as important as poverty in America. Even if their parents are fighting globalization with their last dying employment breath, the kids have accepted it and even embraced it. It is simply a fact of life.

This generation is a natural audience for entrepreneurship. Fully half of college-age students say they plan to start their own entrepreneurial venture in the next five years. That's nearly a third more than the population overall. They see entrepreneurs as visionaries, and they're attracted to the pride and passion of starting something successful. More than 60 percent of students believe they've had a good entrepreneurial idea, and they are driven by the desire to get more control over their hours and their lives.

Marc Ecko is a terrific role model for young people with a drive to create something of their own and the creativity to do what has not been done before.

Born Marc Milecofsky, Ecko's entire life has been one of creative reinvention. While he was still in high school, he began designing and selling hip-hop–inspired T-shirts out of his parents' home in New Jersey. He went to Rutgers University to study pharmacology but was more taken with drawing and design than he was with organic chemistry. With a couple thousand dollars from his friend and his twin sister, he got his start with edgy, graffiti-inspired T-shirts.

He founded his clothing brand in 1993 at the tender age of twenty-one. Within eleven years, his worldwide sales of clothing, shoes, cosmetics, and video games generated more than a billion dollars. In 2007, sales climbed to $1.5 billion.[54] His customers today are like him at the time of his earliest business endeavors—young, hip, and anti-establishment. His counterculture products appeal to white suburban kids and lower-income inner-city youth—one of the few designers able to bridge the cultural gap.

Ecko got all the cutting-edge stuff right: social responsibility, honoring diversity, encouraging creativity, and creating the youth-friendly environment to attract the talent to make it all happen.

The company defined the word "disruptive" in a positive way. They created a business environment of create or die, succeed or go home. They had exceedingly high expectations for their managers and even higher demands for their designers. Unlike many of the dinosaurs of Corporate America still roaming the field, youth or lack of experience was no barrier whatsoever. Talent mattered above all else. Some of their most successful people were still in their twenties and almost everyone was younger than forty. Everyone worked long hours, but they shared a unifying mission to revolutionize cultural tastes in America. And they could see the results of their success on the streets of New York every day. If you could survive this environment, you thrived.

Employees were proud of working for a socially conscious company. They built an environment to inspire this creativity—literally. Ecko's midtown Manhattan office is two stories tall. It has a half-size basketball court and a collection of life-size Star Wars characters. Where else could you post-up a Wookiee and make the world a better (and more excitingly dressed!) place, all before lunch? This is nail-on-the-head stuff for attracting Generation 2020's most creative innovators. If cubicle-land offices suck the inspiration out of the American workforce, it is places like Ecko that pour it right back. And if this was not enough, there were booze cruises up the river, corporate outings to the baseball parks, fashion shows at their offices, and other fringe benefits that made Ecko the place to be for the young, hip, and creative in New York. Those activities may no longer be possible in the antiexcessive, postrecession world, but what is certainly possible is the same sort of personal, informal interaction between executives and colleagues that breeds a tightly knit team. I hope you executives are taking notes.

REACHING GENERATION 2020: THE BEST CORPORATE MISSION STATEMENT

Ecko is one of the most popular brands of men's clothing for Generation 2020. The words below were designed to be communicated to the company's youthful employees to help them embrace the innovative nature of their business, their colleagues, and their customers. It was never adopted, but the passion and intensity it communicates is relevant to any business seeking to employ or sell to this segment of society:

Ecko is passionately irrepressible and disobedient. We celebrate our diversity and champion our freedom to influence, inspire, and impact our generation. We acknowledge and embrace the unknown and uncertain, always choosing focused creativity to boring conformity. Every day we shatter expectations in favor of change, the new and the better. Life at Ecko is always an adventure.

The message I recommended applies to any large, multifaceted company with a predominance of Generation 2020 employees. It sounds like something Bono could have sung, but it's music to the ears of people entering the workforce today:

ECKO = ONE

From many ideas, ONE vision
From many products, ONE brand
From many people, ONE mission
From many priorities, ONE purpose

I interviewed Mark Ecko prior to conducting employee focus groups for his company, and I was impressed with his clarity and candor. It was exactly what Generation 2020 would have wanted to hear from him:

I think of being to our generation what Ralph Lauren was to his generation. Everything that he stood for, culturally and generationally, I want to be able to stand for in a new, contemporary, and significant way to my generation.

I would tell anyone who wanted a twenty-first-century job in a twenty-first-century company with a twenty-first-century mentality to work for Ecko. If they can handle change at the speed of life, it's a great place to be.

CONCLUSION

There is a greater sense of unity and community among Generation 2020 than among any other generation—and it is more than superficial connectivity and social networking. From politics to economics to social causes, they have embraced those who embrace them, and reject those who would seek to divide them. Divisiveness is out. They are acutely sensitive to and hostile against any sort of negative attack by politicians or products, and their message is clear. Don't tell them what's wrong with the competition. Tell them what's right about you.

I close this chapter with the lexicon of the Gen 2020 workplace. If you understand the words that matter, you'll understand the priorities and principles needed to reach them as customers and keep them as employees.

LUNTZ LESSONS

THE LANGUAGE OF GENERATION 2020

Adventure
It's the most positive terminology to describe the shifting priorities and day-to-day difficulties of the typical corporation in these atypical economic times.

Boring Conformity
This generation hates the status quo and is almost as antiestablishment as the youth of the 1960s (though in a less overt and more constructive fashion). A company that defines itself by what it is not and attacks the boring conformity of its competitors will put itself on the right side of the 2020 Generation divide.

Celebrate
This notion comes straight from our interviews and it's purely emotional. Even the most critical, cynical people appreciate the unusual level of intense feeling people put into their work that only "celebrate" can capture.

Champion
Any company that talks about being number one doesn't "advocate" something, they *champion* it. It's a more passionate approach to the concept of "mission and commitment."

Diversity
Diversity is a high priority for the workforce of tomorrow. In fact, within the creative community, it's one of the highest values a company can maintain—particularly when that diversity is regional, attitudinal, and demographic.

Focused Creativity
Creativity alone can be chaotic. Focused creativity is more relevant and more structured. The ideal combination: "flexible, focused creativity." It provides the freedom people want and the results the company needs.

Freedom	Freedom is the core underlying principle that differentiates those who follow conventional wisdom from those who break it. It is also the attribute that so many companies lose when they go from hundreds of employees into the thousands. "Flexibility" in the workplace is a similar desired value, but freedom is a broader, more encompassing term.
Impact	Not many people can claim to work for a company that has a genuine cultural impact on the world around them—an impact they can see with their own eyes every day of the year. It's the lack of impact in big corporations that turns people toward entrepreneurship.
Inspire	"Inspire" is among the most aspirational words in the culture today. More emotional than tangible, it has a transformational and transcendental characteristic that is universally appealing.
Irrepressible	Younger workers are drawn to ideas and companies that, against all odds, simply refused to die and instead have a track record of growth and progress. No matter what the challenge, winning companies always come back fighting.
Passionate	There is nothing more enticing about a workplace environment than the passion people feel about what they do and how they do it—particularly when there is a social-responsibility component as well.
Shatter expectations	The visualization of the phrase is what's important. You don't just exceed expectations. You shatter them to pieces.

7

HOPE I DIE BEFORE
I GET OLD:
What We Really Want Out of Retirement

Will you still need me, will you still feed me, when I'm sixty-four?
—**PAUL MCCARTNEY, WRITTEN WHEN HE WAS TWENTY-FOUR**

The reason grandchildren and grandparents get along so well is because they have a common enemy.

—**SAM LEVENSON**

Bradenton, Florida. This community has one of the highest concentrations of senior citizens in the nation. The local congressman, Dan Miller, once joked that his congressional district was God's waiting room. If you drove through the area on any given day, you were bound to run into a funeral procession or two. Seriously.

I was in Bradenton a few years back to listen to retirees, present them with various alternatives on Medicare, and craft persuasive language for the Republican Party to help them survive their effort to reform Social Security. I learned something that day that changed my outlook toward seniors and retirement. Seniors always carry two things in their pockets: photos of their grandchildren and random dog-eared clippings of news they think is important. The older we get, the easier it is to forget. To be fair, this generation of retirees is better informed about national and international events than their children, and they are more likely to consume more news—even if it is of the old-fashioned paper kind—than their grandchildren. Pictures and clippings may fade, but they never lie—even if our minds start to do both. So if you want to get retirees to engage in a conversation about reforming Social Security or modernizing Medicare, there is only one guaranteed way to do it: Have them look at pictures of their grandkids while discussing the relevant issues.

For most older people, when they're looking at their grandkids, they can't bring themselves to ask the youngsters to sacrifice for them. It just goes against everything that comes with being a parent or grandparent—we do what we have to so our offspring can have better lives, not the other way around. It has been that way since the Pilgrims landed at Plymouth Rock and it will always be an integral part of the American experience. When they have that visual of the new generation in their minds, they're willing to sacrifice much more of themselves so their kids and grandkids don't have to. In fact, the creative minds on Madison Avenue are making a fundamental mistake in their current marketing efforts to retirees across the country. Rather than thinking of their grandparents when they craft pitches specifically targeted to seniors, they should actually be working from images of themselves. Better still, they should use images of their own kids (and therefore, the senior generation's grandkids). This chapter will explore every facet of the senior psyche, including the changing mentality of an increasing number of seniors who have come to realize that "retirement" is just a word rather than a phase of life.

Seniors are particularly protective of their government benefits. To my surprise, when asked about intergenerational sacrifice, younger people are more willing to pay more in taxes to give more benefits to seniors than seniors are to accept fewer benefits so their children and grandchildren would pay less in taxes. Yet knowing just how catastrophic the recent economic setbacks have been on retirement savings and on those living on dividend payments or a fixed income, it's hard to blame the seniors for wanting more benefits or their grandkids for being so altruistic. It's not that they're jaded from years of hard living. It's that they're afraid—very, very afraid.

For marketers, the most important characteristic of the seventy-plus population is the drive to get it all, and get it all *now*. Yes, they are savers, and they are frugal with what they have accumulated. But every day is a mission to accumulate even more—only now it's the small stuff. It's based on basic fear and residual Depression-era instincts that their parents instilled in them. If they don't get it today, they may not get it tomorrow, whether it's money, savings, or the day-to-day necessities of life. They don't have the ability to supplement. What they have is what they have, and they assume they won't be getting any more.

This drives them to some aggressive behavior. Pilfering sugar packets from the lunch counter. Racing to the five p.m. early-bird special at the local restaurant (some things on *Seinfeld* are actually true). Stealing lightbulbs and toilet paper from the budget motel. Even *60 Minutes* commentator Andy Rooney, now in his nineties, admitted he would sneak a leftover roll into his pocket as he left a restaurant.

I invited a dozen middle-class seniors to a two-hour focus group in Tampa a few years back to listen to their opinions about politics. They came not for the discussion or even the $50 incentive payment. They came for the free food. I couldn't hold their attention because the table in the back was bursting with chicken salad, tuna salad, and egg salad. The chance to eat kept beckoning them. If one got up, so did several others. Follow the herd. And since they're old, it would take them an excruciatingly long time to make a sandwich while I fumed. I finally took the platter out of the room so they'd listen to one another. It was the only way to get them to focus long enough to finish the conversation. When the group ended, they demanded the remaining food be returned to them, and I watched them take every last scrap. No food is ever left behind at a seniors focus group.

To understand seniors, you have to observe them close up. Sort of like Marlin Perkins did on the classic 1970s TV show *Animal Kingdom* or Steve Irwin, the late Australian wildlife researcher. And if you pay attention and understand them, you can reach them, please them—and if you can do that, the world is yours since they are the fastest-growing segment of the population.

In this case, size really *does* matter. One of the Madison Avenue whiz kids responsible for some of the worst advertising schlock you see on television today read a draft of this book and e-mailed me quite dismissively, "Who the hell cares what Granny thinks? They've made all their important choices except where to be buried." He's an idiot. He only thinks and sees inside his narrow little box. Do retirees already have their favorite restaurant? Sure. Have they already chosen their preferred brand of automobile and television? Definitely. Aren't they more likely to be downsizing than upsizing? Absolutely. On the decisions that his thirty seconds of program interruption are meant to influence, they are beyond influencing. But the people retiring today aren't like your great-grandparents from decades ago. Many of their decisions are irreversible, but in today's world, they have a host of *new* choices to make, too. And they are the first retiree generation to have a willingness to examine new options and the time and the health to explore those choices.

When Social Security was created in 1935, the average adult didn't even live long enough to collect benefits. Today, they've got twenty years left to live and they plan to live them to the fullest—and that's a lot of purchasing and a lot of consumption. From asset management (they're the richest retiree generation ever) to vacation planning (and the most mobile), they have time, they have (some) money, and they're ready to use both.

SEGMENTING THE RETIREE CLASS

Some people look at older Americans and see a monolithic population of white-haired grannies and grandpas. In reality, there are three distinct groups (or segments) based on their age today and conditions at home during their childhood. If you don't understand the differences, you won't know how to reach them, pitch them, or convince them.

The Greatest Generation (Born before 1929). They may not remember the worst of the Great Depression, but they do remember tough times in the late 1930s and war rationing in the first half of the 1940s. They certainly grew up with a Depression-era mentality. They came of age under Franklin Roosevelt when everyone was a New Dealer, and a majority of them were and are Democrats. Now in their eighties, their health is deteriorating and they're well beyond the point where they could add any income or any savings. They're also living a life of regret. They regret not saving more money, not quitting smoking at an earlier age, and not enjoying life to its fullest. Each day is a struggle, and each dawn brings with it the threat of calamity rather than the enjoyment of retirement. Even the well-off and famous among them feel this way. One Emmy Award–winning TV star from the 1970s and 1980s turned eighty-five recently. Even though he'd remarried and is still performing occasionally, he was despondent about the endgame of his life. "I'm done," he told me. "There is nothing else left to do." That's what the eighties feel like. Their greatest fear is losing whatever is left of their independence, their self-esteem, and their friends.

The War Kids (Born 1929–1939). This is the generation that was just old enough to live through the hardship of war, but they missed just about everything else. They missed the pain of the Great Depression, though their parents suffered greatly. They were out of the house just before their parents bought their first TV. They were out of college just before Elvis and the rise of rock 'n' roll. They were too old for the Sexual Revolution; they missed the computer age and the Internet age; they missed the technological opportunities that people just ten years younger managed to catch. I've seen them line up at senior centers to learn how to use the computer, desperate to keep up, but some of them don't even know how to type. Most are still intellectually and physically active. They want to be needed. They want to contribute, part-time, but no one is asking and they don't know how to offer. McDonald's and Walmart have discovered this great untapped resource. Eventually, the rest of retail will learn.

The Newly Retired (Born 1939–1946). The first wave of the Baby Boomer generation populates this group, but they are a bit older, a bit more traditional, and definitely more conservative. This is the first of the invested generations, and they're screwed. They were taught that the best way to secure their retirement was in stocks and real estate. And now they own homes too big for them that they can't sell and stocks that are worth a lot less today than when they made their retirement plans. It has forced many of them to reconsider the definition of retirement not because they want to, but because they have to. True, they're the first generation to consider "retirement" as a change of careers rather than a change of lifestyle. Some become "consultants," while others have started small businesses, but almost everyone in this age group is still working, if they ever worked at all (women in this age bracket were largely still stay-at-home moms). They're not slowing down; if anything, they're speeding up. The financial clock is ticking, and they have no time to spare.

This brings me to the overanalyzed, much-maligned Baby Boomer generation (born 1946 to 1964) that is determined to wreak havoc on every norm they touch as they head kicking and screaming toward the sunset of their lives. Everything about them is different. They recoil from terms like "seniors" or "aging." Such words may refer to their parents, but not to them. The leading edge of the Baby Boomers, those in their mid-fifties and older, don't see themselves getting "old" in the traditional sense anymore, so any language that reflects the past will be instantly rejected. It requires a brand-new lexicon. Old people *age;* active people *mature.* "Mature" means wiser and more stable, not slower and less independent. It's not a cliché to them: Sixty really is the new fifty. They expect to live longer, explore new opportunities, and embark on new adventures. They're not sitting around waiting for the undertaker, not by a long shot. In fact, they're much more likely to be waiting at Gate B5 to catch the next flight out of town so they can see the world and live the life they couldn't when they were too busy working. Or maybe they're at C11 to catch a connecting flight to Los Angeles on business because they are still enjoying peak earning potential. Or perhaps they are working because they realize they will need more money to maintain the quality of life to which they've become accustomed.

Advertising critics made fun of *Easy Rider* star Dennis Hopper's thirty-second pitch for Ameriprise, but what he says, and the determination with which he says it, deeply resonates with this audience.

"To withdraw. To go away. To disappear. That's how the dictionary defines retirement. Time to redefine. Your generation is definitely not heading for bingo night. In fact, you can write a book about how you can turn your retirement upside down . . . because I just don't see you playing shuffleboard. Do you know what I mean?"

The Boomer generation has been a gold mine for marketers throughout their earning years, and they will continue to be throughout their golden years. Their sheer numbers overwhelm—and beckon to business. The television executives may crave the precious eighteen-to-forty-nine demographic, but it's the pre-retirees who have the cash and are willing to spend it.

The one thing they don't have going for them is the economy. Unlike the soulful declaration of Mick Jagger, time is *not* on their side. Not content with a "traditional" retirement of less, fewer, and smaller, they are redefining the last decades of their lives before they enter them. Sure, some are downsizing, but the majority wants to maintain their current homes and their current lifestyles.* They must accommodate longer life

---

* According to a 2009 study by the Cornell University Center for Hospitality Research, the typical American aged 55 and older still dines out at a restaurant 51 times a year. Half of those visits are to casual dining establishments (top choice: Olive Garden), while almost a third are for fast food (top choice: Wendy's).

WHY BOOMERS MATTER TO MAIN STREET AND MADISON AVENUE

They're *still* more likely to remodel their homes.
Their household *still* owns or leases at least three vehicles.
They're *still* more likely to vote and sign political petitions.
They're more likely to play the lottery.
They're more likely to own a big-screen TV.[55]
They're more likely to take a long vacation.
They're more likely to fly first class and stay in a hotel suite.
They will spend more money next year than all their children—combined.

spans by stretching their savings over more years, and those investments took a hard hit in 2002 and again in 2008. Many chose to have children later in life (often as part of a second or even a third marriage), and those kids are now in their costly college years—just as their elderly parents are having their highest health-care bills. As a result, the Baby Boomers are likely to be working well into their sixties and even their seventies, and often out of necessity. And the postretirement jobs they take are likely to be far different—in substance and compensation—from the careers they leave behind.

Thanks to medical advances, fully 70 percent of Baby Boomers still have one or sometimes both parents alive, and most likely it's Mom. More than half of Boomers think that it is a responsibility to allow an elderly parent to live with them if it becomes necessary—but few people actually do it.

As for financial support, it's a two-way street. According to the Pew Research Center, three in ten Baby Boomers have given money or other financial assistance to a parent recently, while two in ten have *leaned on an elderly mom or dad for money.*[56] At some point in life, a role reversal takes place and the parent becomes more dependent on his or her children. Among Boomers, fully 25 percent say their parents rely more on them than they do on their parents.

When the tech bubble burst on March 10, 2000, we got a hint of the cold chill that would blow over the economy at the end of the decade.

I hosted a focus group of suburban upper-middle-class pre-retirees and retirees in their sixties in Baltimore about a year into the NASDAQ collapse. You know—people supposedly living the American Dream. Each one had a terrible story about watching his or her savings go up in flames as the NASDAQ went into the dumps. One of those stories troubles me even now. One couple had planned for years to travel in their retirement. They sold their house, bought a Winnebago, and carefully plotted the trip of a lifetime—a three-year journey across the country. They were healthy. They were strong. They'd made all the right financial decisions. And as the husband told the group with genuine pride, "My bride is still madly in love with me after almost forty years." He was sixty-four. She was sixty-two. Life was good.

Then the high-tech boom went bust. They were eighteen months into their trip and had made it to the West. The husband recalled, "I did the numbers one night. I did not know how to tell my wife we had to go back." He didn't just mean going back to Baltimore and curtailing their trip. He meant going back to work. The value of their savings had dropped 40 percent. Their retirement was ruined, and he knew he couldn't get it back. He'd had a job that paid more than $100,000 a year. He knew that any new job would pay far less—that is, if he could even get a job. Everyone in the focus group had a hard-luck story. The group lasted twenty minutes beyond the scheduled two hours. Nobody got up to leave. It became a therapy group, and I became the psychiatrist.

As bad as things were back then, they are significantly worse today. That same couple did go back to work, but whatever they managed to earn and recoup since the crash of 2000 was washed away by an even more destructive financial collapse in 2008. Now in their seventies, they can't reenter the workforce, and they are forced to live on a fixed income that is much lower and more restrictive than they ever imagined. They look into the mirror and at each other and ask, "Why us? We played by the rules, we did everything that was expected of us, and yet we are left with half of what we had worked for and saved. Why us?" That American Dream has turned into a national nightmare—and each day this couple and millions more wake up to a very ugly reality that cannot be wished or dreamed away.

◆ ◆ ◆

Birthdays matter—not because of the cake or the song or a reason to eat and drink too much. Birthdays matter because they cause people to intellectualize and emotionalize milestones in a lifetime. The average person born today can expect to live past eighty, and in that lifetime they will have eight birthdays that really matter: 16, 18, 21, 30, 40, 50, 65, and 80. At each of those events, the past will be shed and the future confronted—and, ultimately, accepted. With each passing milestone, however, the focus on the future decreases, replaced by attention devoted to yesteryear. Similarly, the earliest three birthdays are a celebration, while the latter five are often more of a commiseration. It is amazing to me why more consumer product and service companies don't grab on to these important events and attach themselves like glue to paper. Imagine the impact on sales if BMW ran an effective campaign under the banner, "You're fifty. Isn't it time for a BMW?"

No one really appreciates the realities of retirement until the AARP notice arrives in the mailbox a few months after you turn fifty. That's the wake-up call. We don't put ourselves into a retirement frame of mind until we can see it on the horizon, until we are so close that we can smell the scent of the retirement community where we just placed our parents. Yes, many Americans begin saving for retirement earlier in life. They set retirement as a goal. They are aware that it's something that will happen . . . eventually. But to the pre-fifty set, it's easy to feel like there is more time to line up retirement than there really is. When you hit fifty, the switch is flipped. Americans go from thinking too little and being too comfortable with retirement to obsessing and fretting too much over it.

Something else takes over after our fiftieth birthday. Life becomes very self-focused. In our twenties, we're concerned about ourselves. In our thirties and forties, we're concerned about our children and our parents, and a whole lot of self-sacrifice ensues. But by the time we reach fifty, we start to think about ourselves again. This self-centeredness becomes all-encompassing at age sixty-five. It's not a surprise that people feel more vulnerable as they get older. What is surprising is how little the business community has done to connect with that vulnerability. "What does it mean to me?" is a question this group applies to everything.

THE SEVEN MOST FREQUENTLY ASKED QUESTIONS ABOUT RETIREMENT

These are the questions people age sixty and older are most likely to ask people with authority and responsibility:

1. Will I be able to afford health care when I get too old to work?
2. Am I one medical emergency away from bankruptcy and ruin?
3. Is Social Security going to be there for me?
4. Will prescription drugs be so expensive that I'll be forced to choose between medications and food?
5. Will I run out of money before I run out of years?
6. Will I be a financial and physical burden on my spouse or my children?
7. Will I lose my independence and mobility?

There's one attribute that unites all seven questions: control. As you age, you begin to lose control over an increasing number of important areas of life. Younger people look forward to the day when they can do what they want, when they want, where they want, with anyone they want. But that's not reality at all. In fact, the single biggest complaint retirees have is about the loss of flexibility that they once had. They're living on fixed incomes. Their choices are more and more limited. The demands of life are greater. The cost of living is higher. Health is more fragile.

The "peace of mind" that those in the workforce expect to earn upon retirement has been replaced with a gnawing sense of insecurity (maybe that's why Roger Daltrey of The Who hoped he'd die before he got old). With a deteriorating economy, more retirees are having difficulty paying for basics such as food, gas, and medicine, as well as heating and phone services. Half are accepting help from another family member to pay their bills.[57]

For pre-retirees, the situation isn't much better. The economic downturn has knocked them off their plan to put away money for retirement. The raises at work are smaller, the bonuses are almost nonexistent (unless you're on Wall Street), and everyone knows someone who isn't working at all. At the start of 2008, almost 70 percent of people age fifty to sixty-four said they had been on track before the economy slowed down, with savings stashed in 401(k) plans, company pensions, and Individual Retirement Accounts (IRAs). But most acknowledged they weren't saving enough. "Financial security" is the single most important attribute desired by people turning sixty-five. Phrased a better way, "financial peace of mind" becomes even more dear to them. Yet the average retiree has only seven years' worth of savings to stretch over nearly two decades, and one in ten people has saved nothing for retirement, even though they understand they will likely need hundreds of thousands of dollars. The overwhelming majority said they just didn't have enough money left over after paying the bills to sock anything away.

I conducted a study on retirement savings for a major investment firm using a technique I called "reality-based polling" because it was the first survey of its kind to ask people unique questions based on their own personal financial condition. We used computerized calculations of their previous answers to a series of income, savings, behavioral, and attitudinal questions to determine the real value of their savings and their real need for income after they retire based on the lifestyle they wanted to live. We asked them how old they were and how long they expected to live. Our task was to find out whether their money would last from the date of their expected retirement until the date they expected to die at their desired standard of living.

It wouldn't. Not even close. The average person expected to live to age seventy-nine—which at the time of the survey was three years longer than the average American life expectancy.[58] They assumed they'd be retired by age sixty-four, leaving them with an anticipated fifteen years to enjoy life. Here's the problem: Based on their savings and spending, their money would run out after just seven. What made this survey unique is that we called the participants back, one by one, and told them they were going to outlive their savings—sometimes by more than a decade, based on the information they had provided. The most common response was "Oh my God," followed by dead silence. Occasionally they would call out to their spouse to come over and hear what they'd just heard. It made you wince as people came to the realization that their retirement years were in real trouble.

So what does that mean for the great bubble of workers who are moving toward retirement age? Chances are they're going to put off retirement and try to spend less once they finally quit working. This is true of women in even greater numbers.[59] But other than a few service-oriented businesses like Walmart and McDonald's, there are almost no programs to keep people in their late sixties and early seventies gainfully employed and productive members of society. The demand for employment exists among the aging population. The demand for their lifetime of experience does not.

I want to return to a phrase I mentioned earlier: "peace of mind." For the business-minded, think of peace of mind as a commodity. Thanks to collapsing housing prices, collapsing shareholder value, and the collapsing job market, there is a quickly diminishing supply of this commodity in today's economic world. Accordingly, demand is up (and yes, price is, too). If you can wrap your product around the "peace of mind" attribute, you will have met the greatest demand of a large and growing generation. Sell less stress. Sell more security. Sell no worries. Sell the *feeling* that comes with knowing at least one corner of their life, the corner your product occupies, is squared away for the long haul.

WASHINGTON AND RETIREMENT

Political types should not underestimate the bond seniors have with their Social Security checks. If you ask them, they'll tell you it's not a privilege, it's their right. Scratch that. It's more than their right—it's *their money*. It is a sacred promise between workers and their government. People expect Washington to honor the contract that was entered into the day they joined the workforce and the first FICA deductions were taken from their paycheck. It's their money the government took every year, and they have a right to get it back. To them, it is absolutely no different from withdrawing money they already deposited in a savings account—with interest.

Unfortunately, Social Security has created a false sense of security. Today's workers can expect to rely on Social Security and traditional pensions for only a third of their retirement income. The bulk must come from personal savings. Americans believe a civilized society cares for its elders and ensures they have a dignified and decent retirement. We're not talking about penthouse beachfront condos in Boca Raton, we're talking about enough money for food, clothing, shelter, and health. We're talking about security and peace of mind.

Every politician who has made an attempt to reform the Social Security or Medicare system has rued the day, and this is our fundamental problem. There is no shortage of ways to fix Social Security. But there is an utter dearth of political will to make it happen. That's because so many seniors, who vote in such great numbers, are utterly unflinching in their opposition to *any* change in what they currently expect to find in their mailbox.

Rep. Dan Rostenkowski, former chairman of the House Ways and Means Committee and perhaps the most powerful member of Congress in his day, was besieged by cane-wielding seniors in 1989 who were angry about a proposed surcharge on Medicare. The sight of some very old senior citizens attacking him and his car was unprecedented in Capitol Hill history. As awful as his nonrelated legal troubles were at the time—troubles that put him in jail for fifteen months—Rostenkowski has said that day was one of the worst days of his life.

There is no guarantee that Social Security will endure for the lifespan of the younger Baby Boomers, although this group will have single-handedly contributed more money to Social Security than anyone else in history. It's just as well—the trust fund is estimated to run dry sometime in the 2040s. It kind of takes the "trust" and "fund" out of "trust fund" when you can't trust that there will be any funds in it by the time you retire. Boomers correctly worry more about their own personal nest egg—their personal savings and investments—than about the stability of those monthly Social Security checks. Half want to enjoy a comfortable retirement, a third want to maintain their current standard of living, and just a handful expect to "live the retirement of my dreams." To that end, they hope to continue to grow their financial assets and would welcome financial products that would increase their savings, albeit with protection from risk—a lesson learned the hard way courtesy of Wall Street.

HEALTH AND RETIREMENT

Older Americans correctly believe that their country leads the way in medical expertise. And they are rightly pissed off by the fact that more often than not, they can't afford it—or even have access to it.

WHICH OF THE FOLLOWING BEST DESCRIBES THE WAY IN WHICH YOU WANT TO THINK OF YOURSELF WHEN YOU USE HEALTH CARE?

A Human Being	33%
A Patient	27%
A Person	15%
A Customer	9%
A Consumer	7%
The Boss	7%
A Client	4%

America has the best doctors in the world. Kings and sultans and (other) billionaires travel here to be treated for their life-threatening diseases. They don't fly to London, Toronto, or Paris. They don't check into hospitals in countries that proudly boast of nationalized, government-run health care systems. They come to the United States. In spite of its shortcomings, our medical care is still the best in the world, for those who can afford it. If you've just been diagnosed with cancer or learned you need major surgery, whom do you trust? Would you rather have the surgery done at Sloan-Kettering, Johns Hopkins, or the Mayo Clinic, or would you prefer a government-run hospital in England or Germany? For most Americans, it's the doctors right here at home they want most. The problem is that the dreaded Health Care System stands between most patients and the care they need.

Health care *should* be personal. It should be about *people*, not *process*. Doctors (who are people) enter their profession out of a calling to render care to patients (also people). This is how it should work. Unfortunately, older Americans see a gauntlet of greed between them and their care. Their thinking goes like this:

MESSAGE TO HEALTH CARE PROVIDERS: PUT THE HUMANITY INTO HEALTH CARE

Someday some hospital or health plan is going to use the slogan "Putting the Humanity Back into Health Care." Humana has come closest with its "Guidance When You Need It Most" tagline, but no one has directly tapped the humanity attribute. If they make good on that promise, they're going to make a mint. That is the message retirees are begging doctors, hospitals, and insurance companies to embrace.

Health care is about a patient and a doctor, not a set of rules and regulations.

Make it about people, not profits.

Personalize it . . . again.

Talk about *your* doctor, *your* hospital, *your* health care.

And most of all, treat patients like human beings, not numbers on a spreadsheet.

- Insurance-driven costs and qualifiers limit access and affordability.
- Bureaucrats in Washington and in the fifty state capitals think that just because they tailored perfect health-care plans for *themselves,* they can mandate perfect coverage for the rest of us.
- Profit-driven pharmaceutical companies drive up costs and drive out competition for essential medications.
- And personal-injury lawyers sue our doctors and inflate our premiums.

Look at the list of business actors in the previous list. After decades of health care discussions with Americans, I can tell you this: No one believes that insurance or pharmaceutical executives, government bureaucrats, or personal-injury lawyers are really *people.* These are among the most hated professionals in America because they have taken the humanity out of health care.

Politicians and health care reform advocates too easily slip into bureaucratic jargon and wonk-speak. It's a mistake. It distracts from the

WHAT SENIORS *REALLY* WANT FROM HEALTH CARE PROVIDERS

Health care is one of those issues that can send polls off the charts. In my world, 60 percent constitutes widespread support. Anything higher than 80 percent is practically universal, and any results that go above 90 percent should be considered unanimous. These results from a nationwide poll of all adults about health care are, therefore, astounding:

- 97 percent say health care providers should be required to give their patients full information about their condition and treatment options.
- 95 percent say a patient should have the right to a speedy appeal when a plan denies coverage for a benefit or service.
- 95 percent say any basic managed-care plan should be required to allow patients to see specialists when necessary.
- 91 percent say a complete list of benefits and costs offered by a health plan should be required to be provided to every potential patient before he or she signs up for the plan.
- 87 percent say all HMO plans must allow patients the option of seeking treatment outside their HMO, with the HMO picking up at least some of the cost.

principle of prevention and care, and it raises fears that need not exist. Barack Obama gets this. In a focus group of undecided Virginia voters on the night of the second presidential debate, his command of the emotions surrounding health care was obvious. Obama *personalized* it by talking about his mother's battle with cancer, being denied the care she needed, and linking that to the current lack of affordability and accessibility. Obama talked about "health care" at a time when most politicians talked about the "system." It was less a political lecture and more a personal journey, and it worked. There's a lesson here for health care providers. Allison Janney, the actor who played White House press secretary C. J. Craig on *The West Wing,* has been the voice of Kaiser Permanente for almost a decade. Her ads consistently test better than almost anyone else's because she has a conversation with the listener. The words she reads and the stories she tells are fashioned from real-life experiences and real-life health care hassles. People expect you to talk to them in their language.

If the fear about health care is aggravated by the impersonal nature of the communication from the insurance companies, the anger about health care is driven by the impersonal nature of the bureaucracy. Americans have come to resent the accountants in seemingly distant corporate bureaucracies with life-and-death powers to hand down health care decisions that determine what is covered and who gets it. Americans want their health care to be governed by the principle of *good medicine* rather than *dollars and cents*.

The whole purpose behind the creation of HMOs was to provide affordable health care without the bells and whistles. The problem was in its name. What does HMO stand for? Health Maintenance Organization. *Maintenance!* Let me ask you, which would you rather have: prevention, treatment, cures . . . or maintenance? Organizations? Would you rather have your care delivered by an organization or by a hospital? But it gets worse. Think about the other name for the HMO industry. "Managed care." Let me ask you again: Do you want your health "managed," or do you want something more, something better? The marketing

WHAT AMERICANS *REALLY* WANT WHEN IT COMES TO HEALTH CARE

1. **The medical professionals are in charge, not the bureaucrats.** Every American, retirement age or not, believes health care should not be dominated by government bureaucrats or HMO paper-pushers. Both interfere with the delivery of quality care. Instead, doctors, nurses, and scientists need to be in charge so that their patients have the final say over their own health care, and also over costs.

2. **People, not paperwork.** Americans universally hate the forms and procedures necessary to complete before the care is given. To us, every dollar and every hour spent on bureaucracy, paperwork, and waste is not just lost. It's unforgivable.

3. **Health care is about rights, not privileges.** People should have the right to choose the doctor, hospital, medications, and plan that are right for them. They want the right to buy as much (or as little) coverage as they need for their individual situation. Too many politicians are spending too much time arguing that health care is still just a privilege. That might have been true decades ago, but not in today's world. Move on and focus on how best to deliver the care that is our right as human beings—and as Americans.

4. **Power equals portability.** Americans want the *power* to carry their personalized health care plan from one job to another.

5. **An end to waste, fraud, abuse, and mismanagement.** Ask anyone who's had a medical scare recently and who also actually looked at the bills. The first reaction is that someone got it wrong. The second reaction is that the whole system is wrong.

6. **Health care quality is having access to the treatment you need, when you need it.** To say the same thing in the opposite tone: *"Delayed is denied care."* In research I conducted leading up to the 2009 health care debate, nothing scored higher in terms of public priority than the timeliness of health care delivery— and nothing was as frightening to seniors as having to wait weeks for the tests they needed and months for the procedures they required. As one senior from St. Louis told me, her hands and voice trembling with fear, *"I can wait a few weeks for my car. It doesn't matter if the cable guy doesn't come. But if I have to wait weeks for the tests or operation I need, I may not make it."* As Washington debates substantial change to American health care, and as the various insurance plans struggle to keep up with patient demands, they all should know that Americans will not tolerate a sacrifice in the quality of care they enjoy today or the time it takes to deliver that care.

7. **Humanize your approach.** Banished forever should be all talk about the health care *"system," "providers,"* and *"networks."* For everyone reading this book, health care is about *personal health.* What Americans want is a *patient-centered approach.* Start with the person and build a solution from there. Treat them like human beings, not file numbers.

geniuses who named these programs gave them terminology that would better fit accountants than doctors. Call it "coordinated care" instead.

Americans believe that health care costs are inflated from top to bottom. Their only weapon for fighting back is a puny one—searching high and low for the *least* outrageous plan. That is why *affordability* is by far the highest priority for retired Americans—ranking above access, quality, and choice. Retirees want the most value they can get for the health care dollars they have to spend. What they don't want is for Washington to play politics with their health care and their lives.

When you're seventy-five years old, or you have no health insurance, you don't ask if your doctor is a Democrat or Republican. You don't ask if Medicare was a Democratic or Republican program. If you need medication or surgery, you just hope it's available and you can afford it.

Washington can't help itself—the city is rife with politics on everything from financial aid to farming. But when the issue is health, that's life and death, and seniors shudder at the idea of falling into the black hole of the uninsured or underinsured. They're looking for a lifeline to pull them out.

The need for patient-centered health care is evident and the demand for it has reached a boiling point. Fully 70 percent of all Americans—and an even higher percentage of people over age 60—consider our health care system to be either in a state of crisis or seriously troubled and that it requires significant reform. And the biggest problem in health care in 2009? Profits and bureaucrats, *not* issues related to quality.

The demand for reform cuts across all party lines and demographic groups. Americans disagree on the *type* of reform that is needed, but they widely agree that meaningful change must come. As I have written elsewhere in this book, Americans approach political issues based on

WHICH OF THE FOLLOWING IS THE AMERICAN HEALTH CARE SYSTEM'S SINGLE BIGGEST PROBLEM? AND YOUR SECOND CHOICE?

(COMBINED ANSWERS)	
Too profit-driven	60%
Too bureaucratic	39%
Too inaccessible	21%
Too complicated	19%
Too restrictive	13%
Too confusing	12%
Too limited	11%
Too unsafe/intimidating/ unpredictable/ insensitive	**Less than 10%**

personal experience, not out of abstract ideology. They aren't interested in amorphous arguments about the merits of free markets vs. regulation. They're interested in solutions that help them go from *uninsured* to *covered*, from *inaccessible* insurance to *affordable* insurance. Regardless of what ideological side you're on, Americans expect the conversation to revolve around certain fundamental principles, necessities, and expectations—and they will judge the political debaters and the health care providers not by the legalistic and bureaucratic changes they offer but by whether they have individualized, personalized, and humanized health care for themselves and their families.

The *personal* nature of health care is perhaps most evident in the use of prescription medications. Older Americans have an intimate relationship with their pills. They can tell you how much each costs, when to take them, how long before they start to work, and a whole host of other odds and ends. For many who depend on medications to stay alive or stave off chronic pain, those little pills are every bit as important as a vital organ. Medications are ingested, injected, rubbed in . . . you name it. *That's* personal.

Older people pride themselves on the number of medications they take. It's like a pharma badge of honor. I've stood in the back of the room at senior centers and heard them talking about their morning regimen of pill-popping in almost the same incomprehensible language that teens use to text one another. But don't call it medicine or drugs. Based on my language research with seniors, if you want to tack on a high price tag, call them "medications":

- "Drugs" are illegal narcotics or the useless candy that claims it's medicine.
- "Medicine" is what you get over the counter: aspirin, cold remedies, and sleeping pills.
- "Medication" is the product of science, laboratories, and research. Medications are serious and significant, which is why they require a prescription. They're about living longer and living better.

It's no surprise that the cost of medications is so irritating. Seniors simply do not understand and do not accept why a tiny little pill should cost so much. They do not appreciate the research and development that goes into their medication primarily because the pharmaceutical companies (the word "pharmaceutical" represents a more scientific organization than a "drug" company, and therefore deserves higher prices for their products) call it R&D rather than talking about the billions of dollars and the painstakingly detailed research over decades that may—or may not—result in a medical breakthrough.

Here's one area where retirees and their children differ sharply. Retirees want pharmaceutical companies to focus on medications that improve their day-to-day life, while the younger population wants research for new treatments for illnesses that are untreatable right now. Retirees live in the here and now; they don't have the time to wait for the cure for cancer.

The place where retirees and future generations do agree is in pricing—they hate it. For their part, what frustrates the pharmaceutical industry is the lack of appreciation among consumers who, quite literally, are alive today exclusively because of their product. There aren't many companies who can claim that using their products doesn't just improve quality of life but can sustain life itself. Among people age seventy and older, more than 90 percent are on some sort of medication—and many of them are breathing only because a pharmaceutical company had the right pill at the right time.

And yet, older Americans put drug companies in the same reviled ranks as the oil and gas industry—primarily because of what they make, and I mean that both figuratively and literally. Americans understand that companies need to profit to exist in a free-market economy; however, they believe that "obscene" profits are utterly un-American—especially when those profits are drawn from consumers who are over the barrel (no oil pun intended) and have no choice *but* to buy the product, whatever the price. That can be a bitter pill to swallow. Pun acknowledged.

Similarly, prescription medication is now a life-maintaining necessity for tens of millions of Americans. Gas is too. We have to buy it, no matter the price. And when we believe that most of the price underwrites an inflated profit, we get mad—really, really mad. To many Americans, four bucks for a gallon of gas, four hundred bucks for a bottle of pills . . . it's all the same as forty bucks for a gallon of water the day after a hurricane blows through (this actually happens). It's price gouging. There are laws against price gouging, so why not laws that set a cap on the price of oil or medication? We may not be there yet, but at least that's the line of thinking for a significant number of Americans.

But it goes further. Seniors blame corporate greed for the high costs of medication, and they think "Big Pharma" uses its power to generate big profits at the expense of the consumer. They look at the price of drugs in Canada and Europe, and it upsets them that it's cheaper for our neighbors up north and across the pond. They look at the price of generics, and it upsets them when they have to pay the higher patent drug price for medications that are supposed to do exactly the same thing. And so seniors are now more likely than ever to be using generics (a perfectly acceptable outcome) and buying their medications from Canadian pharmacies (against the law).

Drug advertising also irks retirees. They accept ads for cell phones and cars, but not for their medications. They think it drives up the price, and they disapprove of the *It's a Wonderful Life*–inspired visuals of allergy-prone people strolling through fields of flowers and of impotent men leering into the camera while they caress their significant other. These ads work, or they wouldn't be run, but it definitely damages the image of the industry among the same people they should be courting. A larger portion of the industry's advertising budget should be dedicated to commercials that utterly refuse to sell a product but instead play up the innovative and humanitarian aspects of their companies.

People do acknowledge a balance between affordable medications today and the need for companies to invest in researching new drugs for tomorrow. Even in their anger, they haven't given up on the hope that a pharmaceutical company might find a cure for a disease. But they don't want "maintenance" drugs just to keep them alive. They want medications that will *prevent* a health crisis. They make the same link with their health insurance—they'd much rather have preventive care than maintenance.

Americans are confronted with a genuine disconnect between the kind of care they expect and the kind they can actually get for the amount they are prepared to pay. Yes, this is a long way of saying many Americans are hypocrites. People complain that the cost of health care in this country is too high. They complain about their general practitioner who barely gives them fifteen minutes and a cold stethoscope on their chest. Yet they prize the medical specialist. When you face a life-threatening medical crisis, everyone wants the best. Cardiologists are the rock stars of medicine for retirees. They heal the heart, the organ that epitomizes love and more practically pumps our lifeblood through our veins. Cardiologists routinely perform small miracles to bring people back from the near dead.

Unfortunately, many of you reading this book will wind up in the care of a cardiologist if current trends hold true. Every twenty-six seconds, an American suffers a coronary event, and a third of Americans will die from it. Heart disease is the leading killer in this country. More than one million people suffer heart attacks every year. Another sixteen million have heart disease.[60] Heart disease knows no racial, gender, or class boundaries. Most Americans know someone who suffers from or has died from a heart-related illness. Fully six in ten have already lost a close family member—and these percentages are rising. And two-thirds of us believe we ourselves are at risk for heart problems. Heart and stroke medications are credited with saving more than one million lives each year. There are three million more cancer survivors now than there were a decade ago. The pharmaceutical industry needs to do a better job telling Americans what they're doing right. Every day they provide the medications that save people who suffer from heart attacks, strokes, cancer, and other life-threatening diseases. When it comes to communication, to borrow a line from one of the most famous ads of all time, America's pharmaceutical companies seem to have fallen down and they can't get up.

And while Washington is finally trying to do some good to help seniors get the pills they need at a price they can afford to pay, the jury is still out on Medicare Part D. If you don't speak Medicarian, this is the prescription drug subsidy program passed by Congress and signed by President Bush in his first term. Many say that typified Bush's embrace of runaway spending. Most Democrats in Congress criticized the program for not spending nearly enough. They measured the quality of the program based on the amount of the government subsidy. And some Republicans criticized the program for being too complicated. For something that cost its supporters so much credibility, you might have expected the program to deliver more for its target beneficiaries. The lessons learned from the flawed prescription-drug benefit program and rollout offer some valuable lessons for any business or politician who wishes to appeal to what seniors really want.

Medicare Part D presents an ongoing challenge to seniors because of

HOW TO CONDUCT EVENTS WITH SENIORS

1. **Promote the heck out of your event at least two weeks in advance.** Seniors need to schedule around doctors' appointments and social engagements. They also need to arrange for transportation and may need a younger friend or relative to join them to help simplify the information and cut through the confusion.

2. **Don't present them with physical barriers at the outset.** Pick a site that has plenty of easy parking and *no stairs*. Make sure the room has a good audio/visual system so they can see and hear as clearly as possible. People best absorb information in nugget-size bites as opposed to lengthy presentations. We live in a visual age, and they watch as much TV as anyone, so provide some visuals. It will keep them interested and, more important, awake.

3. **Give them a simple, easy-to-read handout that outlines all the major details and dates.** They may forget later, and your brief handout will be a godsend. Question-and-answer format is best. Provide names and phone numbers for follow-up. Websites won't help people who aren't computer literate.

4. **Testimonials are a powerful way of communicating to this audience.** If you have people in their age bracket who have a compelling story to which others can relate, go for it.

5. **As people arrive, pass out forms that ask for each person's most important question and their name.** Pick half a dozen questions you can answer, and make sure you mention the questioner's name when you're talking. Young or old, everybody likes to be recognized by name.

6. **Make sure you have plenty of experts on hand to help.** Think about how many times you've waited in the polling place while a senior citizen tries to figure out the electronic balloting.

7. **Get the name, home address, phone numbers, and e-mail address (if they have one) of each person who attends the meeting.** If there are people who seem especially articulate or interested, ask if they'd like to be "ambassadors" at future programs. Again, it singles them out from the crowd—who doesn't like that?—and it gives them something productive to do.

the myriad options, which continue to confound them. I was brought in late in the game, in 2003, when House Republicans were struggling with the legislation. Seniors told their members of Congress that they would oppose a "one-size-fits-all" approach to Medicare, and they would fight being forced into a plan that only gave them access to generic medicines.

As a result, the plan that was put before Congress had innumerable options—limitless choices with all sorts of individual add-ons. The problem was, for a typical seventy-five-year-old widow, ten choices isn't a choice, it's confusion—and thirty choices is absolute chaos. The politicians didn't understand one of the key principles behind retiree thinking: **Give them the right to choose, but don't actually make them make the choice.** The legislation was an initial disaster when it was rolled out. Younger retirees like to show off their pill boxes, but older retirees get befuddled over which medication to take, and suddenly they were being asked—told, in fact—to make a life-changing decision on a prescription-drug plan right then (written by bureaucrats, for bureaucrats) or risk paying a lot more later. It was a heart-wrenching example of too much "choice" being a bad thing.

The mistakes made by Washington are many. The most important:

- It was so complicated that seniors couldn't figure out how to work their way through the system.
- It was too bureaucratic, requiring too much paperwork and too little human interaction.
- And seniors feared it was just another government program that wasn't going to help them in the long run.

To help older people understand the rules and regulations, we crafted a strategy to present it to an audience eager and struggling for information.

The strategy has applications for just about any presentation to older people because it simplifies the information and gives it to them on their own physical and mental terms.

If the product you are selling to these older Americans is related to financial services, the same rules apply. Simplicity sells, not sex appeal. People are jittery about investing their hard-earned dollars, and financial security is paramount. Ditch the mumbo jumbo; they're not MBAs and the financial jargon confuses them. If you're selling technology, pitch them on "innovation you can use today." If you're selling financial services, they want reliability and experience, not state-of-the-art that hasn't been tested. Learn from the failed attempt to "privatize" Social Security. People didn't want to gamble with what should be the most secure government program in America.

FROM RETIREMENT TO WORK

Retired Americans are as insecure as middle-school girls at a dance when it comes to their financial security. Everyone else seems to be better off (they're pessimists), and it's never going to get easier. No matter how much money they bring home, Americans feel like they're struggling. I've had six-figure executives claim to be middle-class, having no notion that the real middle class brings home about $50,000 a year. No matter how much money they earn, people feel like they're living paycheck to paycheck. Their actual salary is not how they define their status; it is what's left in their pockets at the end of the day—their savings.

Retirees in particular are reliant on savings and investments. They have no means to bring in additional income, so *security* becomes critical. Before the 2008 crash, most people said the best reason to keep working after age sixty-five was to stay active and involved. Perhaps try a job they dreamed about, maybe invest in their own business. Do something they *want* to do, as opposed to what they *had* to do to make money. The money was supposed to be secondary.

But everything has changed. The market collapse bled trillions of dollars out of retirement accounts and people aged forty-five to sixty had to rethink their retirement plans:

- 60 percent expect to delay retirement.
- 20 percent stopped putting money into their retirement nest eggs.
- 25 percent took money out of retirement accounts to pay for their current expenses.[61]

WHAT EMPLOYED SENIORS WANT MOST

1. A chance to use their skills and talents in a new way
2. A friendly work environment that is welcoming and embracing
3. A chance to do something worthwhile, to make a difference
4. A feeling of respect from their younger coworkers

These are some stark numbers. By 2016, AARP estimates the workforce over age fifty-five will grow five times faster than the overall labor force. That's not a trend; it's a paradigm shift in the across-the-board lifestyle of our largest generation. Although seven in ten older workers already planned to work into the golden years, the question now is whether they stay in their current full-time jobs (if they can), segue to part-time work, or strike out on their own.

Some companies are adapting to accommodate these veteran employees with flexible hours, telecommuting, job-sharing, and phased-in retirement. Those that offer health care and other benefits to these workers will attract the best employees. Older workers cite these elements as essential to their ideal job, but they want something more.

There is a whole new crop of eager, experienced employees available for work. The above box shows the attributes business can offer that will attract the best talent among older workers.

These workers are not daunted by learning something new—three-quarters of them say they'd welcome new training or work-related education. They work hard and are the least likely workers to take a "sick day" off when they aren't really sick. Money is certainly important to them, but fulfillment and stability at work is just as important. And they have a sense of responsibility that simply doesn't exist among workers half their age and younger.

Fairness is also important to them. They say work-related age discrimination is a reality, and 13 percent say they have personally experienced it—getting passed over for a promotion or raise, being laid off or fired, being denied access to training, losing out on a job to someone younger.[62] Companies often believe that older workers will "cost more" than younger workers. An AARP/Towers Perrin analysis found it to be negligible to ±3 percent in most industries. Those minimal costs are offset by the deep institutional knowledge and know-how that experienced workers bring to any job, augmented by their motivation to exceed expectations.[63]

One in ten wants to start his or her own business or work for themselves after they retire, and I expect this percentage to grow sharply in the next few years. This age group may be ideally suited to entrepreneurship. Even with shrunken financial portfolios, they have more money at hand than younger people saddled with school loans or raising a family. They have large networks of contacts to tap for information, guidance, and leads. They are more confident and far less afraid to fail than younger people. (Still, fear of failure is a significant obstacle at any age—65 percent of people under thirty have it; 43 percent experience it among those fifty-plus.) But different from their younger colleagues is the fact that whatever project they are tackling, chances are they've done something similar before—or they know someone who has—and that experience is a huge and undervalued asset.

The decision to become an entrepreneur may not be available to everyone, given economic realities. But for those with white-collar jobs or an upper-middle-class bank account, it is a chance to start fresh and do something different. The Small Business Administration launched a website (www.sba.gov/50plusentrepreneurs) for older would-be entrepreneurs. It offers statistics, information, links to outside resources, and a self-assessment test.

There is one form of "retirement" that no one wants to talk about. There are millions of Americans alive today who have no idea who they are, where they are, or that they are, in fact, alive. I've lived it, and it's heartbreaking. My mother is among them. She has had only two windows of awareness in the last couple of years. Once she woke up in her assisted-living facility and didn't know where she was. She had a nurse call me and she pleaded, "Why am I here with these people?" This woman, who used to read *The Wall Street Journal* cover to cover every day and never missed *Wall Street Week* with Louis Rukeyser on Fridays, was strapped into a bed because she was a danger to her own well-being, asking her grown son the same question a four-year-old child asks a parent: "Why?" By the next morning, she was back in her foggy, distant world. It occurred one other time. She "woke up" for about thirty minutes, recognized me on TV, and started to cry. My aunt witnessed it and thought I would be pleased. I wasn't—not at all. My mother had a brief moment of lucidity, and in that moment, she remembered she had a child. Then it was over. It was painful for her and painful for me.

I've seen dementia in the corridors of power in Washington. Sen. William Roth of Delaware was in the Senate subway, confused as to where he was, thinking he was in a building. A kid in the subway looked at me and said, "You realize that senator has the awareness of a turnip, yet he has the power to have us killed?" Sen. Quentin Burdick of North Dakota barely knew he was a senator in his later years. I once introduced myself to him and said, "Senator, it's an honor to meet you." He looked around, and said, "Where?" True story. Sen. Strom Thurmond of South Carolina could break your hand, his handshake was so strong. He could talk on and on about his presidential campaign in 1948. But ask him about the vote he had just cast, and you'd get a blank look as he shuffled off.

These are the people who chose work over retirement, at America's expense.

There may be something to the old adage "You're only as old as you feel." A recent study of people seventy and older found they felt thirteen years younger than their chronological age—and thought they looked it, too. Women were more realistic than men, more likely to fess up to something closer to their actual age.

Feeling young is linked to better health and a longer life.[64] Try not to overdo it, though. Dennis Hopper, shilling for Ameriprise retirement planning, drew more criticism than praise from those who comment on television advertising for a living. *Easy Rider* meets investment guy in a suit—rebel with a portfolio instead of a joint. Mick Jagger in Spandex on tour—again—with the Rolling Stones. Guitarist Keith Richards, his face lined like a road map, still rocking out. They're poster boys for the fountain of youth . . . or, perhaps not. I heard someone at a Stones concert refer to them as "The California Raisins." For retirees, it is a memory of what once was.

But here's something to look forward to: Americans are happier as they grow into old age. Researchers chalk it up to maturity contributing to a better sense of well-being. (Not the Baby Boomers, though. They're the unhappiest, born into a crowded and competitive demographic bulge.)

How many jokes have you heard about retired spouses bickering and picking on each other? How many TV shows have been built around marital disharmony? It's a proven formula and has therefore stood the test of time. From Fred and Ethel on *I Love Lucy* to Frank and Estelle Costanza on *Seinfeld* to Frank and Marie on *Everybody Loves Raymond*, we love to see older couples bicker, and we want it to be just a little more biting than we see in our own lives . . . so we don't feel so bad about it. But the truth is a little more cheerful. Here are more details, thanks again to the experts at AARP:

- 78 percent say they're happier now than when they were working.
- 85 percent say they spend more time doing things together with their spouse.
- 76 percent say they're less stressed than when they were working.

They spend more time with their family. They exercise more. They volunteer more and have more time for hobbies. They eat out more often. They have more time for church and religious activities. They have far more time to surf the Internet.

Yet all is not paradise in Leisure World. One-fifth of them feel more tension with their spouse than when they were working and get irritated by being around each other so much. One-third worry about money. Most say they argue about different things than they used to. Many secretly harbor thoughts of divorce.[65]

In the bedroom, their sex lives start to slow down. Older people have sex a few times a month *or less*, making them the least sexually active group—and that obviously creates less satisfaction. When they actually do have sex, older people spend as much time at it as young lovers do.

They are just as likely as young people to contemplate an extramarital affair *if* there were a guarantee they wouldn't get caught. Especially men over fifty.

A few other provocative tidbits about the sexual interests of the over-fifty crowd:

- 39 percent role-play sexual fantasies—about the same as any age group.
- One in five has engaged in a threesome—slightly less than younger people.
- Watching pornography is commonplace—57 percent have indulged.
- S&M remains taboo—only 7 percent have tried it, far fewer than their grandchildren's generation.

There are many more divorced people in this group, but they're believers in the institution of marriage—only one in five has been married twice or more.

This is an age of restraint for many people. They rarely lose their tempers in public. They don't drink as much as they used to or eat as much. Everything has been downsized, including their appetites. They are the least likely people to make an impulse purchase, although the occasional splurge is hard to resist.

Their lives are about control or, more accurately, doing everything they can to keep it. They don't want to have to depend on their children or, worse yet, become a burden to their children. They don't want to lose their homes and be forced to live with other "elderly" people in a "retirement community" (acceptable), "assisted living facility" (not acceptable), or a "nursing home" (God forbid). That last term can reduce a Korean War Marine veteran to tears.

To them, it means a loss of independence. It means losing the ability to decide what they want to do, how they want to do it, where they want to do it, and with whom they want to do it. They want to have lunch whenever they feel hungry, not because someone tells them to sit down in the dining hall at twelve o'clock sharp. They want to drive their car to the mall whenever they feel like it—and they are humiliated when their driver's license is taken away. Or imagine the furtiveness of having sex in a facility where your room doesn't even have a lock because the staff needs to check up on you every couple of hours?

Control is positive. Dependency is negative. As we gradually lose control, we become more dependent. It is this X-Y axis that seniors watch carefully and fret over. They used to do things. Now things are done *to* them. They're living on fixed incomes. Their choices become more and more limited. They don't have the flexibility, in any sense, that they once had.

There is one arena where the population over sixty exercises enormous control. As I mentioned earlier in this chapter, they are a potent force at the ballot box and, unlike younger people, *they vote*—in great numbers. The Baby Boomers cut their teeth politically on the Vietnam War. They insisted this country would not have separate but equal people. They joined in the march on Washington and stayed active. They learned how to work the system out of a sense of social justice. Now they work the system to make sure no one touches the Social Security and Medicare programs that they've paid into for decades and are about to begin collecting.

Hearkening back to Obama's convention speech, the phrase "enough is enough" struck a loud chord with people over fifty. I told AARP's leadership that it was their mission to take that anger and frustration and channel it into constructive political action in 2008. You could not possibly get too angry on America's behalf. This group, especially, could be mobilized because many had already done it decades ago and remembered those days with passion. But asking them to get involved was not enough. They received requests for involvement every day from religious and community organizations. It had to be a more powerful appeal. First, it required the three essential principles of communication I have addressed earlier in this book: *individualize, personalize, humanize.* And second, it required a sense that whatever they did would have a genuine impact. Have you heard the phrase "Drive for show, putt for dough"? Well, for America's retirees, it's not the effort that matters, it's the reward.

Merely pointing out the problems in the country is not enough. Merely pointing out government gridlock is not enough. This generation has seen it all because they've done it all. The only way to activate this segment of the population is to give them the sense that they will make a tangible difference either with their time, their money, or both. They're fed up with task forces and bipartisan commissions. They're not interested in pressure groups and volunteer operations that have no record of success. As one man in a Detroit focus group put it, "It's like paying for a service you don't get."

Older voters heard the call during the recent presidential election. People in the AARP bracket made up an astounding 53 percent of the vote in 2008. The oldest voters narrowly cast more ballots for their cohort, John McCain. The Baby Boomers split their vote evenly between Obama and McCain. Among everyone else, it was Obama overwhelmingly.

They vote their pocketbook more than any other criterion. They vote for politicians who will protect Social Security and Medicare. They vote against government spending. Seniors, by dint of their sheer numbers and devotion to voting, decide what is spent and what is taxed. They want to get the most out of their tax dollars and pay the least—and they know how to do it.

I first realized the power of the senior vote when I was in high school and the school board had put a referendum on the ballot to fund a swimming pool. I remember going with my parents to the polls on Election

Day. Every variation of walker and cane was in line at the polling place. I didn't see anyone under the age of near-deceased. Not surprisingly, they voted down the pool two-to-one. They must have replaced those pictures of grandkids in their wallets with voter registration cards. We kids didn't stand a chance. This same sort of thing is going to happen on a bigger scale over the coming years. Instead of a small town in Connecticut, the conflict will center on Washington (although skirmishes will erupt in town halls, living rooms, and city councils across the country). Instead of swimming pools, the fight will be over Social Security.

CONCLUSION

The single greatest class conflict we will encounter in America in the next fifty years is not about race, religion, or income. It will be old versus young. Younger Americans still respond to messages about "achievement," "hope," "success," and "opportunity." Their older counterparts will settle for "security," "peace of mind," "predictability," and "well-being." It's the tension between maintaining the same level of benefits to the Baby Boomers that their parents received . . . or changing the system so there will be something left for those who come after. If we can find a way to achieve the hope and opportunity to which Generation 2020 aspires, we should be able to achieve the security and peace of mind that their parents and grandparents deserve.

LUNTZ LESSONS

It is never easy or entirely accurate to generalize about a population of 40 million people and growing. Factors such as marital status, employment, and health play a significant role in attitudes as well as behavior. Nevertheless, there are eight essential strategic imperatives for everyone seeking to communicate to or learn from Americans who are at least sixty-five years of age.

1) **Health.** The older they get, the higher on the priority scale health becomes—because it impacts everything else in their lives. Anything that promotes *"healthy living"* or a *"healthy lifestyle"* will attract attention. It's not just about the health component; emphasizing *lifestyle* and *living* helps them feel that they remain active and in control. That they still have the power to live their lives. That's important, because many seniors' greatest fear as they age is losing their physical independence. Anything that combines a time-sensitive offer with a clearly defined financial benefit along with good health will be read immediately.

2) **Control.** The sense of control is so important because it speaks directly to what seniors fear most: dependence on others. Here, word choice matters greatly. It's not about getting or gaining control; they still have that at age sixty-five. It's about keeping and maintaining and strengthening control over their daily lives—for as long as possible.

3) **"Peace of mind."** For seniors, it's not *"security"* that matters. It's *"peace of mind."* Security says there's something out there, some threat from which they need to be protected. Peace of mind communicates that they have absolutely nothing to fear—enabling them to breathe easier and enjoy life to its fullest.

4) **Financial independence.** Life-spans are increasing today just as investment portfolios are declining. Steep declines in the stock market, in interest rates, and in real estate values are the unfortunate trifecta that create financial distress for those living on a fixed income. Control, peace of mind, and even good health are all linked to freedom from financial worry. Anything that can help seniors to regain the feeling of financial independence that they worked for a lifetime to achieve will grab their attention.

5) **The facts.** Don't tell seniors how to think or how to feel. Don't say you know what they should want or why. If Missouri is the show-me state, then today's seniors are the show-me generation. More than for any other generation, give them the numbers and the evidence and let them decide for themselves. Emotional appeals are far less effective than the head-on approach.

6) **Their grandchildren.** This relationship is their visual connection to the future, a major motivating factor in their lives that gives them the chance to give and receive unconstrained love and affection. The impact is real. The more connected seniors are to their grandchildren, the happier their lives. If you are in marketing, consider using images that are trans-generational, showing active grandparents enjoying active grandchildren.

7) **Companionship and connectedness: the chance to be heard.** Loneliness is an undeniably painful component of the aging process—particularly among seniors in their seventies and older. For some, it is their single greatest daily fear. Senior centers have addressed this challenge for those mobile and healthy enough to travel, but more must be done for those who live alone.

8) **"The good life."** They've worked hard. They've played by the rules. They've saved for their retirement. Now they want to enjoy all that life has to offer. To many, this entitlement to *live well* in reward for a *life well lived* is a sacred, fundamental right—the best illustration of The American Dream. For them, *"the good life"* is just as the Sinatra song says: *"to be free and explore the unknown."* And with life expectancy and years of healthy living expanding each year, the good life becomes more than just a dream. It becomes a compelling desire and an expectation that, if not met, will lead to despair.

CONCLUSION

WHAT AMERICANS
REALLY *NEED* RIGHT NOW

*Twenty years from now, you will be more disappointed by the things that
you didn't do than by the ones you did do.*

—MARK TWAIN

This book has brought you a reflection of the plans and priorities of the
American people as they close out the first decade of the third millen-
nium. I had planned to conclude with the collective wish list of the nation, what 300 million people would ask for if they were blowing out
the candles on their next birthday cake. But with an economy in disar-
ray, expectations for the future in tatters, and hope in such short supply, it would be far more instructive to address what Americans really
need. If we are to put America back on the right track, restore confidence in the future, renew trust in our institutions, and revitalize faith
in ourselves, it will take much more than just satisfying our daily
wants. We have to go back to square one and reexamine who we are
as a people, what makes us unique as a nation, and what truly needs to
get done.

And that requires us to admit what this book has shown again and
again: we are a nation of well-meaning hypocrites:

We want smaller, less intrusive government, yet we want more oversight of the economy and oppose specific budget cuts;

We want taxes lowered, but we won't accept a decline in the quantity
and quality of services and we aren't eager to pay for stuff ourselves;

We say we want to eat healthy, but just look at what we actually consume;

We say we care about the environment, but we won't give up our pickup trucks or SUVs.

In this new economy, we clearly aren't always going to get what we want. Yet the things we need remain within our grasp. That's what my "What Americans Really Want . . . Really Survey" is all about—the nine priorities for the next ten years. It proposes new and different ways for Americans to invest and grow. For example:

Rather than investing in the sanctity of markets, we should invest in the goodness of people.

Rather than longing for the simplicity of the past, we should embrace the technological opportunities of the future.

You may notice that nothing in these two priorities is focused on how to get America back to where it was a few years ago—because where we were a few years ago was unsustainable. I do not call for big government initiatives or clever financial strategies. I do not urge Americans to work and work until they get back the money they lost. That's not going to happen for a long, long time. Rather, I implore Americans to take a different approach to regain our collective confidence based on the "What Americans Really Want . . . Really National Poll" conducted exclusively for this book that captures the spirit of America based on what I know to be true about ourselves and the character of our country.

Here, then, are the nine public needs based on the "What Americans Really Want . . . Really National Poll" conducted exclusively for this book—an unprecedented nationwide survey of more than 6,400 adult Americans conducted from December 2008 through April 2009.

PRIORITY #1—RESETTING OUR EXPECTATIONS ABOUT LIFE, OPPORTUNITY, AND THE AMERICAN DREAM

In October 2007, the Dow hit its peak of just over 14,000. For several weeks in 2009, it was at less than half that record high. If your retirement plan was invested in the stock market, you have probably had to rethink everything. *Reset.*

Home prices today are off 15 percent to 50 percent over the past three years. If you were counting on your inflated home equity to put a child through college or hoping to sell your home to pay for your retirement, it may not be enough. *Reset.*

Tomorrow the price of gas might be $2 a gallon. But it might just as easily be $3. Or more than $4. You can't control it or predict it, or perhaps even afford it. All you can do is react to it. *Reset.*

Our federal government seems intent on proving the only things it can do quickly or effectively are borrowing and then spending more money. From the unconscionable response to Hurricane Katrina, to runaway pork-barrel spending, to the inability or unwillingness of Washington to bail out working families instead of failing bank CEOs, we have witnessed our government's continual and colossal failure to deliver when we need it most. *Reset.*

Seemingly in the blink of an eye, the sense of security and all the expectations we had about where each of us stood financially and where our country stood economically disappeared. Poof. Gone. Like they never even existed. And in fact, I suggest that is how we start to think about it.

I say "reset" because it's time that we accepted the truth and started fresh. The global economic crisis has forced us to realize what we should have remembered all along the way: that the expectations we set in those heady days of high stock prices and overheated home values just weren't realistic. Our government, which has always been long on promises, has shown itself to be short on results. Washington continues to prove that it is too big and too unwieldy to respond in real time, with real results, to real Americans who are really in need.

Please do not mistake this straight talk for pessimism. We still need to dream, and our dreams have their place in our lives and in our culture. But it most certainly is a call to embrace realism so that we can restore a more sustainable optimism rooted in what is, not what we want it to be. This book has outlined the reasons why only 34 percent of Americans think their children will inherit a better America than their parents did, and why only 44 percent think their children will enjoy a better quality of life.

Now, however, it's time to talk about solutions.

Americans must collectively hit the Reset button. This button isn't anything like the Easy button Staples made famous or like the one Hillary Clinton gave to the Russians. There is nothing easy about it. That's the point. The era of easy answers (and easy money) is over. Once we accept the fact that true wealth is much harder to come by and that happiness cannot be indexed on the stock market, we can prepare our hearts and minds for a return to the more basic things in life that really *should* make us happy.

So, what do Americans really need? We asked them, with a special look at Gen 2020, and here's what they said:

Which of the following do you want most? Pick two.
(Combined 1st/2nd Choice)

Ages 18–29	Total	
44%	43%	The Opportunity to Succeed
38%	37%	The Good Life
32%	34%	The Pursuit of Happiness
29%	22%	The American Dream
13%	17%	A Fair Shake
7%	13%	To Be Left Alone
6%	9%	A Fresh Start
19%	9%	Everything I Can Get
7%	8%	A Fighting Chance
5%	8%	A New Beginning

Listen up, Washington and Wall Street. Most Americans aren't asking for "everything I can get." All they're asking for is "the opportunity to succeed" and "the good life" if and when they get there.

We need to return to hometown values more than sky-high home values.

We need genuine peace of mind more than bursting bank accounts.

We need to celebrate the richness of familial relationships, even if our monetary riches recede.

We need communities to make the human connections that a distant federal bureaucracy never can.

We need honesty from elected officials more than handouts from them.

We need to acknowledge that we are a kinder, happier, and more productive nation when we keep God in our lives.

We need to learn how to live on what we have rather than borrow against tomorrow to live a life today that's simply unsustainable.

We need reconciliation between older generations who have paid their dues and younger generations who may be stuck with the check and impatient for change.

We need quality communication; not through handheld devices and twenty-four-hour news, but person to person, employer to employee, and heart to heart.

We need to listen more than we speak.

And we need to remember that it is OK—and, in fact, necessary—to enjoy life even as it becomes more difficult.

All of this becomes possible after we hit that Reset button. We must reset our expectations about the things we thought we'd accumulate . . . the creature comforts we hoped to enjoy . . . the profits we wanted to make . . . the ability of our government to meet our needs . . . and what we really need in life to be truly content. Rather than fixating on what we want, we need to appreciate everything that we have.

PRIORITY #2—RENEWING OUR CELEBRATION OF THE AMERICAN FAMILY

The American family is broken. Not entirely shattered, but certainly broken. When more than half of marriages end in divorce, we have a problem with broken families. When one in three children lives in a home with only one biological parent, we have a problem with broken families. There are countless households where single parents and even responsible older siblings are stepping up and stepping in to fill the void created by the absence of another parent. Unconventional families are doing what they can to make do, but it's an uphill struggle. The strains on time, resources, and money that result from raising a family are increasingly difficult for two-parent households, let alone for single parents. As years of scientific data have shown, good examples are best set and opportunities for children to learn are greatest when they have a mother and a father to teach them. We know we have to do better.

We should find hope in the fact that the American people realize the importance of the family, even if we struggle to protect it. When asked what mattered most to them personally, Americans agree that having "a loving family" is the single most important priority among a list of many high priorities (combined top three answers):

Below you will see 15 personal priorities that people have said are important to them. Pick the three that matter most to you.
(Combined Top Three Answers)

TOTAL

54%	A Loving Family
50%	Good Health
43%	Financial Security
33%	Happiness
25%	Eventually Going to Heaven
24%	A Chance to Give Something Back
17%	Getting As Much As I Can Out of Life
9%	A Great Career
9%	Staying Young at Heart
9%	Doing Something Truly Memorable
8%	A Long Life
8%	Opportunities to Travel
5%	More Time to Do What You Want
4%	Fewer Day-to-Day Hassles
1%	More Choices in Life

Yet there is more assaulting the integrity of the family than divorce and absenteeism. The essential familial ingredients of *time* and *attention* are increasingly rare. The direct relationship between drug and alcohol abuse among our youth and the lack of time and attention from their parents should surprise no one. What is surprising—and deeply alarming—is how parents still continue to engage in behavior that is overtly harmful to their own children.

For a number of years, my research firm did the polling for the Center on Addiction and Substance Abuse (CASA) at Columbia University. Led by Joe Califano—the Secretary of Health, Education and Welfare under Jimmy Carter and a passionate advocate for healthy living—we were encouraged to examine the aspects of parental behavior that might trigger harmful, even pathological behavior in their teenage children. What we learned should be tacked up on every refrigerator door and on the back of every BlackBerry in America. Wake up, America. Here are the six parental behaviors that are most likely to help—or destroy—your own children:

HEALTHY CHILDREN TO HEALTHY ADULTS: THE SIX STEPS PARENTS REALLY NEED TO KNOW

1. **Having dinner with your children.** Nothing says "I truly care about you" more than spending dinnertime with your children at least five nights a week. More than any other day-to-day behavior, parents who dine with their children produce healthier adults because it sends the clear signal that their children are a high priority. Parents who miss dinner—no matter what the excuse—are sending the wrong message, and that message is unfortunately being heard loud and clear.

2. **Taking your children to church or synagogue weekly.** It is no coincidence that the most successful anti-drug and anti-alcohol programs have a spiritual component. If your children are taught at a young age that there is something out there bigger and more important than themselves, they are more likely to respect and appreciate the wonders of life and less likely to destroy it with drugs and alcohol.

3. **Checking your child's homework nightly.** There are two components at work here. Parents' daily participation in the homework assignments communicates that their children matter, and it also serves as an early warning sign if something is off track. Furthermore, children need to see that their intellectual development is just as important as their physical development. The more engaged a child is in intellectual pursuits, the less likely he or she is to engage in harmful physical behavior.

4. **Demanding the truth from your children—and getting it.** Parents who insist on knowing exactly where their children are on Friday and Saturday nights are sending a clear message that not every place, every friend, or every behavior is acceptable. Children who tell their parents the truth are acknowledging those boundaries, but if they would lie about where they are, they are most assuredly

lying about what they do. Deceit in the name of "teenagers will be teenagers" should never be tolerated.

5. **Taking your children on vacation for at least a week at a time.** Long weekends don't qualify because it just isn't long enough to break the daily routine or reconnect the relationship. You need a week without their texting, your e-mailing, and everyone's cell phones. There are no shortcuts here. Switching your portable devices to vibrate is not enough. Turn them completely off so that you can turn your children back on.

6. **Encourage them to participate in a team sport.** Sorry, but individual sports and other group activities such as band and drama don't count. Team members are often even less tolerant of substance abuse than parents—for good reason. When teenagers are forced to depend on one another's physical health and performance, they are less likely to engage in harmful physical behavior. Peer pressure to do the right thing can be a powerful motivating force.

And it's not just a problem with how much time parents give their children; there is also a deficit in how much attention children give their parents. Parents have more competition for the attention and respect of their children than ever before. As chronicled in this book, virtually every American youth has created his or her own universe in the online environment. It's a universe to which they retreat for hours each day. It's a universe where they play not just their own parent, but also their own God. Left unattended, this trend will drive families further apart, as kids look to words and pictures on a screen to shape their worldviews.

Parents cannot undo this trend. Trust me when I say there is no going back when it comes to time spent online. In surveys and face-to-face focus groups, our nation's youth have made their passion about their connectivity to the Internet quite clear. It's how they connect to the world. To them it is a *necessity*. Imagine how you'd have responded if someone tried to take away your car when you were eighteen. Or your phone line. Those are the tools you have always used to interface with your world, your work, and your life. Same goes for the Internet among young people.

Since it's not going away, and because the Internet is full of threats to the family, the best approach is for parents to become a *part* of their online world. Look for opportunities to surf the Web together. Convert their dangerous alone time to affirming together time. The point remains, as it always has, to spend quality time with our children. Even if it means more time looking up baseball highlights on YouTube and less time watching the game on television, at least it's time spent together—you can use it to cajole your kids to play catch with you in the backyard.

Friend them on Facebook or MySpace. Tell them you want to research one of your favorite bands from your own youth, and ask them how *they* would suggest going about it. Then sit down and do it together. Tell them you saw a commercial for Hulu on TV and thought it seemed like a pretty cool idea—then ask them to show you how it works. Because young people are so very protective of their e-universe, and because young people have *always* been fierce about establishing their independence, it won't always be easy. They will reject your involvement if it is purely about telling them what they cannot do, see, or experience. But if this is a natural, periodic activity, it won't seem out of the ordinary. It will all seem "fair"—a key concept among young people. More than just offering an opportunity to monitor their world, it will offer you the opportunity to become a natural part of it.

PRIORITY #3—REESTABLISHING THE RESPECT FOR RELIGION IN AMERICA

From the Pilgrims landing at Plymouth Rock in 1620 to the writings of the Founding Fathers in Philadelphia a century and a half later, the early American experiment with democracy and opportunity has its origins deeply rooted in religion. But in recent years, America is trending toward a new and more troubling experiment. We may soon find out what happens when we *unlink* our freedoms from our faith.

Perhaps we already have. Overall, 82 percent of Americans agree with the phrase on our currency, "In God We Trust," but almost one in five don't. Those four words should be innocuous at worst and inspiring at best, but a growing segment of America rejects them. In fact, in the 2009 Pew Forum on Religion and Public Life survey, the fastest-growing religion is none at all. Fully 16 percent do not affiliate with any belief.[66] If we follow this trend to completion, I believe the result will be an America that is not only less moral, but ultimately more unhappy and less successful.

Despite all of our current economic troubles—and there are many, and they are profound—let us not forget from where we have come and what we have achieved. What made us unique as a nation—and still does—is that we based the founding of America on the cornerstone of a faith in something bigger than ourselves. Over the past 230 years, it is because of our enduring religious beliefs that our culture has put such emphasis on families—often above and beyond the individual—even though our Constitution champions individual rights. Our inherent belief that God has a plan for us has spurred generations to achieve greater success while driving us to leave something better for those who follow. And as faith knows no geographic boundaries, it is also why we have been willing to sacrifice for the freedom of others beyond our borders.

It should therefore be no surprise that almost half of Americans see the Ten Commandments as more personally important to them than the Bill of Rights.

Which of the following matters more to you personally?

TOTAL

52%   The Bill of Rights

48%   The Ten Commandments

What is surprising is that 61 percent of moms with children pick the Ten Commandments—more than any other demographic subgroup in American society; clearly the tenets of spirituality, morality, and values are still welcomed in most homes. On a broader scale, the commitment to intergenerational improvement and worldwide freedom based on core moral principles, while surely imperfect in execution, is a uniquely and admirable American trait. Yet I am concerned that America is on the brink of abandoning it. There is a pragmatic reason to protect America's religious roots: Those who embrace religion are *happier, healthier, and more successful.*

Here are some examples based on the study included in this book, broken out by religious intensity. (Note: religious Americans are defined as those who attend a place of worship one or more times per week and pray once a day; nonreligious are those who "rarely" or "never" pray or attend a place of worship.) Let me be clear: I do not wish to offend non-religious readers. This is simply how Americans believe and behave.

Religious Americans are much more likely to reject the instant-gratification mentality. Two-thirds (66 percent) of nonreligious Americans agree with the statement "If it feels good, do it," despite its selfish, dangerous undertones. By comparison, fully 71 percent of religious Americans *disagree* with the concept of instant gratification. What we have here is a chasm between the value systems of these two American camps. Especially in times of economic uncertainty and a loss of personal direction, we must ask ourselves whether a life in search of instant gratification can possibly yield a lifetime of satisfaction. We must also wonder whether an America with a majority of me-firsts could and would provide for those who are truly in need.

Religious Americans are more likely to prioritize family. One of the best ways to test how a person truly prioritizes his or her time is with the following question: "Assuming you had a surprise day off, which of the following activities would you most want to do?" That's because an unexpected free day allows someone to make up his or her own mind about how to spend his or her own newly found time. No prior obligations to cloud your decision. This day is truly yours, so let's see where your priorities truly are. More than half (59 percent) of religious respondents picked "spending time with my family" as one of their top two choices. By comparison, only 27 percent of the nonreligious picked time with family as one of their top two priorities ("day trip somewhere" came in first). At a time when the American family is facing constant erosion from every angle, we would do well to promote the role of religion, because religion promotes the importance of family.

Religious voters vote religiously. And that doesn't mean they vote based on faith (though many do). We should all agree that voter participation is a prerequisite to a healthy democracy. A clear majority of religious voters (59 percent) replied that they vote in every election, compared with a 43-percent participation rate among nonreligious voters. If nonreligious voters are worried that the religious right holds too much sway in American politics, they might try complaining less and voting more.

Religious employees are more dedicated to their jobs and more fiscally prudent. Almost half (46 percent) of religious respondents estimate that they will continue to work for their current employer for five or more years, compared to just 31 percent of nonreligious respondents. Conversely, more than a quarter of nonreligious workers (26 percent) plan to stay with their current job for less than a year, compared to just 15 percent of religious workers. With spirituality comes job satisfaction. Moreover, while religious people are less financially focused, they save more money than their nonreligious counterparts.

Religious Americans are more satisfied sexually. Yep, you read that right. Fully 61 percent of religious people said they are "honestly satisfied" with their sex lives, compared to a minority (45 percent) of nonreligious people. Just over half (54 percent) of the population at large responded that they are satisfied—so religious folks are, er, outperforming them, too. Jokes aside, there is something to this. For all of our national experience with the Sexual Revolution and freeing ourselves from moral conventions, it is a fact that the people who adhere to those conventions are more satisfied. Unfettered freedom does not translate to genuine contentment. Rather, it seems that faithful commitment does.

Through my research, and by any simple observation of popular culture, it is clear that there is an increasing number of Americans who are dismissive—or worse, hostile—toward religion. This is a mistake. Whether you believe in God or not, the empirical data in support of the positive effects of faith on our nation is indisputable. Americans have turned in the past to religion in times of great national crisis, and our country emerged stronger as a result.

The statistical findings above are simply examples of a larger truth: People who keep God in their lives are more content with their lives. Particularly in these trying economic times, not only are they are better suited to remain at peace with the challenges before them, they are also more prepared to handle them. In other words, God is good for us as individuals and collectively for our society and our country.

PRIORITY #4—REBUILDING THE MUTUAL COMMITMENT BETWEEN EMPLOYER AND EMPLOYEE

Too many Americans are unhappy in their current jobs. This is particularly troubling considering that we spend more time at work than we do at anything other than sleeping. In fact, we spend more time with our coworkers than our families and friends. So, what do American workers *really* need? A few more dollars, surely, but even more important, *more satisfaction, more fulfillment, and more excitement* from their jobs. And rather than more jobs, what Americans really need is more careers. It largely falls on employers to realign their focus to provide these new opportunities rather than taking the trench-warfare approach of hire, fire, and replace.

Our priorities for the American workplace within the next ten years should be both aspirational and inspirational: First, to restore the American worker to his/her rightful place as the most valuable, respected, and sought-after employee in the world. And second, to restore the American company as the most successful and desirable place to work in the business world.

There are many influences that will decide whether we are successful in this goal. Tax policy. Regulatory oversight. Global economic forces. Much of it is beyond the control of individual American workers and businesses. So I suggest that American workers and business leaders start with what they *can* control: their relationship with one another. What matters most, and what must be addressed, is the lack of trust and confidence between employer and employee. As long as that trust remains broken, so too will the foundation upon which the American economy is built.

The obvious issues such as compensation, benefits, working conditions, and hours on the job are perennial sticking points that will always be on the table for employers and employees to negotiate. They are important—but very clearly *not* at the top of the list for most American workers. On the contrary, according to the American Priorities Poll, by an overwhelming 84 percent to 16 percent margin, Americans would choose less money at a job they love over more money at a job they hate. While Americans of every age overwhelmingly choose happiness over pay, the survey shows that the older we get, the stronger our preference for job satisfaction:

AGE	PERCENT PREFER GOOD JOB OVER MORE PAY
18–29	76%
30–49	81%
50–64	88%
65+	94%

The lesson is this: The more we work, the more we realize life is about *more* than just work, more than just a paycheck. Employers should realize this and seize on it. Rather than focusing exclusively on whether your pay scale is competitive with the market, set out to ensure the lifestyle you offer is appealing to the kind of employees you hope to attract.

Of similar importance is the *tenor* of employer-employee relations. We have reached a boiling point in that relationship, and it threatens to vaporize the preeminent status of American business. It's time for an **"Employer-Employee Bill of Rights"** that is signed by both parties that includes the following three commitments:

1. **A commitment to speak and a commitment to listen.** There have to be regularly scheduled two-way "listening sessions, "town halls," "open forums," call it what you will, but they have to be scheduled at regular intervals and time has to be reserved for everyone to speak, respond, and learn.

2. **A commitment to provide genuine work-life choices.** This is particularly problematic in retail, but it's a growing problem in the service area as well. Parents have the right to attend the important functions of their children, and employers should not only recognize that right . . . they should embrace it. Conversely, employers have the right to insist, wherever possible, that employees inform them well in advance if and when they will be absent from work.

3. **A commitment to predictability.** It is simply unacceptable for employers to tell employees to expect a forty-hour work week when they are hired and then ask them to do fifty hours or more—or cut their hours significantly if they're hourly employees. Conversely, employers have every right to demand that employees arrive on time and stay until the appointed hour.

Only by recommitting to the importance of continuous two-way listening, communication, and cooperation can we ratchet down the conflict and increase American productivity and satisfaction.

America's experience with labor unions provides a useful example of what can happen when the dialogue between employers and employees takes on a tone that is too confrontational. Make no mistake: Labor unions had, and I believe still can have, a useful place in our American economy. But somehow along the way we have gotten off track. Too often, Big Labor has squared off with Corporate America in an effort to prove a point, advance an agenda, or just plain make a scene.

Businesses and union leaders alike have adopted a take-no-prisoners approach to negotiations. Well, we know what happens when no prisoners are taken, right? The battlefield is strewn with casualties. And guess who those casualties are. They're not the generals. Not the CEOs, not the corporate boards. Not the labor leaders and organizers. They are the foot soldiers. They are the workers in the company who are supposed to be taken care of by the union. And they are the line managers who are supposed to be taken care of by their company.

These are the people whose very livelihoods are at stake when the confrontation comes to a head, as it too often does. They are the people who might go days . . . weeks . . . even months without a paycheck because of a strike or a lockout. They are the ones who have no guarantee that when an agreement is finally made, things will be better than before. And in the big picture, we know that America has become a less competitive economy in the global market as a result. Especially in today's economy, we can't afford it.

It's not my intention to pick solely on the labor movement. Similar combativeness occurs where no unions are present, but labor negotiations play out on a national scale and therefore make the most identifiable example. So let me offer this example of what happens when we crank up the volume of discontent and drive *down* the results. The story, as told by our survey, is staggering. When given a list of institutions and asked to pick which matters *least* to America's future, Americans chose unions by a commanding margin: 61 percent chose it as one of their top two choices, followed by the media (56 percent). By contrast, only 4 percent chose "business" to be least important. For all the antipathy in this country toward Corporate America—and there is plenty—Americans still recognize the importance of business to our success as a nation.

There has to be a better way. I have worked with Fortune 500 companies who dug in their heels, locked out their employees, and in the process threw away decades of fidelity with the lifeblood of their business—their workers. And I have worked with companies who took sound advice and recommitted themselves to *communicating* with their employees . . . to actually listening and actually responding to their daily needs. From Microsoft to Apple to Google, there are dozens of companies who have created innovative working environments that encourage greater human interaction and less hierarchy. The result is a workforce that demands less, produces more, and is generally happier in their jobs. It's time to take that lesson to the rest of America.

PRIORITY #5—REINSTILLING ACCOUNTABILITY IN AMERICAN GOVERNMENT

This will be the shortest section about American priorities for the next ten years because I have already written at length about the stark need for greater accountability in American government. I keep championing accountability because the American people keep clamoring for it. In survey after survey, year after year, "accountability" is the one word that cuts through all the political haze. In fact, as conditions have deteriorated, the demand for accountability has only grown. If I'm beating the dead horse of accountability, it's only because politicians killed it long ago.

What the American people need from government is elected officials who say what they mean and mean what they say (which is the most popular definition for "accountability"). But even as Americans lower their expectations about *how much* government can do in their lives, they are going to raise expectations about *how well* government delivers on what it promises. They will throw out the party—either party—that continues to promise the world and deliver peanuts.

PRIORITY #6—RESTORING PERSONAL RESPONSIBILITY AND EMPOWERING CREATIVITY AMONG AMERICA'S YOUTH

The days of easy, carefree living are apparently over for Generation 2020. By a remarkable 4 to 1 ratio, Americans are ready to give the *next* generation a swift kick in the ass. Remarkably, the next generation agrees.

What do you think the youth of America need more?

AGES 18–29   TOTAL

| 75% | 79% | A Swift Kick in the Ass |
| 25% | 21% | A Gentle and Understanding Hand |

But there is more to the story. A swift kick alone is not going to help this generation achieve its fullest potential. I have referred to them as Generation Zero because they have seen the worst of life both visually on 9/11 and economically in 2008–09, requiring a significant rebuilding effort to renew their faith in the future. Yet this generation can and should be the most successful, dynamic, and diversely talented cohort in American history. What America's younger generations need from our older generations is probably something in the middle of the two choices we offered in the survey. What they need is a firm hand *and* a gentle guide to channel their creativity and raise them from near economic ruin.

Let's start with where they begin: in school. The fundamental question that has challenged American society for decades is in choosing who gets the attention and the resources: the good students, so that they will become great—or the poor students, so they will become better. The Bush administration put its emphasis on struggling students, but the American people are much more evenly divided:

Which is more important for America . . . that no child should be left behind or that exceptional children should be encouraged to pursue excellence?

AGES 18–29   TOTAL

| 51% | 55% | Exceptional Children Should Pursue Excellence |
| 49% | 45% | No Child Left Behind |

Americans were then asked which high-school subject is absolutely essential for the children of today to learn. What they told us is that those who have most recently completed high school (eighteen-to-twenty-nine-year-olds—our Generation 2020) have differing priorities from the general public:

If you had to choose, which of the following high-school subjects is absolutely essential for the children of today to master well?
(1st and 2nd Choice Combined)

TOTAL	AGES 18–29	
37%	35%	Math
32%	20%	American History/Government
29%	40%	Writing
28%	22%	Economics
23%	20%	Science
19%	19%	World History
11%	17%	A Foreign Language
8%	12%	The Arts (Including Music, Theater, and Visual Arts)
7%	11%	Public Speaking
3%	3%	Physical Education and Athletics
2%	2%	Geography

Everyone agrees that math is important. But look at the disconnect between Gen 2020's desire to learn writing and the general public's emphasis on history and government. Writing presents them with an opportunity to express themselves: to explore, map, and share their own thoughts and pursue their own future. As someone who has enjoyed a highly satisfying career driven by words and language, I find this encouraging. But history and government, to them, represent something of the past. As someone who has also spent my life in the study and appreciation of our system of government and our heritage, I find this troubling. I hesitate to reference the infamous George Santayana quote that "those who cannot remember the past are condemned to repeat it" because it has been so frequently misquoted, misattributed, and overused. But it does apply to a generation that can still name the Three Stooges even though they've been dead for forty years but can't name three members of the Supreme Court.

In fact, each of the school subjects where the Generation 2020 result is higher than the overall population offers a common theme and direction: They are all part of what you might describe as a "liberal arts" education. Young people place a higher premium on learning foreign languages, public speaking, and the arts. This is consistent with their affinity for things global and international, communicative, collaborative, and creative. They have an accordingly lesser emphasis on subjects that are often studied and researched alone: math, economics, and science.

Yes, we should encourage their creativity. As someone who will sift through twenty-five résumés to find even one person worth interviewing, and then interview ten people to find one person worth hiring, I agree that writing should indeed be a top priority. However, we should be concerned that the soft approach of the liberal arts education, which permeates our colleges and universities, is now encroaching on our high schools. We must go in the opposite direction. America's youth should learn concrete skills and useful information, not just amorphous concepts. They not only need to learn how to think, they must also learn how to do. The world—multicultural and fascinating as our young people find it—requires an increasing level of knowledge to succeed. Our high-school students should learn the practical information they need to hit the ground running once they leave home. This includes everything from learning how to manage a budget (which fewer and fewer *college* students know how to do) to learning a skill or trade that can employ them immediately. Many states and schools are already moving in this direction, allowing high-school students to take internships that are more like apprenticeships.

Math and science cannot be allowed to fall by the wayside, either. While our young people are discovering new and creative ways to share their feelings on video blogs, the youth of other nations are learning the skills they need to be the next great generation of engineers, programmers, and scientists. We risk losing part of what has made our nation great if we surrender our position as the world's leader in technology and innovation. Yes, we are the nation that put a man on the moon (forty years ago), and we create more entertainment products enjoyed by more people than all the countries on the globe combined, but will we be the nation that builds the first automobile that doesn't pollute, or the nation that finds the cure for cancer? If we aren't, that will be a sure sign of decline.

PRIORITY #7—RESPECTING THE ACCOMPLISHMENTS, EXPERIENCE, AND CONTINUING RESOURCES OF AMERICA'S SENIORS

A nation that doesn't honor its heroes will soon find itself without heroes to honor. The single most powerful gift we can give older Americans is our respect. Whether they are members of the Greatest Generation, who conquered a depression and defeated world tyranny, or the War Kids, who built the foundation for a modern and prosperous America based on equal rights and justice, we owe older Americans a world of gratitude. Even in deep recession, this country provides more opportunity for success than our grandparents could have dreamed possible. It is by their labor that the foundations for our success were laid. It is their dreams that we must remember to embrace, live out, and enjoy.

Part of demonstrating our respect is to listen. As we confront the problems of today, we should seek the counsel of those who lived through even harder times before. The financial crisis we now face is to the Great Depression what the September 11 attack was to Pearl Harbor. Times are hard now, but they have been harder. What they will share with you, if you'll ask them, is what kind of *character* it takes to survive crises like those we now face, and the kind of sacrifices for family, friends, and country that become necessary when the stakes are at their highest.

We also need to welcome retirees back to the workforce if that's what they want and need. How strange to think that Corporate America would rather invest in the least-business-savvy and least-experienced demographic. So what if these older Americans are working because their promise of retirement was broken? They'll be every bit as motivated as someone half their age—and a lot more disciplined and dependable. Plus, they'll have twice the experience.

The idea that there is a clear line between those who are "retired" and "unretired" is hopelessly antiquated. American seniors used to be able to springboard into retirement. Now most will have to wade in slowly. Employers need to embrace this truth and aggressively recruit and retain talented, mature Americans by providing what they want and need out of a job: opportunities to use their skills in new ways, to make a difference, and a feeling of respect and value from their younger coworkers. Particularly when times are toughest, Corporate America needs to shed its bias toward the least experienced and least business-savvy in favor of those who have the greatest expertise and can make an immediate contribution with minimal guidance. Retirees are a prized and critical resource we cannot afford to ignore.

PRIORITY #8—INVESTING TIME AND COMMITMENT INTO MENTORSHIP

I address the need for investing in mentorship toward the end of the priorities because the mentor relationship can be the tie that binds it all together.

Yes, young people need the foundation of a supportive family to survive and thrive, but many also need the capstone of an accomplished mentor to strive and achieve. Even if the family structure is in place, intact, and providing the necessary emotional support to excel in today's world, members of the family might lack certain knowledge or experience. And where the family structure has broken down, there is even greater need for the attention of an adult who takes a personal interest in the success of a child.

America's greatest need for mentorship is in the communities where broken schools and broken families are breaking the dreams of America's youth. We need caring adults to fill the void in these schools and these neighborhoods that no government program or dollar can replace. There are times when only the care of neighbors in action can bridge the gap between our students' hopes for achievement and their fears of being least, last, and left behind. And we need these neighbors in action to come from all around; even if your suburb doesn't have a problem with neglected young people, the city down the road probably needs your help.

I have discussed the need for younger Americans to find constructive ways to channel their creative energy, as well as the need for older Americans to find ways to remain involved, contribute, and be valued for the experience they have to offer. What better way to connect need with need than through mentorship?

Moreover, the need for mentorship does not dwindle as Americans move beyond school, college, and internships. We have also explored the importance of building fidelity in the employee-employer relationship. An ideal way to do so is to convert "managers" and "employees" into "mentors" and "mentees." Businesses must strive to provide every employee opportunities to learn as they work. Not only does it make the worker feel valued, it also makes him or her more valuable.

We need a recommitment to mentorship because these relationships can meet aspiring Americans' needs on a personal level. Whether it's providing career advice, the right example about how to live a good life, technical training, or just the need for human interaction, mentors have the unique ability to provide tailored attention on an individual level. They need to be an integral part of the American fabric.

PRIORITY #9—REMEMBERING TO HAVE SOME FUN ALONG THE WAY

Have a Big Mac
(With cheese, if you like).
Wash it down with a Pepsi
(Regular, not diet, if you prefer).
Sure, these are "guilty pleasures," but so what?
And now—and this is the important part:
Stop feeling so bad about it!
Americans, please hear me. We have too many challenges . . . too many problems . . . too many *worries* these days to give up on life and forget to have fun. Put differently, I believe that we can't afford *not* to enjoy life, even if it only comes in little slices of fun along the way.

Frankly, we have wrung the fun out of life. You can blame much of this on the media, which pounds us with bad news on an hourly basis. Someone needs to teach them the difference between accountability (which we need more of) and sensationalism, which is destroying not just our short-term outlook but our long-term dreams. The media handling of the Bernie Madoff situation is a perfect illustration. Some media outlets used it as a teaching tool to emphasize the importance of prudent investing, diversification of assets, and always having a skeptical eye toward investments that seem too good to be true. But following his car from his apartment to the courthouse as though it was a high-speed chase? Come on!

You can also blame the economy as it increases the supply of stress and decreases the supply of money (even though they're printing trillions of dollars of the stuff down at the bureau of engraving and printing). True, it's hard to have much fun when your retirement has itself retired and when your job is on the chopping block. It's hard to have much fun when you're genuinely worried about whether your kids will enjoy the same quality of life you have, let alone leaving something *better* for them. There's not much time or money for fun when you're working and paying for your elderly father's assisted-living care and your daughter's college tuition at the same time.

But the economic excuses are masking a bigger societal problem that threatens to undermine America's unique, upbeat nature and can-do spirit. It's not just that we can't afford fun, it's that we feel *bad* for having it when we *can* afford it. We hear doom and gloom from high and low, so we feel the need to repeat it, to become a *part* of it. Better to commiserate with the depressed than be on the receiving end of poisonous publicity. You might avoid telling the neighbors about the trip you're planning to Orlando (or worse yet, Vegas) because who can afford to travel in a time like this? Only rich people who aren't suffering, that's who. And shame on them for it.

Please. This is America. Save up. Comparison shop. And yes, be prudent . . . but please, if you like adventure, don't be afraid to travel. If you enjoy good food, don't forgo that special glass of wine to go with it. If reading is your pleasure, go out and buy that book—in hardcover—that you've wanted to read forever. If you love television, get the platinum DirecTV package. Be proud of it. This is still America, and America is supposed to be a fun place to live. Even if your bleak financial picture really does put many recreational activities out of reach, do not give up on fun. Make time to *take* time. Even if you don't do anything particularly fancy or expensive, a mental break from the emotional grind of our times is a survival essential.

Yes, times are different. It's not about keeping up with the Joneses any longer . . . it's simply about keeping up. But even amidst our new reality, there are opportunities to readjust our outlook and still find the fun in life. I know there are people who used to be *ashamed* to go to Walmart. Today, many of those same people are loading up their carts right next to you and me. They may try to avoid eye contact, but still they bargain shop. There's a reason why Walmart's sales have *grown* during the current crisis.

To these people I say: Why feel bad about it? What's *not* fun about saving a hundred dollars on a new TV? Or thirty dollars on your groceries every week? Sure, the lines at the cash register aren't fun. Neither are the elbows to the face during the biggest sales. But if those thirty extra dollars fund two large pizzas and movie night at home with your family—mission accomplished. These days we need to take every opportunity available to have fun with those who matter most. Walmart's tagline for 2009, "Save Money. Live Better," is more important now than ever before. As we all try to weather this economic storm, it's places like Walmart that are helping us keep the American Dream alive, not destroying it like so many in the media might want us to believe.

I know the nanny-staters among you have been shaking your heads since the beginning of this section. I have done you a disservice by leaving the bitter taste of a fatty burger and sugary soda in your mouth. Some of you really believe we *should* feel bad for every bite of fast food and drop of high fructose corn syrup we consume. But allow me to make the case for balance in life.

We know that our work lives *must* be balanced with our personal lives. And even within our personal lives, there is a time to attend to family business and a time to just plain hang out. Likewise within our work life, the best employers allow employees to have some fun along the way. It builds camaraderie and eases tension. We need balance throughout. It even must be promoted within the discrete areas of life we balance against the *other* areas of life.

The same goes for food. Yes, we eat too much junk food. But that's because we like to do it. And a little comfort food can go a long way during very discomforting times. Just because we eat too much doesn't mean we should eat none. And if we eat a little, we shouldn't have to feel bad about it. We should instead find the fun in it.

Tell me, would America be a better, happier place if we banned all fast food and replaced it with tofu? Or replaced Big Macs with brussels sprouts? Pepsi with prune juice?

In the same way, we simply *must* balance the weight of the economic crisis with the emotional lightness that comes with having fun with friends and family. We are right to worry about and plan for our futures. But we would be wrong to forget to have fun along the way. We simply won't make it a better tomorrow if we don't take time to enjoy life today. Take it from me. My entire life has been lived in the name of delayed gratification. You can do better. Make it a *priority* to remember to have a little fun along the way.

We would do well as a nation to remember the importance of taking responsibility for our own lot in life. But I also think there is a danger in putting *too much* pressure on the individual. I do not mean that government should pick up the slack (and neither do most Americans). Our public institutions are weakening and are in no condition to be relied upon except in times of crisis.

Rather, I think it is appropriate to call for a new era of *familial responsibility*. This world is too big and too daunting for any one person to go it alone. Government institutions are likewise too big and too distant to truly solve problems on a personal scale. And standing alone, any one person operates on the edge of the knife, with economic ruin on either side. But the family is the perfectly scaled security net for every human being. No one can know a person's needs as well as his or her family does. And no stranger, bureaucrat, or even dedicated social servant will have the kind of compassion that motivates the sacrifice it sometimes takes to get a person through the toughest times. The classic line is really true—"we all need somebody to lean on." And the best somebodies are those who have the special relationship that family ties engender.

I believe the solution to the challenges raised in this chapter and this book are all within our grasp. I have spent my career getting to know the American people. I know what keeps us at our best and what reveals us at our worst. These actions and efforts are all within our collective character. They will work. And if we work together to achieve them, the America we see in ten years will be richer in spirit—a wealth far more significant than material gains.

APPENDIX:

The What Americans Really Want . . . Really Survey Results

From December 2008 through April 2009, my firm interviewed more than 6,400 Americans nationwide to understand what really makes us tick and what truly matters most in our lives. It is the most comprehensive survey of its kind.

Take this unique opportunity to see where you stand, whether you are in the solid majority or the narrow minority.

Now you're going to see several statements and I want you to tell me whether you agree/disagree with each one.

1. I'm mad as hell and I'm not going to take it anymore.

TOTAL

72%	**Agree**
33%	Strongly Agree
39%	Somewhat Agree
17%	Somewhat Disagree
10%	Strongly Disagree
28%	**Disagree**

2. If it feels good, do it.

TOTAL

54%	**Agree**
14%	Strongly Agree
40%	Somewhat Agree
22%	Somewhat Disagree
24%	Strongly Disagree
46%	**Disagree**

3. Live free or die.

TOTAL
88%   **Agree**
54%   Strongly Agree
35%   Somewhat Agree
10%   Somewhat Disagree
2%   Strongly Disagree
12%   **Disagree**

4. I want it all and I want it now.

TOTAL
35%   **Agree**
9%   Strongly Agree
26%   Somewhat Agree
32%   Somewhat Disagree
33%   Strongly Disagree
65%   **Disagree**

5. The best things in life are free.

TOTAL
61%   **Agree**
27%   Strongly Agree
35%   Somewhat Agree
20%   Somewhat Disagree
20%   Strongly Disagree
39%   **Disagree**

6. The Ten Commandments are a good guide to live by.

TOTAL
89%   **Agree**
60%   Strongly Agree
29%   Somewhat Agree
8%   Somewhat Disagree
3%   Strongly Disagree
11%   **Disagree**

7. In God we trust.

TOTAL

82% **Agree**

60% Strongly Agree

22% Somewhat Agree

8% Somewhat Disagree

10% Strongly Disagree

18% **Disagree**

THE 2020 GENERATION

8. If you could be a teenager in any decade, which would you choose?

TOTAL

32% 1950s

17% 1960s

16% 1970s

13% 1980s

7% 1990s

16% Right Now

9. What do you think the youth of America need more?

TOTAL

79% A Swift Kick in the Ass

21% A Gentle and Understanding Hand

10. Which is more important for America . . . that no child should be left behind . . . or that exceptional children should be encouraged to pursue excellence?

TOTAL

55% Exceptional Children Should Pursue Excellence

45% No Child Left Behind

11–12. If you had to choose, which of the following high-school subjects is absolutely essential for the children of today to master well? And what is your second choice?

TOTAL	1ST	2ND	
37%	17%	20%	Math
32%	19%	13%	American History/Government
29%	17%	12%	Writing
28%	16%	12%	Economics
23%	9%	13%	Science
19%	8%	11%	World History
11%	5%	6%	A Foreign Language
8%	3%	5%	The Arts (Including Music, Theater, and Visual Arts)
7%	3%	4%	Public Speaking
3%	1%	2%	Physical Education and Athletics
2%	1%	1%	Geography

(IF YOU ARE THE PARENT OF CHILDREN 17 YEARS OLD OR YOUNGER)

13. If you had to choose, which is more important to you as parents?

TOTAL

43%	That Your Kids Do Well Spiritually
23%	That Your Kids Do Well Intellectually
14%	That Your Kids Do Well Professionally
10%	That Your Kids Do Well Financially
10%	That Your Kids Do Well Socially

14. Which of the following scares you most for your kids? You can only pick one.

TOTAL

41%	Drug Abuse
25%	Sexual Promiscuity
25%	Academic Failure
10%	Alcohol Abuse

GOVERNMENT

15–16. Now you're going to see a list of a dozen major American institutions. I want you to indicate the institutions that are **most** important for America's future. (1ST/2ND CHOICE COMBINED)

TOTAL	1ST	2ND	
51%	31%	20%	Schools
26%	18%	8%	The Church
24%	12%	12%	Federal Government
23%	11%	12%	The Military
22%	9%	13%	Business
13%	4%	9%	Local Government
12%	5%	7%	The Courts
11%	5%	6%	Financial Institutions
9%	3%	7%	Hospitals
4%	1%	3%	The Media
3%	0%	2%	Police
3%	1%	2%	Unions

17–18. Please indicate the institutions that are **least** important for America's future. (1ST/2ND CHOICE COMBINED)

TOTAL	1ST	2ND	
61%	41%	21%	Unions
56%	25%	32%	The Media
27%	19%	9%	The Church
14%	6%	8%	Federal Government
8%	3%	5%	The Military
8%	2%	6%	Financial Institutions
8%	1%	6%	Local Government
5%	1%	4%	The Courts
4%	1%	4%	Business
3%	1%	2%	Hospitals
3%	1%	2%	Police
2%	0%	1%	Schools

19–20. Which of the following values is the most important? (1ST/2ND CHOICE COMBINED)

TOTAL

45%   Liberty

33%   Opportunity

30%   Justice

28%   Democracy

24%   Equality

16%   Pursuit of Happiness

15%   Fairness

9%   Privacy

21. Which of the following matters the most to you? (1ST/2ND CHOICE COMBINED)

TOTAL

66%   Freedom of Speech

40%   Freedom of Religion

20%   Freedom to Own a Gun

18%   Freedom from Unreasonable Search and Seizure

16%   Freedom to Petition the Government

12%   Freedom of the Press

12%   Freedom from Cruel and Unusual Punishment

9%   Freedom to Peaceably Assemble

5%   Freedom to Have a Quick and Speedy Trial by a Jury of Your Peers

2%   Freedom from Having to Incriminate Yourself

22–23. From the same list, which of the following matters least to you? (1ST/2ND CHOICE COMBINED)

TOTAL

47%	Freedom to Own a Gun
29%	Freedom from Having to Incriminate Yourself
25%	Freedom of the Press
19%	Freedom from Cruel and Unusual Punishment
17%	Freedom to Peaceably Assemble
17%	Freedom to Petition the Government
17%	Freedom to Have a Quick and Speedy Trial by a Jury of Your Peers
14%	Freedom from Unreasonable Search and Seizure
11%	Freedom of Religion
1%	Freedom of Speech

RELIGION/VALUES

24. Which of the following matters more to you personally?

TOTAL

52%	The Bill of Rights
48%	The Ten Commandments

25. And which is more important? You do need to choose.

TOTAL

65%	Morals
35%	Values

26. And which do you think is the worst vice affecting Americans as a whole? You can only choose one.

TOTAL

64%	Greed
8%	Gluttony
7%	Envy
7%	Sloth
6%	Vanity
5%	Rage
4%	Lust

JOBS

27. Honestly, now, what is more important to you . . .

TOTAL
91%   The Opportunity to Succeed
9%   Protection from Failure

28. Would you rather make a lot more at a job you hate or a lot less money at a job you love?

TOTAL
84%   A Lot Less Money at a Job You Love
16%   A Lot More Money at a Job You Hate

29. Looking into the future, if you had to guess, how much longer do you think you'll still be working for your current company? (among full-time employees only)

TOTAL
18%   Less Than a Year
12%   1 Year
14%   2 Years
16%   3 or 4 Years
15%   5 to 9 Years
26%   10 Years or More

30. Which of the following annual incomes for an individual would you say is the MOST you can make and still be considered "middle-class"?

TOTAL
9% $50,000
27% $75,000
20% $100,000
10% $125,000
15% $150,000
7% $200,000
8% $250,000
3% $500,000

31. And if you lost your job tomorrow, how long would your savings last before you ran out of money? (among full-time employees only)

TOTAL

23%   I Have No Savings

19%   A Month or Less

23%   Two–Three Months

14%   Six–Nine Months

9%   A Year

4%   Two Years

9%   More Than Two Years

32–33. Assuming you had a surprise day off, which of the following activities would you most want to do? (1ST/2ND CHOICE COMBINED)

TOTAL

43%   Spend Time with Your Family

32%   Day Trip Somewhere

25%   Spend Time with Friends

15%   Reading Books/Magazine

15%   Clean up the Home

13%   Catch up on a Hobby

12%   Do Nothing at All

10%   Use the Computer

10%   Take a Long Nap

8%   Exercise

6%   Go Shopping

6%   Go Play Sports

5%   Watch Television

PERSONAL PERCEPTIONS AND BEHAVIOR

34. Are you . . . than the average American?

TOTAL

24%   A Lot More Intelligent

66%   A Little More Intelligent

9%   A Little Less Intelligent

2%   A Lot Less Intelligent

35. Are you . . . compared to the average person your age?

TOTAL

10%   A Lot More Attractive

51%   A Little More Attractive

35%   A Little Less Attractive

4%   A Lot Less Attractive

36. Which of the following is most important to you?

TOTAL

43%   A Little More Money

30%   Fewer Day-to-Day Hassles

17%   A Little More Free Time

10%   More Choices of the Things You Want

37. If you had to choose, which of the following would you rather be?

TOTAL

46%   Rich

27%   Physically Strong

18%   Powerful

6%   Sexy

4%   Famous

38–39. Here are some various situations you may face that require you to wait. While some you may experience often and others only occasionally, which of these do you find most annoying when it does happen to you? (1ST/2ND CHOICE COMBINED)

TOTAL

79%   Being Put on Hold by a Customer Service Representative

31%   Waiting to Go Through Security at the Airport

29%   Waiting at the Supermarket Checkout Line

29%   Waiting at a Department Store to Pay for Your Items

25%   Waiting to Make a Left Turn at a Busy Intersection

5%   Waiting to Check in at a Hotel

THE FUTURE

40–41. Which of the following do you want most? (1ST/2ND CHOICE COMBINED)

TOTAL

43%   The Opportunity to Succeed

37%   The Good Life

34%   The Pursuit of Happiness

22%   The American Dream

17%   A Fair Shake

13%   To Be Left Alone

9%   A Fresh Start

9%   Everything I Can Get

8%   A Fighting Chance

8%   A New Beginning

42–44. Below is a list of a number of significant issues, problems, and challenges facing the United States today. If you had the power, which three—in order—would you fix first? (COMBINED ANSWERS, TOP THREE)

TOTAL

31%   Restoring National Economic Stability

31%   Restoring Values and Morality to Society

29%   Preventing Terrorism

29%   Improving Schools and Education

26%   Ending American Dependence on Foreign Oil

22%   Restoring Political Accountability

22%   Curing Cancer

22%   Lowering the Tax Burden on Working Americans

13%   Ending World Poverty

13%   Closing the Widening Gap Between Rich and Poor

12%   Global Warming

12%   Restoring Personal Financial Security

10%   Strengthening Social Security and Medicare

8%   Ending Race and Gender Inequality

7%   Restoring Respect for America Around the World

5%   Ending Racial Inequality

5%   Fighting Crime and Illegal Drug Use

3%   Rebuilding Our Roads, Bridges, and Highways

45–46. And here is a different list of problems and challenges facing Americans today. If you had the power, which would you fix first? (1ST/2ND CHOICE COMBINED)

TOTAL

51%   Restoring Personal Responsibility

37%   Ending the Culture of Entitlement

34%   Loss of Moral Values

22%   Restoring the Work Ethic

20%   Ending the Culture of Disrespect

13%   Lack of Pride in America

13%   Loss of Civic Engagement and Community Commitment

11%   The Loss of the American "Can-Do" Spirit

47. And which of the following would scare you most about your long-term future?

TOTAL

30%   Your Health Deteriorates

27%   You Lose Control Over Decisions Affecting You

18%   You Run Out of Money

11%   You Won't Go to Heaven

10%   Being Alone

3%   Your Kids Hate You

48–50. Below you will see 15 personal priorities that people have said are important to them. Pick the one that matters most to you. (COMBINED TOP THREE ANSWERS)

TOTAL

54%   A Loving Family

50%   Good Health

43%   Financial Security

33%   Happiness

25%   Eventually Going to Heaven

24%   A Chance to Give Something Back

17%   Getting as Much as I Can Out of Life

9%   A Great Career

9%   Staying Young at Heart

9%   Doing Something Truly Memorable

8%   A Long Life

8%   Opportunities to Travel

5%   More Time to Do What You Want

4%   Fewer Day-to-Day Hassles

1%   More Choices in Life

51. And honestly, now, are you satisfied with your sex life?

TOTAL

54%   Yes

46%   No

NOTES

INTRODUCTION

1. "Lunch with the FT," *Financial Times*, December 6, 2008.
2. Starwoodhotels.com/corporate/careers/who/history
3. 2008 Brand Keys Customer Loyalty Engagement Index, www.brandkeys.com
4. *Condé Nast Traveler* magazine, Readers' Choice Awards, jetblue.com
5. "As Las Vegas Slumps, Wynn Doubles Down," Tamara Audi, *The Wall Street Journal*, Oct. 30, 2008

CHAPTER 1

6. New York Times 10-K SEC Filing, 2009, and "Fall in Newspaper Sales Accelerates," Tim Arango, *New York Times*, 4/27/09.
7. LMSR Survey of 2,000 apartment renters in New York, Los Angeles, Chicago, Washington, DC, Miami, and San Francisco, 2008
8. Coffee Statistics Report 2008, www.coffee-statistics.com
9. 2008 National Coffee Drinking Trends Summary, NCA Market Research & Resources
10. "New Dunkin' Spots Say Chain Beats Starbucks on Taste," Emily Bryson York, *Advertising Age*, Oct. 22, 2008
11. OnStar ad, Nov. 20, 2008, *The Washington Post*
12. Pew Internet and American Life Project, survey of 1,102 adults, Nov. 1, 2007–Feb. 5, 2008
13. Pew Internet and American Life Project Networked Family Survey, 1,267 respondents, Dec. 13, 2007–Jan. 13, 2008
14. Rasmussen Reports, 1,000 adults, Nov. 17–18, 2008
15. Harris Interactive Poll, 2,454 adults, July 9–16, 2008
16. American Beverage Association, "What America Drinks," 2005
17. Cigarette Smoking Drops to Lowest Level in 25 Year Trend, Harris Interactive Poll, 1,010 adults, Feb. 5–11, 2008
18. "Suave's Message to Moms Connects," *USA Today*, Oct. 23, 2006
19. "Cheetos Joins Super Bowl Ad Parade," *Adweek*, Jan. 29, 2009
20. Organic Trade Association, 2007 Manufacturers Survey, www.ota.com
21. Beer Institute, Shipment of Malt Beverages and Per Capita Consumption by State 2007
22. U.S. Census Bureau, Statistical Abstract of the United States, 2008
23. Netflix.com, July 25, 2008, Q2 2008 financial results

CHAPTER 2

24. *The Wall Street Journal*, Feb. 9, 2009
25. Fordvehicles.com/thefordstory
26. www.well-beingindex.com
27. *Forbes*, March 30, 2009, p. 29
28. Bureau of Labor Statistics, American Time Use Survey 2007, www.bls.gov.tus/

CHAPTER 3

29 "Hints of Hope in Jobless Data Even as Rate Jumps to 9.4 percent," by Peter Good-
    man and Jack Healy, *New York Times*, pg. A1.
30. Ibid.
31. 2008 American Honda Motor Co., publicpolicy.honda.com, *The Washington Post*
    ad, Nov. 5, 2008
32. Luntz survey, 2008
33. "Grocery Conflict Rooted in Last Strike," Jerry Hirsch, *Los Angeles Times*, April 23,
    2007
34. "Growing Sense of Outrage Over Executive Pay," Heather Landy, *The Washington
    Post*, Nov. 15, 2008
35. Ibid

CHAPTER 4

36. Edison-Mitofsky exit poll for the television networks and the Associated Press,
    17,834 voters, Nov. 4, 2008
37. "One-Way Media Lost the Election as Cable, Interactive Dominated," Michael Lear-
    month, *Advertising Age*, Nov. 10, 2008
38. "Poli-fluentials: The New Political Kingmakers," Carol Darr, The George Washing-
    ton University Graduate School of Political Management Institute for Politics, De-
    mocracy, and the Internet, October 2007
39. Zogby International survey for the Congressional Management Foundation, 9,536
    respondents, 2007
40. Ibid

CHAPTER 5

41. Pew Forum on Religion & Public Life, Religious Landscape Study, 35,556 respon-
    dents, May 8–Aug. 13, 2007
42. Ibid
43. Ibid
44. The Harris Poll, working with the Marriott School of Management at Brigham
    Young University, 2,513 adults surveyed online, March 11–18, 2008
45. National Council of Churches USA, 2008 Yearbook, NCC press release, Feb. 14,
    2008
46. "Billy Graham: A Spiritual Gift to All," *Time* Magazine, May 31, 2007.

CHAPTER 6

47. *Communication Arts*, March/April 2009, p. 28
48. "The Politics of Sex Survey," *Playboy* magazine, 2/08
49. Josephson Institute, survey of 29,760 high school students, released Nov. 30, 2008
50. "What Are They Talking About," Betsy Towner, AARP Bulletin Today, Oct. 1, 2008
51. eBizMBA, based on Inbound Links, Alexa Rank, and traffic data from Compete and Quantcast.
52. CareerBuilder.com survey for employers, 2,546 hiring managers, June 1–13, 2007
53. Editorial Projects in Education Research Center, released by America's Promise Alliance, 2008
54. Marc Ecko Enterprises, FAQ at www.marceckoenterprises.com

CHAPTER 7

55. Mediamark Research Inc, Spring 07 Survey of the American Consumer, 26,000 interviews, March 2006–April 2007
56. Pew Research Center survey, "From the Age of Aquarius to the Age of Responsibility," 3,014 respondents, Oct. 5–Nov. 6, 2005
57. ICR survey for AARP, 1,628 employed respondents at least 45 years old, Sept. 3–21, 2008
58. National Center for Health Statistics, "Health, United States 2007, Table 27"
59. ICR survey for AARP, ibid
60. American Heart Association, "Heart Disease and Stroke Statistics," 2008 update
61. ICR survey for AARP, ibid
62. Synovate Inc. survey for AARP, "Staying Ahead of the Curve 2007," 1,500 workers ages 45–74, April 13–May 21, 2007
63. Towers Perrin analysis for AARP, "The Business Case for Workers Age 50+," released Dec. 21, 2005
64. University of Michigan Institute for Social Research, survey of 516 people 70 and older, over six years
65. Opinion Research Corporation survey for AARP, "Retired Spouses: A National Survey of Adults 55–75," 1,064 adults ages 55–75, Nov. 1–26, 2007

CONCLUSION

66. The Pew Forum on Religion & Public Life, "U.S. Religious Landscape Survey," 2009

INDEX